HIP-HOP
IS HISTORY

HIP-HOP
IS HISTORY

QUESTLOVE
with Ben Greenman

AUWA Books

MCD / Farrar, Straus and Giroux / New York

AUWA Books
MCD / Farrar, Straus and Giroux
120 Broadway, New York 10271

Copyright © 2024 by Ahmir Khalib Thompson
All rights reserved
Printed in the United States of America
First edition, 2024

Library of Congress Cataloging-in-Publication Data
Names: Questlove, author. | Greenman, Ben, author.
Title: Hip-hop is history / Questlove with Ben Greenman.
Description: First edition. | New York : AUWA / MCD / Farrar, Straus and
    Giroux, 2024. | Includes index.
Identifiers: LCCN 2023057423 | ISBN 9780374614072 (hardcover)
Subjects: LCSH: Rap (Music)—History and criticism. | Hip-hop—History.
Classification: LCC ML3531 .Q47 2024 | DDC 782.421649—dc23/
    eng/20231213
LC record available at https://lccn.loc.gov/2023057423

Designed by Gretchen Achilles

Our books may be purchased in bulk for promotional, educational, or business use.
Please contact your local bookseller or the Macmillan Corporate and Premium Sales
Department at 1-800-221-7945, extension 5442, or by email at
MacmillanSpecialMarkets@macmillan.com.

www.auwabooks.com • www.mcdbooks.com • www.fsgbooks.com
Follow us on social media at @mcdbooks

1   3   5   7   9   10   8   6   4   2

CONTENTS

HIP-HOP
IS HISTORY

INTRODUCTION

I am writing from the summer of 2023, the year that has been officially designated as the fiftieth anniversary of hip-hop.

The designation stems from the date, mythic but also real, of an August 11, 1973, back-to-school party in the Bronx, held in the rec room of an apartment building at 1520 Sedgwick Avenue, planned by a Jamaican-born teen named Cindy Campbell (she made the decorations and made up a pricing structure—a quarter for girls for admission, fifty cents for boys, and concessions that included seventy-five-cent hot dogs) and featuring Cindy's older brother Clive, nicknamed "Kool Herc" as a result of his imposing physical stature ("Herc" was short for "Hercules"), furnishing entertainment that consisted of a DJ set in which he spun funk records using a novel technique that foregrounded the beats (or breakbeats), isolating them and repeating them in ways that not only provided a new space for dancers (or breakdancers) but also constructed a frame over which Herc could stretch extended raps or commentaries.

I have my quibbles with picking this date as a birth date, for reasons I will explain, but no one can question the fact of hip-hop's birth, because no one can question what followed: decades of innovation, achievement, energy, artistry, and history, meaning decades of life. History is never simple. It's layers upon layers. But what exactly is this miraculous, mercurial genre that has given so much to me and so many other artists, and to which we are trying in turn to give something back?

Big question. Long answer to follow.

The story begins just after Thanksgiving of 2022, leftover turkey still in the refrigerator. My manager Shawn Gee and the television producers Jesse Collins and Dionne Harmon came to me. They had a question: "The Grammys want to do something for Hip-Hop 50. Would you lead it? How do you feel about putting something together?"

I am the king of "yes," and the victim of it, too. Out of muscle memory and habit I agree to a job before I think about what it actually involves, what I'm getting myself into, and what I might need to get myself out of. "Of course," I said. "No problem whatsoever. I can do this in my sleep."

But sleep was exactly what didn't happen. I got right to work trying to tell the story of the genre, first by building playlists and sourcing history. I knew I would need headliners, big artists, and I would also need important artists who might not have sold quite as much, not to mention artists of the moment. That meant Jay-Z, Snoop Dogg, Public Enemy, Drake, Griselda, Cardi B, Coi Leray, Coast Contra, Jack Harlow, Meek Mill, and all points in between. About five hours into the sourcing, it felt daunting, but with a window of possibility. About ten hours into the sourcing, I realized that the segment—whatever it ended up being—had to have a time limit, and that this fact created a second fact, which was that I would have to demote some artists and cut others out. I would have to make hard choices and play favorites. This whole thing, which had the potential to be a landmark event, could also result in angry faces in a ring around me. Was I being set up for failure? Instantly, I felt a twinge of regret for having said yes.

In truth, it was an accumulated twinge. I had, the previous March, won the Oscar for directing *Summer of Soul*, a documentary about the Harlem Cultural Festival, also known as the Black Woodstock. I created the movie in a relatively calm atmosphere that was ironically enabled by the broad international crisis of pandemic. I was doing different things, living upstate, sketching on weekend mornings, getting further into meditation. But in the wake of the Oscar, I was also in demand. People were seeking me out to direct more movies. I said yes to one offer and yes to a second, and before I knew it I was down for a half dozen commitments. I remember a conversation with my ex-girlfriend, one of the last ones before we broke up. She was dismayed. "You learned absolutely nothing in the last two years," she said. "You told me that the less work you do and the more time you have to breathe, the more the stars aligned. You were working only on the things you wanted, and that felt good."

"Right," I said.

"So what's with all the new work?" she said. "You basically just regressed. You relapsed the way a drug addict would. Pandemic was calm in a way but when real life came back you went right back to hiding in your work." She started to say something else but stopped. What she said instead was devastating. "I guess you'll have space and time for this relationship in, like, 2032."

Then and there, I told myself I would never again agree to do anything without taking time to assess it first, to see what the time-management landscape looked like, to think about who other than myself might be affected.

But she was right to tell me that I was wrong, and I was wrong to think that I would listen to myself, and here I was having committed to a Hip-Hop 50 Grammy tribute that had the potential to burn a bunch of bridges while I was standing on them. One of the bridges that it started to burn was the relationship itself. The 2032 estimate now looked optimistic. That relationship, which had spanned the pandemic, started to end, and I did what she knew I'd do all along. I moved forward into more work. Specifically, I started on the Grammy tribute project. I made a demo. I put together an audio map of the hip-hop genre over the half century from 1973, going from the earliest Bronx DJing to Jimmy Castor to "Apache" and moving through all of it, every song and artist I loved, all the ones I listed above and all the ones I didn't, until I got to GloRilla or Ice Spice or whoever I thought best represented 2023. I made what I thought were all the hard choices. By the time I was finished, it was thirty-three minutes and forty-two seconds. I knew that the Grammys weren't going to give me that much time but maybe I could get close. I called Jesse and Dionne and asked them how long I would have.

"Ten minutes," they said. "Maybe eleven."

I thought they were joking. I was sure they were joking. How could anyone pare down the entire half century to a segment that short? On top of everything else it would require me to deliver disappointment to artists, telling some that I could use only a snippet of their greatest songs, telling others that I couldn't use them at all. And what about the artists who were no longer sharp performers, or who I knew wouldn't be warmly received on TV or social media? Would I have to write them out of history entirely? That's when it hit me: they had suckered me into being the bad cop!!! "Is that why you came to me? To make me the bad cop?!?!"

They started laughing. But the laughing didn't last that long. "These things that you're bringing up," they said, "sound like YPs instead of OPs." Meaning: your problem, instead of our problem.

A day later I called Dionne back. I had worked with her on the Oscars when I was the de facto orchestra and a quasi host. I gave her a level-with-me talk. "Even though I'm a creative I am also a suit," I said. "So don't shield me like I'm an artist. Tell me the truth. How much time do I really have?"

"Ten to eleven," she said.

"Come on," I said. "You can tell me."

"I am telling you," she said. "There are other parts of this celebration. We're going to give Dr. Dre an award. You have ten to eleven minutes for your segment."

Jesse and Dionne are the Ashford and Simpson of production. I know when to go to Dad for some things and Mom for some other things. I rolled out my appeal. "Dionne," I said, "I need you to come through for me. You gotta find me five more minutes. Can you give another segment a haircut?"

"I'll see what I can do," she said.

She called me back the next morning. "I've got good news and—"

"You didn't say bad news," I said.

"I got you more time," she said.

"How much? Seventeen? Sixteen? Eighteen?"

"You have thirteen minutes," she said. She delivered the news like she had gone out and gotten venison that was going to feed the household for a month. It was spoken in triumph and a kind of finality.

In the wake of that call, I thought about reindeer games. I always do. It's one of the metaphors I have used more than almost any other. The Roots, since our inception, often felt that hip-hop was a party and we were invited late or not at all. We didn't get to participate in everything that it had to offer, even though we had the talent and the desire. Gatekeepers turned us away for one reason or another: not perceived as hard enough, not making the right kinds of hits at the right time. Being Rudolph came to be my skeleton key for everything. In this situation, though, I wasn't Rudolph. I was Santa. I was the gatekeeper.

The first challenge was to see who I could entice to participate. A tribute is a strange beast. Each artist gets only a little time onstage, and no artist feels like he or she has any real time in the spotlight. Given that, how do you make a pitch to any artist to give up a work-day for two or three bars or even three words? Not to mention how would I figure out for myself who to include and who to leave off my wish list? The way I wanted to do the tribute was chronological, which eliminated some of the ego, but not all of it, in part because there was so much of it.

Shawn Gee had a thought early on. "This is what you do," he said. "You represent one demographic. You pick one New York god, one LA god, one Midwest god, one from Atlanta, one from Texas." Easier said than done. Who was New York? Was it Big Daddy Kane?

Was it KRS-One? Rakim? I did at least a week and a half of distilling and got it down to a fair and decent representation. Then the asks went out. Lots of people were instant no, right out of the gate. Some of it I understood. They were on tour already, or were on a movie set. And there were more than a few fuck-the-Grammys nos as well. The amount of bridge-burning that rappers feel the Grammys have done to them over the years creates and extends that idea. I got it, at some level—the respect hasn't always been there from the Academy—but if I got that call I would have been like Sonny the Cuckoo from the Cocoa Puffs commercial.

Even when I understood the demurrals, I didn't necessarily accept them. I worked on people. To teach myself, I pulled up the *We Are the World* documentary (the original, not the "Al Jarreau is a crazy mofo" version) and watched it twice to see how Quincy Jones operated. What were the words he used? What was his tone? He reprimanded some of the stars, went rough on others, brought people together. I started to adopt Quincy's language. I broke out, "We're coming together for the culture," and, "Let's check our egos at the door." There was a broader argument, too, the one that I made in *Things Fall Apart* and *Summer of Soul*, which was that we don't want a disposable Black culture. We don't want everything we made to fall by the wayside.

None of it worked. As a matter of fact, I had even more drama on my hands. The process of inviting groups started to work—or not work—the way that the Rock and Roll Hall of Fame worked. Lots of these groups hadn't been groups for decades. Some hadn't been in each other's presence that long. And in some cases, the original group's name had been transferred to members who hadn't been part of the original picture. That was another can of whoop-ass that had the potential to be opened right on my head. I was reporting hourly to the Grammy group thread, telling them that in addition to working out production and song choice, we were juggling dozens of egos. I made two requests: first, that we were going to need extra security, not just because of beef between rappers but because of beef within groups; and second, that we were going to need a life coach to talk people off the ledge.

And there were ledges. I almost climbed onto one myself when I heard the news, a few weeks after I started putting out asks, that LL Cool J was moving forward with his own version of a fiftieth anniversary tribute. His genesis was almost comically straightforward. He was at a party and had a conversation with the president of CBS, who brought up the concept, sparked to the idea of LL running it, and told him to have a good evening. It was like the movie *Boomerang*, where Lady Eloise (played by Eartha Kitt) runs her cosmetics empire without exactly running the company. At the top tier, wishes are articulated, but no plans are put in place. I heard a little bit about the LL version, but I figured that it would dissipate, which is why I was unprepared when Jesse called together the entire team for an announcement: "Guys, we have a situation on their hands," he said. "Apparently, LL Cool J has been promised that it would be his segment." Moans and groans all around. "We kind of have to share the moment with him."

The news landed on me like a brick. I was already dealing with the headache of how to chop my half hour down to thirteen minutes, and here was a new element (LLement?). It was explained to us that LL was willing to work together, but I knew him, and knew what kind of strong alpha figure he was. What flashed into my head was a quote from *Friday*: "It's just like it's both ours." My first thought was to text Shawn to tell him it wasn't going to work, that I needed to drop out. But my baby/bathwater instincts got to me. I don't like throwing away work that's already done. And when I reached out to LL, he didn't make an alpha move. Instead he was gracious enough to hit me right back and ask after my thoughts. I gave him my mix. "This is great," he said. "Let's roll with this."

Meanwhile, actual negotiations were still in progress. Sometimes I was going to the artists, other times assistants or managers. I had never seen a world so built on defense. What I mean by that is that during a week of conversations, I never saw a single proactive creative decision made. Rather, everything was a reaction to someone else's decision. "Who all going to be there?" was the most common question I heard. I knew why: they wanted me to make adjustments to remove the people they found unsavory. I tried to accommodate. I went back to Mom and Dad. We made calls to management or label heads. Sometimes we managed to get the water under the bridge. Sometimes we had to push people out to keep someone else's peace. That was just the seating arrangements, the way you'd work out a wedding between two warring families. Then there were secondary questions: "How many dancers does blah blah blah have?" I should have said, "I signed an NDA and I can't say." But my naive ass answered, and that led directly to games of chicken, hints that maybe an artist wouldn't show up. It was like a scene from an 80s action movie where the hero had to solve a Rubik's Cube before the building exploded. I did, barely, just in time for rehearsals. My partner in music direction for the event, Jazzy Jeff, worked with me to get the band ready for the medley, first in Electric Lady in New York. Then we went west to SIR Studios in Los Angeles. We had four days to go.

Much of rehearsals was just as fun as you would expect. LL Cool J and Run are storytelling geniuses, and they showed it off regularly. They could have a *Prairie Home Companion* of hip-hop folklore. Just one example: LL named Chung King Studios. It used to be John King Studios, but there was a dope Chinese restaurant around the corner. One day LL looked up from his take-out carton. "You should call this place Chung King," he said. "I only come here because of the food."

But that didn't mean that it went smoothly. The four-day rush to the Grammys was cut in half by logistics, meaning that we spent two full days mapping out entrances and exits for vocalists, making sure that Eighties Rapper X didn't run into her nemesis on the way out of the building. We had two artists drop out because of COVID and another with a family issue. We had stuck-in-their-ways rappers who resisted in-ear monitors, which made it impossible for them to hear as I counted in the track. And then we had one particular artist who we were sure had sent a body double. This performer showed up in a full-face mask and sunglasses. Me and Jeff wondered if it was really who it was supposed to be. "I'm going to go and find out," I said.

The security guard stopped me. "Nah," he said.

"Hi," I said. "I'm Questlove. I'm the musical director of the event."

"I know who you are," he said.

"I just want to powwow," I said. "I talked to the manager, the assistant. But not once to the actual artist."

The security guard took a beat. "Yeah," he said. "Nah. That can't happen." All the while, the artist is there in the back corner of the room, hoodie, sunglasses. To this day I am still not sure whether we got the real artist or a hired double.

Suddenly it was game time. Grammy night. First Lady Jill Biden was a presenter at the awards, and any time you have someone presidential, whether White House or White House–adjacent, you have to go through a certain level of sweeping just to get in the building. Historically speaking, rappers and metal detectors are not good friends. Off the top of my head, I can think of at least four acts that have had crippling things happen to their careers because of metal detectors. Working out that whole mess was endless. It exhausted me, but it also gave me one of the greatest laughs of my life, when Stro Elliot turned to me and said, "We've seen this before"—pause—"*30 Rock*." He was talking about the episode where Liz Lemon briefly dates a conservative Black guy, decides she doesn't like him, and tries to tank the relationship by bringing him to the Source Awards, where she thinks she can prove both that she is not racist and that he is unpleasant. Everything that happened in that episode happened on Grammy night, but it wasn't on my mind until Stro mentioned it. Even thinking about it now gets me laughing. Thank you, Stro.

The last rapper cleared security. I finally made it to relaxation. I could rest for a bit, put clothes on, walk the red carpet, tell a joke to Taylor Swift, and go to my table, where I was sitting with Jazzy Jeff, Shawn, Tariq, his wife Michelle, some others. I wanted to just chill out and see Bad Bunny, who was opening the show with performances of "El Apagón" and "Después de la Playa." The second I leaned back in my seat, my phone buzzed. I looked at Shawn to see that he was going for his phone, too. Both of us had gotten Code Red texts that we needed to report to the directors' booth all-caps-and-nine-exclamation-points IMMEDIATELY!!!!!!!!!

Shawn got up and went. But I couldn't move. It wasn't because of fatigue. It was because of where I was sitting. Bad Bunny wasn't performing onstage per se. The way the tables were set up, he was playing in the space between the tables. I was in the camera's eyeline. They sent a crew guy out to me, and Jesse started guiding him, like Ving Rhames in *Mission: Impossible*. "Weave around camera fourteen. Go behind Beyoncé, quick. Now bend down." It took seven minutes to join Shawn and Jesse in the booth.

"What's the emergency?" I said.

"Well," one of the Grammy guys said. The way he said it, I knew that it was bad news. "One of your acts is already en route home. He felt disrespected because one of the security people disrespected someone in his party."

"Let me talk to them."

"You're not hearing me," the guy said. "He's en route."

My brain was catching up, slowly. "What exactly happened?"

Evidently this said rapper was late getting to his table, and he got caught in the Bad Bunny sight line cross fire. A security guard stopped him with a hand. "You can't be roaming like this," he told the rapper. Somehow the guard's hand also found its way into the vicinity of the rapper's girlfriend's breasts. Groping was alleged. "Fuck this," the rapper said, and left.

I couldn't accept that one of my acts had vanished. Jesse and Shawn and I called the CEO of his label, his manager, his friends. We called everyone but Barack Obama to beg him to please turn around and come through. But by the time we reached anyone he was back at his Calabasas mansion watching the telecast. An hour and fifteen minutes to stage, and we were down a man.

I had to talk to six different parties to clip the missing rapper's performance segment. But it was a live show. I had to wait for commercial, then run to the light person and explain that hey, after this performance, before this one, we have to delete these cues on your computer. Then I had to run to the pyro person and give the same explanation, except that I had to wait because the commercial was over. At the next commercial it was off to the choreographer, who had to break the news to some soon-to-be-heartbroken backup dancers. Then the graphics person, then the camera person. It took me forty-seven minutes to make the rounds to each person to eliminate forty-three seconds of the medley. All the while, I was getting pissed. This person was not being considerate of the fact that when you head home, it's not just about you. There are other considerations. There are *nothing but* other considerations. The only silver lining was that I could now bring the medley in under thirteen minutes without much trouble.

It was 6:55 (West Coast time) by the time that nightmare dissipated. Then the nominees for Best Rap Album of the Year were read. One of them was Kendrick Lamar, meaning that the winner was Kendrick Lamar. Anyone should have been able to predict that. Pulitzer Prize–winning Kendrick Lamar? It doesn't take much to know that he has it sewn up. Which, of course, came to pass. But one of the other nominees? He didn't have the gift of foresight. He was pissed. He wanted to go. He was, of course, one of the rappers in the medley. "No, no," I said. "Please be considerate of your favorite artists. You don't know how much trouble even one small change can cause. It took me forty-seven mi—" I blinked and he was gone. Didn't even let me get the full sentence out. The full word, even.

Now it was 7:04. I was supposed to be dressed and in my spot at 7:13. I knew exactly what to do. "I need four minutes," I said. I found a closet backstage in the arena. I ran into it and then out. "I need a chair."

"What are you doing?" Jesse said. He looked stricken.

"I need to go in there and meditate so I don't panic."

I sat in the closet and went to YouTube to do an exercise called Breath of Fire. Over the pandemic, I had done breath work and meditating, and I had learned that fear and excitement are the same thing, more or less, with the only difference being that fear was excitement without breathing. When you take breathing away you are in the grip of your fear. When you breathe, you convert it to excitement. I did Breath of Fire for three minutes while the people outside the door stood looking at each other like I was fucking crazy. I could hear their judgment through the door.

I was out of there twenty seconds early. Already people were yelling, "Places." I ignored them. "This is what we're going to do," I said. "We're going to get in touch with Lil Uzi Vert." Even though he was from Philadelphia, I didn't know him well enough to text him. To reach him, I was going to text either Jay-Z or DJ Drama, a fellow Philadelphian who was part of his label. I played it through in my head, trying to figure out who was the less likely rejection. Jay, I knew, was the king of the no, so I texted Drama instead. "Hey," I wrote, "I got two minutes and thirty seconds left. Please give me the number of whoever is sitting next to Uzi." I have learned over the years that you never go to directly to the artist. You go to the person who has his ear. I called that number. "Look," I said. "I know you were one of my initial nos. But I need something from you." Beside me someone screamed that we were one minute to stage. I ignored the scream and kept going. "Brother," I said. "After GloRilla performs, you will hear 'Just Wanna Rock' played. Your song. At that moment, I want you to bum-rush the stage and do the dance move and the hook. Can you do me that solid? I have lost two core people and need the bailout." It was a message forged and calibrated by excitement. Whenever Black people use "brother," that's the equivalent of being on their knees begging. I pressed send. And just at that second, as the rainbow disc was spinning, my phone battery went out. I didn't know if the message was sent or not.

I also reached out to LL Cool J as a fail-safe. "LL," I said, "when

I raise my hand, give a motivational speech about hip-hop." He was the best at those hip-hop-is-worldwide speeches, Bronx to Bali to Baltimore to Berlin. I wanted a classic *Friday Night Lights* moment. "Can you hear me?" I said. He put up his hand in response. Good: I knew that at the very least I would get an inspirational moment from LL.

Now it was the medley, for real for real. Black Thought, aka Tariq Trotter, kicked off the proceedings with an introduction that was also a kind of invocation. "Fifty years ago," Tariq started, "a street princess was born to be an icon. The art form took the entire world by storm. How she do it? Her influence? Constantly raising the stakes each generation. Domination by whichever means it takes to go from spark into a flame that became public domain. And she prefers to be referred to by her full government name."

He stopped, and Grandmaster Flash started, Flash being Joseph Saddler (in government name terms), the Barbados-born and Bronx-raised DJ who built on the innovations of Herc, Grandmaster Flowers, Pete DJ Jones, and others, and formed what can fairly be thought of as the first rap group with three vocalists (Cowboy, Melle Mel, and the Kidd Creole: none government names).

What followed was hip-hop history, played live. The weeks of hell turned into heaven. Run-D.M.C. performed "King of Rock," LL Cool J and DJ Jazzy Jeff performed "I Can't Live Without My Radio" and "Rock the Bells," Salt-N-Pepa performed "My Mic Sounds Nice," Rakim performed "Eric B. Is President," and Public Enemy performed "Rebel Without a Pause." Then there was a pause, Black Thought and LL returning to perform "El Shabazz," a one-minute-and-change cut from LL's 1985 album *Radio* that is one of the earliest hip-hop skits, the interstitial spoken-word pieces, often comic, that populate the genre's albums. This one basically told listeners to turn the record over and hear the other side. That was my instruction for the tribute as well. Then we resumed with the night's historic roll call: Posdnuos from De La Soul, Scarface, Ice-T, Queen Latifah, Method Man, Big Boi, Busta Rhymes, Missy Elliott, Nelly, Too $hort, the Lox, Swizz Beatz, and Lil Baby.

This was a real unveiling. On top of that, the biggest artist, Jay-Z, was an integral part of it. It wasn't because he was in the medley—he wasn't, on account of his segment later in the telecast—but he was on camera throughout, from his table in the crowd, mouthing along to every word of every song. It was the best collaboration I had ever done with him, and he wasn't even onstage.

The whole time, I was trying not to manifuck myself. That's something I learned from my life coach, Lauren Zander. If you put something out into the world, you can manifest your future, but if you put something negative out there, you can manifuck yourself. Those voices were creeping in on me. Maybe they should have let LL do it. Maybe Dre would have been in control. I was dreading the last act, GloRilla, not because of her, but because of what came after. She only had sixteen bars but they were the longest bars in human history. I went through every variation of "He's not a jolly good fellow," "he" being me.

When the moment came, we played "Just Wanna Rock." I didn't see Lil Uzi Vert, so I put up my hand. "Give the speech now, LL!" I said. I heard nothing. I said it again, still got nothing back. "Why can't LL hear me?" I said. I was screaming into the mic, which meant that anyone with ears heard me. That meant every rapper. No speech. And the night was over. I was like Prince in *Purple Rain* after he played "Purple Rain," desperately unsure how his masterstroke had landed with the audience, terrified that he had just tanked his career and his life. I threw my sticks down. I threw my in-ears to the floor (and they're expensive). I went running down the hall crying, tears mixed with sweat, ripping off my shirt, mad as hell, twice as sad, wanting to go home and eat, wanting to shut it all out.

A minute after I got to the dressing room, a pack of jubilant motherfuckers came into the room. "Man," they said. "This is dope!" Were they mocking me?

I wiped away some sweat (tears) and saw that they were doing the Lil Uzi Vert dance. "What are you all talking about?" I said.

"He killed that shit."

"Who?"

"Lil Uzi Vert."

"Lil Uzi Vert who?"

In the churn of the first artist dropping out, stage positions had shifted. Whoever was entering left would instead enter right, and vice versa. That I knew. But I hadn't realized that the second artist dropping out had returned things to their previous state. I was looking at the wrong part of the stage when (if I could believe what I was being told) we launched into "Just Wanna Rock" and Lil Uzi Vert jumped up, rushed to the stage, and danced. I didn't believe it until James Poyser showed me a video from his phone.

"He got my text?" I said.

A guy who knew Lil Uzi Vert tilted his head in confusion. "What text?"

I explained what text. "Nah, man," the guy said. "He didn't get any text." As a matter of fact, no one believed me until I recharged my phone, and then when they saw the text sitting there, not transmitted, everyone flipped out completely. But I knew what had happened. I had done Breath of Fire and then the universe had sent the text.

There's an epilogue. There's always an epilogue. I left to get my red-eye flight back to New York, stopped near LAX for some sushi at a supersecret place I know, made the plane, slept, and woke up just as I was landing at 6:00 a.m. Exactly at that moment, one of my teeth fell out. How apropos, I thought. My body was keeping the score.

Luckily for me I knew of a dentist to the stars. I went directly to his office, where he replaced my tooth.

As I was falling into the gas, I remember asking myself one question: Was it really worth it? Even as I said the yes that would lead me to Lil Uzi Vert's triumphant moment, I was acutely aware that there might be repercussions. Why couldn't I just let things be and work on my movie career? Trying to throw my arms around the entirety of hip-hop was like running with the bulls. Why would I want to put that white outfit on? Why would I want to lose all my fucking teeth?

This book is both that and not that. It is another attempt to explain the amazing, beautiful, chaotic genre that has given me everything and taken almost as much. But it is not eight weeks filled with stressful rooms and Zooms. Instead, it is my own space, my own computer, my own time, my own thoughts. Hopefully it will put all my teeth back in.

My last book, *Music Is History*, picked out songs from across my life span and mapped them to important events. Here, the title spins a little differently. When you say that hip-hop is history, you are asking people to ask you a question right back. What do you mean by that? Do you simply mean that it is historically significant, or are you also building in a counterargument that the genre has run its course in some important ways? I would say yes, and I will continue to say it throughout the book.

I also want to add some invisible words to the title. There's a long one to start with: *Hip-Hop Is (Revisionist) History*. What I mean by that is that the entire life span of this young, vibrant genre has been marked by assessments and reassessments, declarations that proved to be untrue in a year's time, or ten, and opinions that cracked open like eggs to reveal newer opinions inside of them. There are so many classic albums that I just didn't get when I first heard them, so many classic artists I misunderstood at the time, so many classic moments I misread that have taken me decades to read correctly. And even that is equivocal: this is history as filtered through my sensibility, which means that others may well disagree.

For example, let's look at the so-called origin story of hip-hop, that back-to-school party that Kool Herc's sister set up in August 1973. Identifying that party as the first seed is problematic, at least. In part, of course, Herc was drawing on existing Jamaican music traditions, like toasting, where Jamaican vocalists performed over

American R&B records. You can see relatively direct lines between Caribbean-born African Americans and the first wave of hip-hop. But for me, it also draws on traditions in Black music that stretch back at least a decade earlier. I think of Ray Charles taking the Southern Tones' "It Must Be Jesus," outfitting it with secular lyrics, and creating "I Got a Woman." The rebellion in that act, the march straight into the heart of popular secular music, cannot be underestimated. Nor can the fact that social and racial advances in the 1960s went hand in hand with music. When people talk about all the *Ms* that shaped that decade—Martin, Malcolm, Medgar—they should include Motown. And King, too—not Martin, but James Brown's record label. In 1967, the year that Aretha released the feminist Black pride anthem "Respect" on Atlantic, and dominated the charts through spring and summer, Brown came along in the autumn with "Cold Sweat," which helped to create the breakbeats that would later be broken out of soul music and used as the building blocks of hip-hop.

Big stars helped forge attitudes and philosophies, but others poured concrete for a foundation. Who can forget the afro-poetic artists of the late 1960s and early 1970s? There's Gil Scott-Heron, who released songs like "The Revolution Will Not Be Televised" and "Whitey on the Moon," manifestos in cool. There are the Last Poets, who devised and developed a genre they called, unfortunately, "jazzoetry," but who laid much of the groundwork for the sensibility of hip-hop, especially on the 1973 album *Hustlers Convention*, recorded by one of the Last Poets, Jalal Mansur Nuriddin (born Lawrence Padilla), under the pseudonym Lightnin' Rod. There were the Watts Prophets, who came out of LA at the height of the Black Power movement and released two early influential records, mostly spoken word in nature—*The Black Voices: On the Streets in Watts* and *Rappin' Black in a White World*. (They are very specific documents of the times, with statistics pulled from the headlines and almost essayistic mentions of SNCC, the John Birch Society, urban rot, and more. The second record has a broader palette, partly as a result of female vocals by Dee Dee McNeil, who was a contract songwriter at

Motown and sings the almost-title song, "Black in a White World," and "What Is a Man," which popped up twenty-five years later in John Singleton's *Higher Learning*.) There was Imhotep Gary Byrd, a Buffalo radio personality who released the proto-rap classic "Every Brother Ain't a Brother" in 1970 and then cowrote with Stevie Wonder, among others (he furnished the lyrics for "Village Ghetto Land" and "Black Man" on *Songs in the Key of Life*). His radio voice, in my mind, was the inspiration for a whole slew of MCs, from Wonder Mike of the Sugarhill Gang to Jimmy Spicer to early Chuck D.

Other inspirations came in from all directions. If you're thinking back through the forerunners of hip-hop, you can't leave out Curtis Mayfield, for helping to construct a progressive spirituality out of street thinking on *Super Fly*. You can't leave out Melvin Van Peebles, for pioneering Black independent filmmaking (and inspiring a generation of entrepreneurial and aesthetic breakthroughs) with *Sweet Sweetback's Baadasssss Song*. You can't leave out Bo Diddley. And Maya Angelou. And Nikki Giovanni. And Jayne Cortez. Dick Gregory. And Jesse Jackson. And and and.

Some of the forebears were events, not people. Take the New York blackout of July 13, 1977, when the city went dark and countless pieces of equipment, from turntables to mixers, were liberated in the looting that ensued. There are a million other factors, too, from the way that the punk revolution overthrew the existing rules of rock and roll (and pop and soul), clearing the way for aggressively new thinking, to the specific dynamics of New York club culture, including discos and gay dance clubs. None of this should minimize Herc's party. It's just that hip-hop didn't come from one place, and it didn't go to one place. It went everywhere.

Following it was a challenge, and a pleasure. That process supplies the second invisible word in the title: *Hip-Hop Is (Recurring) History*. I have a theory about hip-hop, which is that you have to keep coming up with new theories. As I see it, change in the hip-hop world starts on the twos and the sevens. What that means is that once rap was up and running, it tended to change every half decade or so, lagging slightly behind the cycle of decades. So hip-hop remade itself over the course of 1982, held steady for a little while, changed again in 1987, held steady, changed in 1992, and so on. In my mind, each half decade is a country unto itself, in many ways. Each has its own drug of choice. The genre first bloomed in the bright light of disco's cocaine years, moved on to the forty-ounce era (1982–1987), then passed through crack (1987–1992), weed (1992–1997), ecstasy (1997–2002), sizzurp (2002–2007), molly (2007–2012), pain pills (2012–2017), and opioids (2017–2022), before arriving in the tragic fentanyl present. As you see, one period ends in the same year the other begins, which makes sense: history doesn't know that you're about to rip the last page from the calendar. There are periods of transition. This book should be read straight through, of course, with feet up on an ottoman, but if you are pressed for time or returning for rereading, you can also pick a single section. These sections, and the periods they describe, aren't just pharmaceutically distinct. Each period had its own style, its own subjects, its own technology, its own culture. There are obviously many minor and even some major changes that happen at unpredictable times and do not respect this schedule. But the twos and the sevens are a useful framework. What is hip-hop without a rhythm?

This brings us to the third invisible word in the title, shorter than "revisionist" or "recurrent," like most words. *Hip-Hop Is History*, true, but if you'd prefer, *Hip-Hop Is (Two) Histories*. From the seventies through the early nineties, I was a hip-hop fan, a kid in Philadelphia who became a tween in Philadelphia who became a teen in Philadelphia who became sort of a young adult in Philadelphia. But there is a point in the early nineties when I put certain parts of my life either behind me or off to the side—jobs I had worked but didn't want, college plans that intrigued me but got in line—and became a professional musician. In hip-hop. From the moment I met Tariq Trotter in school, we moved as a pair toward what turned out to be destiny, and what turned out to be the Roots. Once that die was cast, I was not just an observer of events but also a participant—and even those moments when I was a participant shifted from outsider to insider. In some ways, *Hip-Hop Is History* is about growing into the genre.

Things in hip-hop change every five years, yes, and I am one of those things. If I was an on-the-scene participant from the early nineties onward, I reached a point where I had to step back. Several points, in fact. My approach to the genre that gave me my livelihood and much of my life changed as I aged. I watched new stars come up. I listened to styles come and go. I watched people depart this earthly plane. The pace of growing slowed. Roots, once down in the ground, prevented rapid movement. In my youth, I loved this genre, so much that I willed myself into it. I learned what I could. I tried to learn everything. At some point, I realized what all experts do, which is that their expertise is far more limited than they know. There were subgenres that I didn't fully understand and then subgenres that I didn't even know. I was convinced that I needed to keep my brain flexible. I was going to be Quincy Jones rather than . . . I don't know, my dad. But how would that happen? There wasn't a straightforward playbook. In a way this is a book about aging and my increasing awareness that I would have to learn new ways to learn. And in some ways, then, *Hip-Hop Is History* is also *Hip-Hop Is (My) History*. That's the fourth word, the shortest, and in some ways the sharpest.

So read this book with those invisible words visible in your mind. This book is not an encyclopedia. It can't be an encyclopedia. It would be fifty years long. It is a book, with the length and weight and scope of a book. As I look back across the first half century of this genre, so many figures have come and gone. So when I discuss Biggie primarily in the context of what he represented at the 1995 Source Awards, that isn't to minimize his discography or his skill. When I discuss the Pharcyde primarily in the context of what they (through J Dilla's production) taught me about the role of humanity in hip-hop, that isn't to ignore the joys of their music or their wild stage show. When I have left people out, that isn't to dismiss them as unimportant, only to say that choices had to be made, and these choices—as in the Grammy salute—were subject to the flow of narrative and argument. It's less omission than mission.

Finally, I should mention that one of the most challenging (and interesting) parts of writing this book was finding the right level—not of expertise, but of explanation. I have thought about hip-hop every day, give or take, for the last forty years. Many of those days have also included in-depth conversations. I have touched on some of them within this book. But the conversations didn't need to include background history or additional context, since I was having them with people who were every bit as obsessed as I was. I could just dive right into talking about Slick Rick covers and quasi covers and whether Snoop's "Lodi Dodi" or Mos Def and Talib Kweli's "Children's Story" carries with it more of the spirit of the original (and how Boogie Down Productions' "9mm Goes Bang" and Brother Ali's "Nine Double 'Em" fit into the equation), and it might be a fascinating dive, but one that would resonate with only three to eight readers. A book needs to reach thousands and thousands or else it's just turning out the sounds inside my head. I have taught college classes, so I have learned this lesson before—that sometimes (often) you need to tell other people things that you already know, that the point isn't trying to be the smartest person in the room because you're not even sure what rooms you'll be in, that a common (to me) fact told well can be as satisfying as a new piece of information discovered.

Teaching classes, whether those formal ones or informal ones (social media posts, text chains, the playlists I make for people whether they like it or not), has also taught me that there's a real advantage to giving people parting gifts, not just in the form of insights and arguments, but in the form of helpful recommendations. Each section includes not only history and analysis but also a large list of songs. Consider those lists spurs for further listening. But also consider the fact that even these lists have their rules. In compiling them, I have followed the *Thriller* principle. What that means, in short, is that some songs are too obvious to add to the list. Public

Enemy's *It Takes a Nation of Millions to Hold Us Back* would be near the top of my list of best hip-hop records (most revolutionary in its day, influential over time, most pleasurable to hear end to end), but that doesn't mean that I am going to put ten of its songs on my list for the 1987–1992 period. Instead, I have tried to make picks that will push readers deeper into places they might not otherwise explore.

So that's the rough blueprint for the book. I wish you a smooth—or at least smoother than the Grammys—ride.

—QUESTLOVE, 2023

1979

WHAT YOU HEAR IS NOT A TEST

1982

A new form of music is born, and everyone who witnesses its birth is reborn.

How are new art forms born? First, they are preborn. Rap was a product of what preceded it, and while some of those earlier influences are obvious, others are not as well understood. As I said in the intro, I don't totally accept the Kool Herc party as a hard-and-fast origin story. There were artists before him that did some of the same things that rappers would later do, whether it was raging against the establishment or prioritizing rhythmic vocals over melodic ones. But even artists like Gil Scott-Heron or the Last Poets tell only part of the story. They may have been "rapping" over jazzy musical beds, but they were not exactly part of the direct gestation of the new genre. For that, you have to drop into a disco, and drop in on disco music. I'm speaking here not of the later, watered-down disco that became a go-to move for uninspired record producers everywhere, but the original, pure, awesome disco. I'm speaking of Philadelphia International Records, for example. That music was rejected by much of America for reasons that had nothing to do with its aesthetic quality. It was rejected in part for reasons of homophobia and racism, the fact that it was pushed forward by gay Black producers and DJs. As an underground phenomenon, it was revolutionary and also reviled. That led, on the one hand, to the mainstreaming and watering down of disco and, on the other hand, to an evolution of the music. The first significant evolution was boogie, which was disco's heir in one way and disco's undoing in another. The plan with boogie, I think, was to put the brakes on disco by slowing it down, literally. Boogie's aim was true. Between Leroy Burgess, Kashif, and then Leon Sylvers especially, a form of music evolved that was disco, essentially, but without the same cultural context. That was the music that morphed into rap and then into what we now know as hip-hop. Male MCs felt safe working with it and then working past it. So who made the first rap song? What was the Big Bang of the new genre? It's hard to say, but it's easy to say why it's hard to say. We all know of artists and artworks that stepped forward from all that was there before and identified a new horizon in the process. Remember when Picasso pushed forward the idea that a figure in a painting could be seen from different angles at the same time? Minds. Were. Blown. But in most cases, artistic works evolve along a continuum. What was the first jazz song? Was it "Livery Stable Blues"? Was it "Dippermouth Blues"? How about the first rock song? Was it "Rocket 88"? Was it "Good Rockin' Tonight"? Hip-hop is a genre, and as I have explained, a genre that came not out of nowhere but out of somewhere, and several somewheres at the same time. Because of that, locating the first rap song is not a simple matter. There are at least a handful of works that accelerated the process of peeling away from boogie and minting a new thing. But the absence of historical clarity does not mean the absence of consensus, in the sense that if you stood out in the street with a clipboard and asked a thousand passing to name the first rap song, you'd hear the same answer from the vast majority of them. What answer? Read on.

My sister Donn and I were washing dishes after dinner. We had the radio on, which was not uncommon. This would have been in the fall of 1979. Hurricane David had just ripped through the Dominican Republic, killing thousands. The United States had banned the importation of tuna from Canada. The sports cable network ESPN was a newborn, as was the future rapper Flo Rida (then Tramar Dillard). I didn't know any of that back then. I was eight years old, and all of my available attention was focused on the radio. It was tuned to WDAS, which was classed as an R&B station but which was about to extend that definition in historic ways.

And so, one Thursday evening, WDAS announced and then played a new song by a group called the Sugarhill Gang. At the time, in my mind, I saw it as one word—Sugarhill, like a place—and in fact that's how it would be written on the record. But Sugar Hill was more properly two words. It was named that way for Sugar Hill Records, the label that had assembled, recorded, produced, and released the Gang, and the owners of that label (the husband-and-wife team of Joe and Sylvia Robinson, with interest and partnership from various other industry figures. They did business with some prominent "friends of ours," including the "entrepreneur" Morris Levy, who lent his muscle to help with distribution. For more on those business tactics, consult Fredric Dannen's *Hit Men*) had named it after the Sugar Hill neighborhood of Harlem, a serene and leafy rectangle that runs from 145th to 155th Street, Edgecombe Avenue to the east,

Amsterdam Avenue to the west. It's long been cited both as one of Harlem's crown jewels and as effective counterprogramming for any reductive, racist views of the place. Langston Hughes wrote about it in 1944 in *The New Republic*: "If you are white and are reading this vignette, don't take it for granted that all Harlem is a slum. It isn't. There are big apartment houses up on the hill, Sugar Hill." Named for the sweet life, it inspired the Robinsons when they started their record label.

Initially it was thought of as a disco label, as that was the dominant Black dance music of the time. But one of the acts they signed was a trio from Englewood, New Jersey—right on the other side of the Hudson River from Harlem, less than ten miles away in fact—that didn't exactly do the things that disco was supposed to do. They didn't sing, for example. Instead, they told comic stories over the groove, at great length and with great enthusiasm. By later standards, they weren't virtuosos, and as it turned out, some of the stories they were telling were borrowed from others without permission, not to mention the central bassline. Those are footnotes upon footnotes. The main text, at least back in September of 1979, was their new song, "Rapper's Delight."

My sister and I heard it announced and then we heard it. The effect was instant. It was as if we had been plugged into an intergalactic power source. I was coming in relatively unaware. I was well-versed in music. Even though I was an eight-year-old chronologically, I was musically thirty-two or so—by that point I could name engineers and rhythm arrangers and all the members of the Commodores not named Richie. I knew that the engine moving the song forward was Chic's "Good Times," which had been burning up the radio all summer and had in fact hit number one on the charts in August. But I was unprepared for the presentation. "Now what you hear is not a test," said a man at the beginning, and he was absolutely right. Over the Chic foundation, the three men in the group started talking, but not quite talking; chanting, but not quite chanting. They were doing something new, something that was named by the title. They were rapping. They introduced themselves: Big Bank

Hank, Master Gee, Wonder Mike. They juggled nonsense syllables. They named dances. They told entertaining stories. We were transfixed. We had never heard anything like it. No one had. Usually in those cases, when a song came on the radio that demanded our attention, we would hold a tape recorder up to the speaker to preserve it for posterity—and by "posterity," I mean us. But in this case we didn't want to miss a moment.

I played through an internal debate: run for the tape recorder, risk missing a moment, or stay and hear it all but leave with no proof that this had ever occurred. I made my peace with missing a moment. I ran. I got back with the tape recorder and pressed record right at the moment that Wonder Mike famously reminisced about his recent trip to a friend's house for dinner. He was not satisfied with the cuisine as served: he found the macaroni far too soggy for his taste, the peas too mushed, and the chicken positively ligneous. (That's a word that means "like wood"—I didn't know it back then, and in fact, if I'm being straight, I didn't know it until about two minutes ago. But ligneousness was one of the major ways that the food at Mike's friend's house just wasn't no good.)

If I had turned the radio down during the song—though I never would have done that—I would have heard it being played in homes up and down the block. That night, other kids called me to share the excitement. I have talked often about the way in which white soft rock music was a kind of social lubricant for me in school. Acts like Ambrosia, Air Supply, Dan Hill, Chris Rea—those were the songs that seemed to seep into every corner of the public consciousness. People would be singing them at school. As a result, I had to learn them so as not to be unlearned. They gave me, if not social status, social acceptance. The day after "Rapper's Delight," there was a seismic shift. I went to school after a long night practicing and found that I could re-create the lyrics. More importantly, a few other kids found out that I could. That led to more and more and more finding out. My friend Aantar represented me in this new career: he would get me snacks, or the promise of a few minutes talking to a girl I liked, in exchange for a performance of the lyrics.

The world had been turned upside down. Before "Rapper's Delight," I had known "Good Times" because it was a number-one hit, but mostly my thoughts had bent toward Michael Jackson. *Off the Wall* had dominated our thinking, from "Don't Stop 'Til You Get Enough," a single since summer, to all the other songs that rose into view when the album came out in August. We were doing "Rock With You," "Workin' Day and Night," "She's Out of My Life." This was all before the "Don't Stop 'Til You Get Enough" video, which took over our minds all over again. And then this other thing came zooming in from the sky, like a missile, hit the ground, but when it exploded, there was not destruction but new possibilities. One principle that will come up again and again is the impermeability of virtuosity. Michael had abilities that were not easily transferred to children sitting at home by the radio. We could—we did—try to sing like him, and to dance like him, but that required, as it turned out, otherworldly talent, not to mention years and years of tireless practice. The Sugarhill Gang had a brilliance all its own, but all it required to replicate was a good memory and a night of dedication. I had those. That led to something more complicated and intimate, which was a true shift in identity. I discovered that rap and hip-hop made me popular, but also that I responded to it. It was like a battery snapped into a toy. I saw that I was something different with this kind of music, something more. That meant that to become more myself, I had to acquire it. (I say that "Rapper's Delight" was a beginning, but it wasn't *the* beginning. "King Tim III" by the Fatback Band, the first real rap record, had been out for months at that point, though I would be fifteen before I knew what a Fatback was or gave it its proper due.)

As a kid, you strategize constantly, though you may not think of it in those terms. You may think of it just as living, as being, as surviving. At the time, I was only eight, but I had an older sister who was in high school. A high school girl meant high school boys ringed in a circle around her, with interest in getting even closer. One of them, Stephen Savitz, understood that one of the most efficient ways into Donn's heart was through her adorable little brother. He befriended me. He would take me for food, ask me if there was anything I wanted. Why, yes, there was something I wanted. Stephen and I went to a record store on Chestnut Street, a Listening Booth. I didn't just want the 45. I wanted the long version, the twelve-inch, which ran a full fifteen minutes. Stephen Savitz served as my purchasing agent. It cost $3.17 ($2.99 plus tax). It was the first pressing and it went immediately into my collection, in the sense that it was my collection. It remains there today, amazingly enough. After that, I went back to the record store regularly, so I could transfer new rap singles from store to home. But after that first one, I was on the hook for the cost. Either Donn wasn't giving Stephen enough attention or he had discovered other, better uses for his money: food, say, or records for her. As a result, my primary mission between record store trips was scrounging up enough change. I found coins on the ground. I found them on the counter. I palmed them while pretending to add them to the collection plate in church.

When enough change accumulated, back I went, for whatever else the record store had to offer, in what remained of 1979 and in 1980, too. There was Fatback, again, and "King Tim III," but there was also "To the Beat Y'all" by Lady B, who was one of the earliest Philly rap acts. The song is hard to find today on streaming services, but it was everywhere back then, a moment of true local pride. Everyone of a certain age in that certain place acquired and memorized the record: "I got eighteen years experience I'm the master of karate / I said don't nobody mess with me and I don't mess with nobody." Lady B was also a presence on the radio, where she had a Saturday-afternoon hip-hop show on WHAT 1340 AM. I would tape the entire show, one to four, which helped me line up my record purchasing for future weeks.

I know that I got "Love Rap" by Spoonie Gee. Spoonie was one of the first and best stars of the genre. Born Gabriel Jackson in 1963 in Harlem, he had been raised by his mother and then, after her death in the midseventies, moved in with his uncle Bobby Robinson, who ran a record store and record label. Jackson began to learn his way around MCing. As Spoonin' Gee, he recorded a track called

"Spoonin' Rap" for a label called Sound of New York, USA, and then went back to his uncle's label, Enjoy Records, where he recorded "Love Rap." During that time, he also founded the Treacherous Three with Kool Moe Dee and L.A. Sunshine, but when he became a solo star, they added Special K to preserve their threedom. (It wasn't a demotion, though. Spoonie stayed affiliated with the Treacherous Three, to the point where, when he recorded with them, they were billed as Spoonie Gee and the Treacherous Three.)

I got Funky Four Plus One More's "Rappin and Rocking the House," another Enjoy release by a band that would decamp for Sugar Hill, and a group that featured a pioneering female hip-hop artist—the Plus One More was MC Sha-Rock, born Sharon Green. (Female acts were not uncommon in the disco that preceded hip-hop, and so not that uncommon in the earliest days of the hip-hop that followed disco.)

I got Sequence's "Funk You Up," a Sugarhill release that not only featured a female MC but was by an all-female group—one of the members was future soul superstar Angie Stone, here known as Angie B. They also appeared on "Rapper's Reprise (Jam-Jam)," a label summit record that united them with the Sugarhill Gang and contains one of the best early couplets: "The rap I have controls your will / Which is typical of Sugarhill." They also did a record with Spoonie Gee, "Monster Jam."

I got Disco Dave and the Force of the Five's "High Power Rap." This song sits at the center of various kinds of confusion, at least where record obsessives are concerned. It was sometimes credited to Crash Crew, sometimes to Crash Crew Disco, sometimes to Disco Dave and the Force of the Five MCs (the five consisted of Reggie Reg, Barry Bistro, G-Man, MC La Shubee, and E Mike C—the DJ, DJ Darryl C, counted as neither Dave nor MC). On top of that, this is one of the first examples of rhyming over a record—they didn't want to use a house band so they looped and taped over it. This put them way ahead of most sampling technology, four years or so.

"High Power Rap" came out on Mike and Dave Records, though the group would be on Sugar Hill within the year. But Grandmaster

Flash and the Furious Five also released a track that interpolated the same song: "Get Up and Dance," which had been recorded back in 1978 by a Mississippi-based funk and disco band named Freedom. "Get Up and Dance" was an early star among samples and would continue to be used over the years. De La Soul would use it for the "Buddy" remix, and probably the greatest return would come from SWV's "Anything," featuring the Wu-Tang Clan, on the *Above the Rim* soundtrack. Grandmaster Flash and the Furious Five made good use of it, but the way they credited it was, frankly, insane. The song that they built with the sample of "Get Up and Dance," by Freedom, was called . . . very strange drumroll . . . "Freedom." It would be like Run-D.M.C. recording "Walk This Way" and then calling it "Aerosmith" instead, or MC Hammer recording "U Can't Touch This" and then calling it "Rick James" instead. (Weirdly enough, Sugarhill did it too: the title song of their *8th Wonder* album was based on a song called "Daisy Lady" by 7th Wonder.)

I got "We Rap More Mellow," by the Younger Generation, which Lady B played often on WHAT. The song interpolated Stephanie Mills's "Put Your Body in It," a straight-up funk monster, and illustrated an ironic principle: the more hip-hop tried to move beyond disco, the more disco it sounded. The song not only was a sonic cousin of Grandmaster Flash and the Furious Five's "Superrappin'," but turned out to be the actual Furious Five, minus Grandmaster Flash, and not exactly undercover. They named themselves in the lyrics, one after the other: Melle Mel, Kidd Creole, Scorpio/Mr. Ness, Keef Cowboy, Rahiem. I didn't understand why they weren't credited normally and didn't find out for years. (As it turned out, they were a studio project of the producer Terry Lewis—not the one who would later be in the Time and help mastermind Janet Jackson's career—and had a rotating cast. The Furious Five were only the first performers to step into those Younger Generation shoes.) The song had a section near the end that confused me a little: "We are the best as you can see / So eliminate the possibility / That to be an E-M-C-E-E / Is not a threat to society." I spent maybe more time than I should have untangling that double negative.

I got "The 'Micstro,'" a top-drawer early rap song whose credits also stumped my young brain. The song title was clear enough, even though it had a word in inexplicable quotes. But who was the artist? On the label it looked like Radiänce, or maybe Radiänce featuring DJ "R.C." but I saw other labels that said RC LaRock. Whatever. Didn't really matter. That record hit.

I got Kurtis Blow's "Christmas Rappin'," which was the first rap song to be released by a major label (Mercury) and definitely the song that Argyle would have been listening to in the limo if *Die Hard* had come out five years early.

All of these records went in a bin, one leaning on the other. I didn't always think of it as buying and building history. But it was.

One of the other historic rap songs of 1980 wasn't exactly a rap song. In those days, the genre was coming into focus. There were rap-adjacent sounds in disco, in go-go, in funk. And then there was one glorious New Wave song, if in fact that's what it was. I am talking, of course, about Blondie's "Rapture," which arrived on the earth after Deborah Harry and Chris Stein accompanied a friend to a party. The friend was Fab Five Freddy, born Freddy Braithwaite, a Brooklyn-born graffiti artist with a foot in the music world. Freddy's father had been an accountant who had worked with and befriended jazz artists like Thelonious Monk and Randy Weston. Max Roach was his godfather. Freddy, as a young man, stood at the crossroads of various strands of the emerging hip-hop culture: street art, fashion, and rap parties. Harry and Stein, introduced to rap performance, were hooked, and determined to make a rap song of their own.

The result was "Rapture," which went on their 1980 album *Autoamerican*. The album in general looked back across the history of Black music for inspiration: to blues, to jazz, to reggae. (The first single was a cover of "The Tide Is High," which had been a hit for the Paragons, a rocksteady group with future solo superstar John Holt as lead singer.) But "Rapture," the strangest and longest song on the album, wasn't about the past at all. It was about the future. And people liked the future. The song reached number one.

I bring up "Rapture" not just for its historic credentials, but for its personal significance. I had a cousin who liked walking around, chest puffed out, reciting the lyrics to "Rapture." Except that he thought the song's title was "Fab Five Freddy," because those are the first words of Harry's rap portion. And he also bungled the next lines. The real ones were "Flash is fast, Flash is cool / François c'est pas, Flash ain't no dude." His were garbled. I pointed it out. A point for Ahmir. But then he Flashed back. He had, he said, a twelve-inch of Grandmaster Flash and the Furious Five's "The Adventures of Grandmaster Flash on the Wheels of Steel." I did not have it. "Prove it," I said. He did.

With the proof, we went to my father's turntable, which was like getting into the temple at the beginning of *Raiders of the Lost Ark*—another classic pop-culture product from that same year— and standing in front of the idol. It was equally forbidden to touch. But we touched. And like in *Raiders*, it brought down the entire temple around us. I think I was grounded for a week. And like in *Raiders*, it was worth it. The song is more than the golden idol. It's the ark itself, or maybe the Holy Grail. It's seven minutes of Grandmaster Flash operating a trio of turntables, mixing and scratching his way through a stack of records. One of them was an old spoken-word record that featured the sci-fi hero Flash Gordon. The rest were history. "Good Times" was there, along with "Rapper's Delight," of course, and Queen's "Another One Bites the Dust," whose bassline was inspired by "Good Times"; but there was also a museum's worth of early rap classics, including "Apache," "Freedom," "Monster Jam," and "8th Wonder." There was even a strange late-1960s instrumental, "Life Stories," which had been put together by Robert Moog, the father of the synthesizer. That record opened my mind the way that "Rapper's Delight" had. I started to see that hip-hop was not just a place of clever lyrics and borrowed rhythms and melodies, but an entirely new way to make things. Musique concrète had been around since the 1940s, but not in my house.

We took the record off the turntable. But it never came off the turntable of my mind. For months I tried to re-create what Grandmaster Flash had created, not on my dad's equipment—even I wouldn't have dared do that—but on two little toy turntables that I had in my room. My dad wasn't thrilled. He wanted me to focus on the drums. He was worried that all the turntablism would ruin the records. And he didn't understand how anything new could come from spinning all these old circles.

Okay, so this new genre of rap music wasn't just fun party music. It could be real compositional art. Got it. But no sooner had I understood this than Grandmaster Flash and the Furious Five came back with another record that tipped me into another epiphany. This was the next summer, 1982, when they released "The Message." "They" is a strange term here. The song was credited to the full group, but in reality the verses were written by Duke Bootee and performed by him and Melle Mel. And what verses they were. "The Message" painted a bracing but bleak picture of inner-city America in 1982. Broken glass, the smell of urine, "rats in the front room / roaches in the back," junkies, repossessed cars: and this was just the beginning. The song got more bracing and bleaker after that, as it explored the effects of this poverty, the psychological disabilities, the skewed worldview, the girls forced into the street life, the boys who drifted into violence and crime. The result was a blinkered consciousness, a life as a "stick-up kid," a prison sentence, and a prison suicide. All of it was wrapped in a catchy chorus—"It's like a jungle sometimes / It makes me wonder / How I keep from going under"— and minimalist music. "The Message" landed on me hard. I had never before wanted to listen with such glee to something so bleak and heartbreaking. There had been songs before that explicitly handled social problems. Curtis Mayfield's "Pusherman" had, but the energy of the music and the nonthreat of his falsetto vocals softened the blow. "The Message" softened nothing. It electrified me but it also shocked me. I didn't understand much of what was happening in the song, the realities of street life that were being sketched out. But I thought about the song all the time over the years that followed, and thought about them in sharper focus in key moments. Richard Nichols, the Roots' manager for decades, had a story of his own, from his time, about seeing the movie *Shaft*. He was just a kid back then, around the same age I was when I heard "The Message," and he was growing up, like I would later, in Philadelphia. His older sister went with him to the movie. *Shaft* had many things in it. It had a Black private dick that's a sex machine to all the chicks, for starters. It had crime. It had punishment. It had mustaches. It also had scenes with big buildings in New York that housed mostly Black people. Those buildings stuck in Rich's mind. When the movie ended, he was walking up the aisle out of the theater with his sister. He tugged at her sleeve and asked her if she remembered the tall buildings from the movie. "Yeah," she said, "the projects." Oh, he said, if that's what they're called. "It is," she said. Okay, he said, well, where are the projects in Philly. She laughed. "You live in them, you dummy," she said.

The last minute of the song was especially vivid, and especially bleak. It's a skit where Mel and Cowboy get together on the corner to shoot the shit: trade local gossip, check in with the rest of the group, talk about their plans for that night. The conversation is interrupted by cops. "Freeze!" they say, and then "Get 'em up" (meaning your hands), and then, after being told by Mel and Cowboy that they are down with the Furious Five, "What is that, a gang?" and then, "Shut up," and then, "Get in the car." This final minute of the song was an update of Stevie Wonder's "Living for the City," but again it was so bleak, uncompromising, and so cold at its heart. The first time I heard it, my father heard it, too, and for ten minutes it pulled him down off his anti-rap stance. It also encouraged my father to sit me down for the all-important talk that Black parents have with their kids, the advice about how to navigate the world of law enforcement and its threats. He ticked off a list of acceptable behaviors: speak clearly, keep hands on the wheel, nothing tricky or aggressive, don't give anyone a single reason to think of you as a body to harm.

When Mel and Cowboy talk about their evening plans, they lock in on one in particular. "We could go down to Fever, man. We could see Junebug, man." They mean DJ Junebug at the Disco Fever. The Disco Fever was the hottest Bronx club at the time, and Junebug, born Jose Olmeda Jr., was the place's regular DJ. He was also a drug dealer, one of the early examples of the intertwining of those two worlds, and one of the early examples of how they could come together in ways that were not only ready-for-the-party but tragic. A little more than a year after the release of "The Message," Junebug and his girlfriend Linda, who worked as a bartender at Disco Fever, were murdered. Here's how the news had it, stark and factual: "The tied-up bodies of a Bronx disc jockey and his girlfriend were found in his apartment Sunday, Bronx police said. Jose Olmeda, twenty-four, was apparently stabbed to death in his third-floor apartment at 3540 Decatur Ave., and Linda Harris, twenty, was found drowned in the bathtub." Sometimes you can't keep from going under.

1982

LOVE BOUGHT
YOU CLOTHES

1987

Black America realizes that hip-hop is a new way to talk to ourselves, and the conversation really gets going.

Hip-hop was born out of disco and boogie and became an important post-disco music. We know that because that happened only a chapter ago. But by 1982, innovators were reassessing the foundation of the genre. It was too overgrown, too fancy. Minimalism was coming, and it was coming through Queens. The prime mover of hip-hop during this period, Russell Simmons, was devoted to a stripped-down aesthetic that extended through his music and the fashions of the artists he worked with, the most important being Run-D.M.C. The hard B-boy beats and postures they promoted, more rock-adjacent than dance-adjacent, shifted the ground under hip-hop, changing the way that the music was seen and heard, not to mention bringing in a new audience of urban and suburban teenagers. There were also new lyrical lines being drawn around those changes. We have talked about the way that cocaine defined the earliest era. By a few years into this B-boy era, it had a different status. White lines, don't do it, because this was also the era of the forty-ounce malt liquor bottles. Forties were a staple in Black neighborhoods, in part because of their inherent qualities (size, alcohol content) and in part because inner cities were an explicit target for marketers. The Reagan years were notoriously hostile to inner cities, and hip-hop of this period is filled with observations of, and from, those neighborhoods—artists hanging on stoops, looking around, writing down what they saw even before they could commit it to wax. It was a journalistic duty but also a political one and also an intensely personal one. D.M.C. has discussed his daily ritual of that period: "My routine for the early days was I would get up, go grab my 40 ounce, go to the studio, lay down our records, leave and go home with Joe, and Jay would stay with Larry and Roddie in the studio to put the damn album together." Joe was Joseph Simmons, also known as Run, the group's other MC. Jay was Jam Master Jay, the group's DJ. Larry was Larry Smith, the pioneering hip-hop producer. Roddie was Rod Hui, the engineer and mixer, who was instrumental in those early days. And D.M.C.'s forty ounce was Olde English 800. D.M.C.'s account of his heady early days has a dark undercurrent, of course, because what started as recreational drinking developed into full-blown alcoholism, to the point where he was drinking a case of malt liquor a day by the early nineties, was admitted to the hospital for pancreatitis, cleaned up temporarily, started drinking again, and finally came to terms with his drinking as a symptom of mental illness. But that story comes later: at this point, it is part of his impression rather than his depression. The other main move here was to begin to brand hip-hop as a rebel music. Many early songs were party songs, about inclusion and fun. Run-D.M.C. practiced some level of urban realism, but they weren't looking to be classed as outlaws. Then, in 1985, Schoolly D released "P.S.K. What Does It Mean?" The song, the first blast of what would come to be known as gangsta rap, attracted shock and contempt from the press. The *Los Angeles Times* had a typical reaction: "If parents have bad dreams about the Beastie Boys or Run-D.M.C., Schoolly D is a full-blown nightmare." The same article suggested that there was no daylight between Schoolly D's records and his life, which was a compelling but preposterous theory; when the Beastie Boys met Schoolly D, they were disappointed by his lack of thuggishness. Still, "P.S.K." begat *Licensed to Ill* and Ice-T's "6 in the Morning," one of the first rap songs to have "nigga" in its lyrics, and a million other songs that located hip-hop outside of polite society, even if its practitioners were inside of it. (Ice-T, for example, grew up in upscale communities like Summit, New Jersey, and View Park–Windsor Hills in Los Angeles.) One of the songs that best captures the era, strangely, isn't even a hip-hop song. It's Sting's "Englishman in New York," which is a portrait of the gay icon Quentin Crisp and his life as an elderly man in Manhattan. In the song, Sting tried to illustrate the diversity and energy of the city by moving through different musical landscapes: there's a bit of jazz, a bit of rock, a bit of hip-hop. His take on hip-hop comes just after the two-and-a-half-minute mark, when massive hip-hop drums burst into the arrangement. When I first heard the song, it struck me as super-corny: a big here-comes-trouble moment. But I also remember having conversations with people who said, "Whoever mastered that shit, man, they're going to win music." It distilled the genre down to one single, signal sound. Two decades later, "Englishman in New York" became the basis for a hip-hop adjacent song: the Black Eyed Peas' "Union," featuring Sting. "Union" is a plea for everyone coming together, "all for one and one for all," for erasing difference in the name of world peace. Conspicuously missing from the song: those drums.

Hip-hop was making strides. I was listening to everything I could, and I noticed that rap was going places it hadn't gone before, which meant that it was going places that no one had gone before.

Set course for "Planet Rock."

Back when I was a kid, the local NBC station showed *Soul Train*, which was syndicated at the time, in their 1:00 to 2:00 a.m. slot late Saturday night / early Sunday morning. I went to bed as instructed, right on time, but with the understanding that my clock-radio alarm would rattle me awake at 12:45 a.m. so that I could walk to the TV, watch *Soul Train*, and then climb back upstairs to go to sleep. In theory, that happened immediately. Ahmir walks to bed, Ahmir falls asleep. In practice, I had to be gentled back to sleep by the radio. In those days, 2:00 a.m. radio was the experimental edge of things, where DJs would explore the edge of jazz, world music, and live tracks. They let it all hang out. During those years, I heard a song that was bizarre synth music, completely compelling, pure hypnosis on the airwaves. I tried to tape the song, which was by someone or something named Kraftwerk, but then the *Soul Train* syndication schedule changed and I wasn't allowed to be up so late and that was that. Three years later or so, I was at a neighborhood party, a birthday thing at a local skating rink. Rinks had DJs, and the DJ at this particular rink for this particular party was the older brother of the friend whose party it was. He played your basic roller-skating music, "Celebrate" by Kool and the Gang, "You Dropped a Bomb on Me" by the Gap Band, and then a song that I had never heard before, except that I had heard it on late-night radio after *Soul Train*, more than once. I went to the DJ booth and asked my friend's older brother what that song was. "You want it?" he said. He held out the twelve-inch. "Here." It was "Planet Rock." It sampled the Kraftwerk song I had heard, which I learned was called "Trans-Europe Express." That party and that twelve-inch made my day, my year, and part of my life.

Set course for "White Lines (Don't Do It)."

Released in 1984 by the no-longer-top-of-the-heap Sugar Hill label, the song was credited to Grandmaster Flash and Melle Mel, which was a little short of true. Grandmaster Flash had broken off from the group by then, at least for touring purposes, and he was involved in a protracted legal battle with the label. In reality, "White Lines" was a Melle Mel solo track. It had a driving bassline—furnished by label session player Doug Wimbish, later of Living Colour, covering (without proper attribution) a song called "Cavern" by a band named Liquid Liquid. Even with the bassline, it wasn't a driving song. The white lines were cocaine. The song was about the seductive nature of the high, the economics of the drug trade, and the lack of social justice in prosecuting drug offenses (a street kid gets arrested with drugs, he goes to jail; a rich businessman gets arrested, he's out on bail immediately). I later learned that Melle Mel was still doing coke while he was preaching against it.

As a footnote, years later I was talking with LL Cool J, born James Todd Smith, and he told me that his first idea for a rap name was J-Ski. "Oh," I said. "And?"

He shook his head. "My grandmother wouldn't go for it," he said.

My brain was racing. What did his grandmother have to do with a rap name one way or another? Was she some kind of name genius?

"Because of the drug thing," he said.

Now my brain was losing the race. I had no idea what he was talking about.

"You know," he said. "Ski is snow. And snow is . . ." He paused. I must have looked like a person being asked directions in a language he didn't understand. "And snow is coke."

I think I nodded, but it was like a whole education had been delivered to me all at once. All the ski names were cocaine names? Kool Rock-Ski from the Fat Boys? MC Will-Ski from the Bizzie Boyz? Skee-Lo, who covered the Schoolhouse Rock song "The Tale of Mr. Morton"? Lovebug Starski? Joeski Love? Chill-O-Ski (that's Busta Rhymes's first rap name)? Ski Mask the Slump God? Skiifall? I can't say that all (or any) of these rappers had that thought, but now I had it. It connected to my mind. (Ironically, Big Daddy Kane—more on him later—was not cocaine-related.)

Set course for "I Feel For You."

When hip-hop started to encroach upon the charts, other artists came around to it. "P.I.M.P. the S.I.M.P." on Rick James's 1983 album, *Cold Blooded*. It's credited to Grandmaster Flash, though again, that's just the group name, and it's Melle Mel doing the work. It was a billing issue—record labels wanted to say that they had scored a duet with hip-hop's biggest name, and Grandmaster Flash was still that at the time. (Prince's protégée Ingrid Chavez later reversed the title for a song called "Simp the Pimp," an unreleased Lenny Kravitz diss track she wrote after she claimed he claimed too much credit for writing Madonna's "Justify My Love.")

"Unity," a 1984 collaboration between Afrika Bambaataa and James Brown, was a step further, in the sense that it was a legitimate fusion. Look at the cover photo. It's J.B. and A.B. holding hands. The extended single had six different mixes, and between them were interludes where the two performers made small talk. Even those interludes communicated James Brown's reaction to his excitement at seeing his ship land on another world.

But none of those songs worked the way that "I Feel for You" works. The song, which Prince had originally written for the singer Patrice Rushen, had been repossessed when Rushen turned it down. Prince's version anchored his second album, the eponymous one, in 1979. Three years later, it went back into the female vocalist camp when the Pointer Sisters covered it on their *So Excited!* album. But Chaka's take was something else, meaning something better. She didn't need this song. She was already an icon for the records she made with Rufus, and then all over again with "I'm Every Woman." But how could you resist a bona fide summit with Melle Mel rapping, Stevie Wonder contributing harmonica, and even a sample from "Fingertips Pt. 2"? Arif Mardin is credited as a producer, though I wonder about the contribution of David Frank, from the System. The rumor is that Melle's vocal hiccup at the beginning was a happy accident that got left in. It works as pop. It works as a B-boy anthem. It works as Stevie Wonder update and also Stevie Wonder cameo. It works as Prince popularizer. There's almost no way it doesn't work.

The song went right up the charts in 1984 but hit a wall at number three. Why? The two songs over it refused to budge. Number one was Wham!'s "Wake Me Up Before You Go-Go." Number two, which was itself kept out of the top spot by Wham!, was Prince's "Purple Rain." Right after Chaka's version, another female "I Feel For You" was unleashed upon the world, this one performed by Rebbie Jackson, Michael's oldest sister, on her *Centipede* record. This one restored some of the tempo but had none of the world-advancing synthesis of Chaka's cover, and Rebbie's ad-libs leave more than something to be desired. She had more luck with the title track, written by Michael, which had a creepy-sexy video to go along with it. (Remember how Michael would turn into a panther in the extended "Black or White" video? She turns into a tiger in "Centipede.") "Centipede" also got some play as a future hip-hop sample, turning up on Brand Nubian's "Let's Dance," which featured Busta Rhymes, who would team up with Rebbie's little sister Janet the next year for "What's It Gonna Be?!" I'm not sure, but I know that it's not gonna be Rebbie's cover of "I Feel For You."

In many ways (most?) this period is the story of Run-D.M.C. That story starts in Hollis, Queens, a middle-class largely Black neighborhood whose previous most famous resident was . . . let me see . . . Was it Art Buchwald, the political columnist and humorist who chronicled the ins and outs of Washington, DC, for decades (and also, late in his career, successfully sued Paramount Pictures for boosting his script treatment and turning it into Eddie Murphy's *Coming to America*)? Was it Gloster B. Current, who was the deputy executive director of the NAACP in the 1960s and the owner of one of the coolest names I have ever seen? (The winner of that competition, of course, will always be Thelonious Sphere Monk.) Was it the calypsonian Lord Burgess? Whoever it was before Run-D.M.C., after Run-D.M.C. it was Run-D.M.C. The group was initially ushered into the spotlight of the fledgling hip-hop scene by Russell Simmons. Simmons had a little brother, Joseph, and early on Joseph Simmons worked as a DJ for acts like Kurtis Blow. Even though Joseph was Russell's brother, he came to be known as "DJ Run, Son of Kurtis Blow." Meanwhile, another Hollis resident named Darryl McDaniels got interested in writing rhymes, though he was initially reluctant to perform; he met up with Simmons and the two of them began to hang out in Two-Fifths Park, sometimes rapping, sometimes watching the DJ competitions that took place there. One of the hottest DJs in the park was Jazzy Jase, born Jason Mizell. Simmons (Joseph) and McDaniels kept trying to convince Simmons (Russell) to record them, and though he did, occasionally, he didn't see the upside. College followed high school (Run at LaGuardia, D.M.C. at St. John's), but rap dreams remained, and eventually Russell relented. The result was a debut single, "It's Like That," which came out in the summer of 1983 on a small New York indie, Profile Records. The lyrics, by Run, had been originally written for Kurtis Blow and took a clear-eyed look at the frustrations of urban life, particularly empty pockets. It wasn't as bleak as "The Message," but it was less philosophical, more concerned with daily realities. The first verse started with "Unemployment at a record high," and the second with "People in the world tried to make ends meet." The third verse was even more specific: "Money is the key to end all your woes / Your ups, your downs, your highs and your lows / Won't you tell me the last time that love bought you clothes?" The message was straightforward, almost prosaic, and it was matched by the production by Russell Simmons and Larry Smith—a Queens musician who had played bass on Kurtis Blow's "Christmas Rappin'" and "The Breaks" and partnered with Russell on a number of early hip-hop productions, including Jimmy Spicer's "Money (Dollar Bill Y'all)." (Fifteen years before Diddy did it, Russell appeared on the record, doing the hook.) Smith had been experimenting with more and more stripped-down music, mostly furnished by the Oberheim DMX drum machine with the occasional horn, and Run and D.M.C. traded off lines. (My first encounter with the song came strangely. Sister Sledge made a guest appearance on *The Jeffersons*. They were playing a singing group called the Satins, and they were appealing to George Jefferson to back them. When they were asked to give a taste of their talent, they performed a snippet of "It's Like That." Before that, it had just been that rap song that my cousin Markie listened to. After that, it was legit.)

The B-side, "Sucker M.C.'s," was even more spare musically—no horns here—but lyrically it's a gold mine, a rich oral history of the group's early days. It's subtitled "Krush-Groove 1" because it emerged from the laboratory of Orange Krush, a band that included at various times Smith on bass, Davy DMX on guitar, Trevor Gale on drums, and a variety of other members like Kenny Keys, Eddie Colon, and Ron Griffin (his younger brother, William, would earn fame a little later as the rapper Rakim—maybe you've heard of him). Orange Krush released one single, "Action," in 1982, which didn't do much at the time but has become an important historical artifact. "Sucker M.C.'s" didn't show off the band, obviously, but it solidified their place in history.

The minimalism wasn't just in the arrangements. They were stripped down in other ways, too. Black music through the end of the seventies had been characterized by glam-funk excess: hairstyles, jewels, a surplus of fashion choices. Run-D.M.C. was straight B-boy style: sneakers and tracksuits, chains and hats. They could have come right off the street into the studio or onto the stage. This was the beginning of a revolution of addition by subtraction, and also a complete change in the way that hip-hop songs were conceived and executed. In the earliest days of hip-hop, songs were long. They were songs for parties, for building energy, over six minutes, seven, ten. In construction and spirit, they emerged from the tradition of elongated James Brown jams, of Zapp's "Dance Floor" or Funkadelic's "(Not Just) Knee Deep." "Rapper's Delight," which aspired to pop punch, was nearly five minutes long on its album version, though there was a shorter single edit. (There were longer versions, too, running out over six minutes, seven, one close to fifteen.) "Sucker M.C.'s" was 3:09, started and finished in the span of a traditional hit single, which meant that it could fit comfortably on radio if radio would have it.

"It's Like That" proved that Russell Simmons had been wrong and Run and D.M.C. were right all along, as did the second single, "Hard Times." "Hard Times" had started life as a Kurtis Blow song, co-written by Russell Simmons, that had appeared on Blow's self-titled 1980 album and provided a social-lament template for songs like "It's Like That." Rather than faithfully re-create Blow's song, Run-D.M.C. illustrated their own style, the skeletal music, the shouted vocals. The B-side was "Jam Master Jay," which announced the arrival in the group of a third member: their old friend Jazzy Jase, renamed and ready for battle.

Those singles did well enough to create demand for an album, and Run-D.M.C. complied. Just before the debut was scheduled to come out, they released a third single, "Rock Box." Whereas the first two singles had moved toward minimalism, this one blew that formula up. During the sessions for the record, Run-D.M.C. heard a rock band playing in another studio—it was supposedly the American heavy-metal group Riot—and had a brainstorm that involved inviting in a friend named Eddie Martinez to play hard-rock guitar on the song. The aesthetic move here was clear: by fusing stark B-boy rap and screaming guitar, Run-D.M.C. hit upon a formula that let them appeal directly to middle-class kids (a group that included them), and more specifically, white middle-class kids. They also filmed a video for the song that featured Professor Irwin Corey, a longtime staple on the downtown comedy scene, and that video started getting played on video music channels.

The second album, *King of Rock*, was a breakthrough in many ways. Before it, rap records weren't released on CD. They didn't generally spawn three top-twenty singles (the title song, "You Talk Too Much," and "Can You Rock It Like This"), supply much of the soundtrack for a movie (*Krush Groove*), or go platinum. This time there was also a video with an underground New York comedy figure—Calvert DeForest, who played Larry "Bud" Melman on *Late Night with David Letterman*.

Run-D.M.C.'s "Walk This Way" was born during sessions for the group's third LP. It got underway with a shift in the production team. Run's brother Russell Simmons was still there, but instead of Larry Smith, the new record brought on as a producer Rick Rubin, a Jewish kid from Long Island who had cofounded Def Jam records with Simmons. Rubin was very much a disciple of the Run-D.M.C. sound, to the point that his first production credit for LL Cool J, on the *Radio* album, read "Reduced by Rick Rubin." Before Rubin, Run-D.M.C. may have had the will to target the pop charts. With him, they had the way. During the sessions for the follow-up to *King of Rock*, which would come to be called *Raising Hell*, Rubin took out Aerosmith's 1975 album *Toys in the Attic* and played it for Run-D.M.C., who freestyled over the opening section. (It made sense: Steven Tyler and Joe Perry have both talked about how they were going for something funky, a little bit of New Orleans sound, like the Meters, a little bit of James Brown.)

Rubin encouraged them to create an entire song in that spirit, threading the main riff throughout. Neither Run nor D.M.C. loved the idea, but they soldiered on and made a song. The finished song went on the final track list for the new album, though none of the creators—not Run, not D.M.C., not Jam Master Jay, not even Rubin—thought it had the potential to be a single, in part because they weren't sold on the concept, and in part because an association with Aerosmith wasn't exactly a selling point in 1986. They had mostly fallen apart due to drug issues in the late seventies. Joe

Perry and Brad Whitford both left the band. *Rock in a Hard Place*, in 1982, didn't do much critically or commercially, and the album that brought back Perry and Whitford, *Done with Mirrors*, came out in 1985 to mixed reviews and middling sales. What was Aerosmith in 1986? Not what they had been.

Even with these reservations, "Walk this Way" got picked as a single from the new album. Not the first single: that was "My Adidas," which in my mind remains the strongest song from the album and maybe their best song ever. To me, it was the perfect encapsulation of the Run-D.M.C. formula. Russell Simmons imagined them as a minimalist project: minimalist palette for their outfits, minimalist arrangements for their sound. "My Adidas" was this, which meant that it was no kind of crossover. It was hip-hop in its purest sense. It also led to an amazing moment at Madison Square Garden when Run told everyone in the crowd to hold up one sneaker. Adidas went up. The band had made sure that Adidas executives were in the crowd to see it. The nearly immediate result was the first hip-hop shoe endorsement.

"Walk This Way" came out as a single on July 4. Some people called it a cover version, which didn't quite seem right. A collaboration? A reinterpretation? A whole new song that used parts of a whole old song? But there was an additional wrinkle almost immediately: "Walk This Way" had a video.

Up until then, the video world had been hard for hip-hop artists to crack. MTV had a mostly justified reputation for showing as limited a number of Black artists as possible. If you ask around, you will find an (uninformed) opinion that the number was zero. It was not. There were some. The Specials included Black musicians, and MTV showed their videos. Prince's "1999" was on the channel. Michael Jackson's "Billie Jean," helped along by tactical bullying from the Sony president Walter Yetnikoff, became a major presence, as did all successive Jackson videos. And Run-D.M.C. had even cracked into programming with "Rock Box." All along the way, though, people started to notice that the balance was way off, and some of those people who noticed were prominent white artists with the ears of executives. At some point in the mideighties, David Bowie gave an interview in which he called out the channel on the carpet, wondering why they had such a racially narrow definition of pop music, and Little Steven, trying to pitch the network on his "Sun City" project in late 1985, hinted that his video might be a way of getting multiple Black artists on the channel in one fell swoop.

Even as MTV started to balance itself, Black-and-white-wise, hip-hop was an outlier. Again, it wasn't that the channel considered hip-hop verboten. But the exceptions were instructive. One of the videos in heavy rotation in the channel's earliest years was Blondie's "Rapture," which featured the legendary graffiti artist and downtown staple Fab Five Freddy. "Rapture" was shown during the channel's first day, in fact, which means that Fab was among the first Black performers to crack the programming. Run-D.M.C. had been pioneers here, too. "Rock Box," their 1984 single, had come with a video. A strange video. It opened with a lecture by the comedian Professor Irwin Corey, then in his seventies, where he attempted to explain rap. The monologue was nonsensical and then some, with mentions of the Andrews Sisters, incandescent light bulbs, and fugues. As he spoke, there were black-and-white insets of a young white kid laughing. Was he laughing at Professor Irwin Corey? Maybe, but it turned out that he was also waiting for Run-D.M.C. They arrived in their car, went to a club (Danceteria, on Twenty-First Street), and then performed to a mixed downtown audience—some Black people in the crowd, but lots of white people, including that kid. Along the way, the video attempted some early computer effects, silhouetting the group inside a TV set, isolating them on a blue background, and then swapping their heads. The video, in general, seemed to be trying something that was different from, or maybe even the opposite of, the desired effect of "My Adidas." It was making an argument that Run-D.M.C. was palatable for white America.

"Walk This Way," in its video form, upped this ante. The group shared the screen with Aerosmith, or at least Steven Tyler and Joe Perry. (The rest of the group was played by actors, or musicians from other groups hired to perform the role of Aerosmith for the video.) The video starts in an Aerosmith sound check or rehearsal. The band's next-door neighbors, Run-D.M.C., are pounding on the wall to protest the loud noise. Aerosmith doesn't care. Steven Tyler counts in the song. Joe Perry plays the riff. But just when Tyler is about to sing, Run-D.M.C. starts rapping instead. Hijinks ensue, including a hole punched in the wall, a guitar poked through that hole, and then the two groups uniting onstage. (There's a close-up of the band's Adidas, of course.) The second that video hit, it was clear that Run-D.M.C. would be going mainstream. MTV moved it immediately to the heaviest rotation, meaning that it showed as much as twelve times a day. The song ended up charting at number four, the first rap single to go top ten (it was also a higher position than the Aerosmith original, which had peaked at number ten).

The next song from the album was "You Be Illin'," which went top thirty, and then came another rock-rap track: "It's Tricky," whose video had no downtown comedians in it. Just kidding: it had Penn and Teller, who operate a three-card monte game that takes no prisoners until the frustrated marks call in the cavalry, in the form of Run-D.M.C. (The song, which bit a piece of the Knack's "My Sharona," resulted in legal action twenty years later when the band sued over the use of the sample, claiming that they had never heard "It's Tricky" until 2005. That seems unlikely, though I am not a judge. The case was reportedly settled.)

A few years before, Run-D.M.C. had set benchmarks for hip-hop albums, hip-hop videos, and the cooperative crossover between hip-hop and rock. Now they did it again, at a higher level. Everyone noticed. Part of that everyone was *Rolling Stone*.

I had been an obsessive reader for years. As a music kid in the seventies, it was the big dog, a kind of Bible. In the mid- to late eighties, there was some competition, some of it significant. *Spin* came along in 1985. *The Source* began life in 1988, first as a newsletter. But *Rolling Stone* still had the majority of mindshare, at least when it came to my mind.

Unlike MTV, *Rolling Stone* had never demonstrated any resistance to giving Black artists their due. Tina Turner had been on the cover of the second issue ever, and the cover subjects of early years included Sly and the Family Stone, Miles Davis, Chuck Berry, and Jimi Hendrix, even Sun Ra. They knew what everyone knew, which was that rock music was a melting pot that contained everything from cutting-edge psychedelic guitarists to teen-oriented artists from the fifties to jazz visionaries who were trying to keep pace.

Through the mideighties, Black artists continued to grace the magazine's cover, from Prince to Stevie Wonder to Michael Jackson. Tina Turner was still there, after all those years. Marvin Gaye got a memorial issue after he was shot to death by his father over a missing insurance letter. (It was April 1, 1984, a day short of Gaye's forty-fifth birthday, the cruelest month—and joke—in many ways. Run-D.M.C.'s debut had been out for only a matter of days.)

But even *Rolling Stone* couldn't quite come to terms with the idea of a rap star on its cover. Their hesitance was part of a broader set of concerns that wondered whether this new art form (sometimes it was said with invisible quotes, "art form") might not quite be music in the old guitar-bass-drums sense. And no one really read it as racist in the narrow sense, or could, because what about all those other Black artists? It was helped by the fact that the Black superstars of the time were increasingly making pop-friendly, chart-friendly records intended to stand alongside the music of white superstars. What were the differences and distances when you compared Phil Collins to Lionel Richie? Even Prince, a visionary innovator, noticed when touring behind his *1999* album that certain white rock acts, from the J. Geils Band to Bob Seger, were doing huge numbers on the charts with fairly conventional dance rock or sweeping ballads. That helped to shape *Purple Rain*, where songs like "Let's Go Crazy" and "Purple Rain" responded directly to the sounds Prince heard out on the road (and specifically to Geils and Seger respectively). Hip-hop didn't seem to want to make nice with the mainstream.

Until, of course, "Walk This Way" did. With the video in heavy rotation, not only running alongside white rock acts but prominently featuring one of them, something had to give. And it did.

In December 1986, Run-D.M.C. became the first rap stars to land a *Rolling Stone* cover.

I have written about this cover story before, in my book *Music Is History*, and at length, and so I won't revisit it in great detail here. But I do want to reiterate that the story was strange, in the sense that it spent an awful lot of energy reassuring its readers that the members of Run-D.M.C. were safe Black people whose music could be normally consumed by mainstream white teenagers, don't worry, don't worry. The article took pains to distinguish Hollis, "a neighborhood of one-family homes and well-tended gardens," from "Watts or Harlem." It even took the time out to note that Run was (gasp) capable of filial pride: "'My father is a great person,' says Run, sounding like a true product of the middle class."

To see that issue as a Black teenager in 1986 was exciting at first: here was a historic act, heroes in a new kind of music, breaking through to a broader audience in unprecedented ways. But the more I went through the article, the heavier my heart became. At a distance of nearly forty years, I understand a little better what might have been involved in the article. I have seen the hip-hop world declare itself unthreatening for the benefit of mainstream listeners, with varying degrees of success, and I have also seen the exact opposite, where hip-hop acts stand firm on their guns-and-drugs credentials, sometimes even firmer than firm, exaggerating them cartoonishly for Super Fly points, and try to collect white ears that way. It's a complex issue, but knowing more doesn't make my heart any lighter when it revisits the December 1986 *Rolling Stone* cover story.

The other move, equally important in the context of the eighties, equally offensive in a sense, was to separate Run-D.M.C. from rap violence. In the tour from that summer, there had been incidents in New York and Pittsburgh and Long Beach, California. Sometimes the articles would, when discussing the shows, call them "'rap' concerts," as if that second set of quotations around the word "rap" would help protect white readers. Promoters started talking about pulling back on live shows, to the point where they would eliminate them entirely. The controversy reached Washington, DC. Tipper Gore, the wife of Al Gore and the founder of the PMRC (Parents Music Resource Center), an advocacy group that combed music for especially sexual or violent lyrics (it started with Prince's "Darling Nikki"), told whoever would listen that "angry, disillusioned, unloved kids unite behind heavy-metal or rap music, and the music says it's OK to beat people up." Lots of people listened.

Even Run-D.M.C. listened. But they heard a misdirect and misrepresentation. The violence, they knew, was being caused by gangs in cities who were coming to the show to work out beef with other gangs. The group could have whitewashed the issue entirely to help them with their climb up the chart. But Run handled it directly, calling out the gangs but also declaring that something could be done about them. Moreover, he was already doing it, as he explained to the *Los Angeles Times*: "We've had beautiful shows all over the country. We haven't had any major problems. There are always bad kids in the audience, but I've been touring for four years, and I've never seen anything like this. These gangs are running your town. These weren't our fans. They were scumbags and roaches! These gangs came to try to kill people and get on the news. We played Detroit, which is a tough town, and we got respect from the gangs there. They knew not to mess with us. I got onstage and told them, 'You don't come to fight here. This is my turf and I want respect.' So they cross their hands over their chest and say, 'OK. This is Run's show. I won't mess with anyone till I get outside.'" It's like that.

In the wake of Run-D.M.C., other groups appeared in the sky—or, if they had already appeared, they now became visible as parts of constellations. Superstars create star systems.

The first group to strike while the iron was hot was the Beastie Boys. Point of fact, they struck before the iron was even turned on. The Beasties had begun life, famously, as a New York hardcore band that featured Michael Diamond and Adam Yauch, along with John

Berry (who would leave the band in 1982) and Kate Schellenbach (who would go on to found Luscious Jackson). The name, Beastie Boys, came to them (probably at Berry's suggestion) after a number of other names that reflected a number of other configurations. They were briefly BAN, briefly the Walden Jazz Band, briefly the Young Aborigines. (Later on, they would claim that "Beastie" stood for "Boys Entering Anarchistic States Towards Inner Excellence," but that's retconned. At the time, it was just a name. Some other people have proposed that they invented it so that, if they ever succeeded, they would be shelved in record stores just ahead of the Beatles. As far as I know, this is unproven.) In 1983, they added a third member, Adam Horovitz, and released a single, "Cooky Puss," that was rooted in pre–Jerky Boys prank calling—it opens with the dial tone and the touch-tone going out to a local Carvel. It was mostly just brat-comedy, juvenile jokes about "pussy crumbs," but there were also gestures toward hip-hop, turning the idea of itching into the idea of "scratching," meaning turntabling. There was talking, but not much rapping. Even so, the group liked the direction, and they started to think of themselves as a brat-rock/rap hybrid. That involved hiring a DJ for some performances, and that DJ was none other than Rick Rubin.

Rubin was in the process of cofounding Def Jam, and he started to produce singles for the Beasties at the same time that he was moving the East Coast rap aesthetic forward with acts like LL Cool J and Run-D.M.C. The earliest Beasties singles were among the earliest Rubin productions—"Rock Hard" was second only to T La Rock's "It's Yours"—and they had a similar feel to what Run-D.M.C. was doing over on Profile in one important respect. Back in the early days of hip-hop, everyone had radio-jock-itis; MCs sounded smooth and fluid, like they were holding down a drive-time slot. Run-D.M.C. were the first rappers to yell on a record. Nobody yelled before that. After that, lots of people yelled. The Beasties yelled especially. "Rock Hard" used (without permission) the central guitar riff from AC/DC's "Back in Black," which made it an early example of another Rubin trademark—take the biggest, loudest, dumbest rock riff and build from there. By now, the Beasties were well into the process of re-conceiving themselves as a rap group, which involved taking on new names. Yauch was MCA (as he would explain later in "No Sleep Till Brooklyn": "Born and bred in Brooklyn, the USA / They call me Adam Yauch but I'm MCA"). Diamond was Mike D. Horovitz was Ad-Rock. Early songs piled up. "Rock Hard" had a B-side called "Beastie Groove" and there was also "Drum Machine," a one-off side project credited to MCA and Burzootie (that was Jay Burnett, an engineer and percussionist who played on a billion records, including Arthur Baker productions like Hall & Oates's *Big Bam Boom*).

When the Beasties first appeared, we didn't really know that they were white kids. (By "we," I mean me. Maybe I also mean some of my friends, but all I can say for certain is that I thought this and no one stopped me.) If anything, we believed that they were Puerto Rican. There was something about the nasal quality of their vocals that suggested South Bronx. Those earliest singles didn't clarify matters, and even their first big moment in the spotlight—an opening slot for Madonna on her Virgin tour in the late spring and early summer of 1985—failed to tip off hip-hop fans, who for the most part weren't going to see the Madonna shows. The story of that gig is worthy of a short film all on its own. Madonna's manager, Freddy DeMann, wanted a rap group to open for Madonna, who had been a part of New York's club culture and had an appreciation for the music. He called Russell Simmons and inquired about the Fat Boys, who were riding high on the strength of their debut and readying a sophomore album. Simmons was connected to the group through Kurtis Blow, who produced the records, and he had promoted them, but he was not their manager, when he used a combination of playing dumb and playing smart to move DeMann off the spot. "What about Run-D.M.C.?" he said. It sounds like a no-brainer when you say it that way. But Run-D.M.C. were stars with a star price, and when the dust settled, Simmons had sold DeMann on another group: the Beasties. They opened those shows with a half hour set of a half dozen songs. Rubin was onstage as a DJ. They antagonized the audience and got them ready for Madonna.

That was 1985. Then it was 1986, and they had an album on the way. The first single was "Hold It Now, Hit It," which included two distinct versions of the song, the one that would end up on the forthcoming album and the one that changed the world. That's the so-called "Acapulco" version (it's a willfully snotty corruption of a cappella, meaning that it stripped out the music and kept their vocals). The opening of the song is lifted from Kurtis Blow, specifically from the first few lines of Kurtis Blow's "Christmas Rappin'" (a poetic voice starts reciting Clement C. Moore's "'Twas the Night Before Christmas," and Kurtis interrupts with "hold it now, hold it—that's played out"). The Acapulco version kept the horn bridge, which was lifted off Kool and the Gang's "Funky Stuff," but other than that it was just the three Beastie voices. But that was plenty of music. You had Ad-Rock furnishing the high end, Mike D in the middle, and MCA holding down the bottom. That version—raw, propulsive, using existing hip-hop techniques but also trying something new— captured DJs so completely that most people never got to hear the flip, which was the album version. When they did, they were—and by "they" I mean me—disappointed beyond belief. What were these drum machines strung like cobwebs over this perfect song? I hated that sound. Years later, I bought the drum machine that Rick Rubin used, not for a Garden of Evil, but because deep down I felt bad for it. It wasn't trying to hurt anyone.

That first Beastie Boys album came out in November 1986, six months after *Raising Hell*. It was a thunderbolt. Two extra singles, "Paul Revere" (a story of the Beasties' origin cowritten by Run-D.M.C.) and "The New Style," had preceded the album's release, and they had done some damage on the dance/R&B/hip-hop charts, but the big moment came about a month after its release, with its fourth single, "(You Gotta) Fight for Your Right (to Party!)." It went top ten on the charts and became an anthemic distillation of everything that the Beasties represented: bratty partying, sticking it to authority, being loud and crude and hilarious. In addition, it made it permanently clear that the group wasn't Puerto Rican, which also made it clear that hip-hop was having its Elvis moment, meaning that it had located white stars who could carry the music to places it hadn't previously gone. The Beasties weren't tourists. They came to rap genuinely, if through a different path than other acts. And they were mindful of their connections, their community, and the (still-new) legacy of the genre—the album included not only "Paul Revere" but also another Run-D.M.C. song, "Slow and Low."

While the Beasties embraced the connection to Run-D.M.C., other groups diverged, either purposefully or accidentally. Boogie Down Productions revolved around the friendship of the MC KRS-One and the DJ Scott La Rock. KRS-One, sometimes Blastmaster KRS-One, was Kris Parker, except that he was really Lawrence Parker, and Kris was already a nickname, short for "Krishna," because people thought he was always seeking spiritual wisdom and had taken an interest in Hare Krishnas. Part of that spiritual searching may have come from his rough childhood: his Barbadian father hadn't been around during his childhood and he bounced from home to home, mother's boyfriends, stepfathers, repeated domestic abuse, until he set out on his own when he was sixteen. La Rock was Scott Sterling, also a child of divorce but more stable and successful, a standout both academically and athletically. In fact, La Rock had already been off to college, at Castleton State in Vermont, where he was a varsity basketball player, and was back home after graduation, working at the Franklin Armory Men's Shelter in the Bronx. That's where he met KRS-One, who was living there. The two of them became friends and then creative partners, and they soon added Derrick Jones, aka D-Nice—he was from the Sterling side of the equation, sort of, a cousin of a security guard at the shelter.

Despite the relatively wide age difference (La Rock was three years older than KRS-One, who was five years older than D-Nice), the group started making music. More importantly, they started making Bronx music. They released the single "South Bronx," a declaration of location and of purpose. The song wasn't a standalone, but a response to MC Shan, a Queens rapper who had released "The

Bridge," produced by Marley Marl, the year before. "The Bridge" sung the praises of MC Shan's neighborhood and his borough, and KRS-One took offense. Were the Queens rappers suggesting that they were the ancestral home of hip-hop? Because everyone knew that was the Bronx. KRS-One, never particularly subtle, laid out the issue cleanly in "South Bronx": "So you think that hip-hop had its start out in Queensbridge / If you popped that junk up in the Bronx you might not live."

The Juice Crew was no stranger to beef and answer records. Back in 1984, a Brooklyn posse of rappers and dancers, UTFO, had released "Roxanne, Roxanne," a song about a young woman's reluctance to accept their overtures. The group's name stood for Untouchable Force Organization. (Yes, I know, what's the *T* for? Well, a British hard-rock band had already taken UFO, so they added the some-what pointless *T*.) UTFO subsequently canceled a TV appearance on a show produced by various Juice Crew members; Marley Marl and Mr. Magic, among others, were inconvenienced and annoyed. A fourteen-year-old girl overheard their conversation, stopped to chat, and the three of them cooked up an answer record, "Roxanne's Revenge," in which the fictional character from the original song mocked UTFO. UTFO pushed back with "The Real Roxanne," in which the Roxanne character was voiced by Elease Jack, and after that it became an open-source war. Every local producer or female MC got into it, and there were dozens of Roxanimosities aired out. The whole thing was an unprecedented mix of open-source dozens, viral before there was such a word, and one of the most enjoyable early chapters in hip-hop history. The Bridge Wars, as they came to be called, were something different, one region asserting itself against the claims of another region, which is also the definition of war. And yet, what's wrong with regional pride and an insistence on accurate history?

Bridge conflict intensified. MC Shan released "Kill That Noise," which didn't mention Boogie Down Productions by name but made several references to the conflict ("Those who try to make fame on my name die," "If you knew at the time what you were saying / You wouldn't be on your knees, praying"). By that point, Kris and Scott had put an entire album together, *Criminal Minded*. Kris has always made a big deal about the fact that Boogie Down Productions was the first rap group holding guns on their album cover. But really what he was doing was taking a different kind of shot, putting reggae into the mix as a compositional element. Hip-hop had always been rooted in island music and Afro-Caribbean identity, from Kool Herc (he came from Jamaica) to Grandmaster Flash (Barbados) to KRS-One himself (also Barbados). Figuring out how to introduce dancehall rhythms into hip-hop paved the way for Slick Rick, among others.

Even though the musical blueprint spanned the globe, the album's concerns were often local. One of the standout songs was "The Bridge Is Over," which not only bit back at Queens but actually sampled "The Bridge." At the end, KRS-One has a message for them. In some ways, it's par for the course for hip-hop beef, though he was establishing the formula: you're old, you're tired, your music is bad, you'd better stick to bragging about your sneakers. What makes the whole thing at least a little strange is that it is set to the melody of Billy Joel's "It's Still Rock and Roll to Me," the most mainstream of mainstream rock/pop songs. The song's not sampled but it's essentially reperformed with KRS-One's lyrics instead of Billy Joel's. The conflict fizzled a bit after that, though other artists tried to get involved.

(As it turned out, the beef wasn't just about regional pride. It was at least a little bit about personal pride. Even before Boogie Down Productions was a going concern, Kris and Scott had made a demo called "$ucce$$I$the Word" and had played it for Mr. Magic. Mr. Magic brushed it off brashly. He rated it as less than nothing. That, even more so than the idea that history might be misrepresented, pushed Kris forward into beef. I finally asked D-Nice to play me that legendary demo. It was horrible. BDP was doing a not-very-credible pop rap, kind of like the Force MDs or the Fat Boys. Damn, I thought. Kris wanted us to go through life thinking he played this futuristic paradigm-shifting classic for Mr. Magic and he hated it? Mr. Magic was right!)

In part, of course, the conflict ended because real life happened. D-Nice was jumped by some men who thought he had been creeping on their girls. He was the youngest in the group, remember, still only a teenager, and he sought out Scott La Rock, then twenty-five, to help settle the matter. D-Nice and Scott La Rock and some of their friends drove to the Highbridge Homes to find the guys who had jumped D-Nice, and then drove home. Shots were fired at their Jeep. La Rock bumped his forehead on the dashboard in the confusion, unaware that he had in fact been shot in the back of the head. He was brought to Lincoln Hospital, just a few miles away, but died.

Boogie Down Productions lasted for a little while, essentially as a KRS-One solo project. The second record, *By All Means Necessary*, also showed Kris with a gun. The difference is that this was a historical gun. Kris was posing like the famous photo of Malcolm X, whose famous quote, slightly misquoted here (Malcolm said, "By any means necessary"), gave the record its title. The contents followed suit, with more socially conscious songs like "My Philosophy" (in part a memorial for La Rock), "Stop the Violence" (self-explanatory), and "Jimmy" (a pro-condom song in the age of AIDS).

But it wasn't all big thinking. In "My Philosophy," Kris questioned those who were commercializing hip-hop, rapping, "It's not about a salary, it's all about reality." Some people felt that he was criticizing Run-D.M.C., not his original Queens nemesis, but a Queens nemesis nonetheless. That theory was supported by another song, "Nervous," where the Run-D.M.C. connection was more overt. By this point, Run-D.M.C. had gotten their endorsement deal with Adidas. Kris mocked them by opting for another brand. "How many people got Nikes on?" he asked. "If you got your Nikes on, put your feet up in the air. / If you don't got Nikes on / I think you need to keep your feet down." This probably had less to do with Kris's own brand preferences than with the fact that the tide had turned in the sneaker world thanks to a Brooklyn-born, North Carolina–raised basketball player named Michael Jeffrey Jordan. Air Jordans had debuted in 1985 and quickly taken over the shoe world.

KRS-One continued to release records under the BDP name and then under his own name. In 1990, on a record called *Edutainment*, he released a track called "Beef" that questioned the karmic (and medical, and financial) wisdom of eating cows. By then he was a vegetarian, occasionally pescatarian, a lifestyle he has continued to advocate for. But was he talking only about meat when he said, "When will this poisonous product cease"?

New York–area rap classics were stacking up quickly back then. In 1986, the same year as "South Bronx," a duo from Long Island called Eric B. and Rakim released a single called "Eric B. Is President." Eric B., Eric Barrier, was the DJ and provided the music. Rakim, born William Michael Griffin (he was close to the famous R&B singer Ruth Brown) was the rapper. The single, recorded at Marley Marl's home studio, was like nothing everyone had ever heard but was, at the same time, everything everyone wanted.

Eric B. had no shortage of innovative musical ideas. He was the first to use Fonda Rae's 1982 deep funk cut "Over Like a Fat Rat," which turned up later on songs by De La Soul, Grand Puba, Kool G Rap, and others. This isn't surprising. He had started without Rakim, working as a DJ, sometimes on the air at WBLS, and put out a call for an MC to round out his project.

Rakim answered the call and then some. Lyrically, the song was nothing revolutionary, though as it hit its marks—declaration of lyrical prowess, claims of superiority over the competition—it did so with a high level of skill and dexterity. The opening couplet ("I came in the door, I said it before / I never let the mic magnetize me no more") announced them by way of suggesting that they had been around for a while (not true) and that they were capable of a scientific precision (true). Tangled up in the narration of process was a pop answer record. Janet Jackson's "What Have You Done for Me Lately" had been released earlier that year, and it wasn't received as a simple pop record. The music, and especially the drum sound, was hard enough to take seriously, which meant that it was hard enough to push back against. "Eric B. Is President" suggests that Janet's song was misguided in its relationship dynamics, that she wasn't just asserting control but acting entitled. "She was comin' on like she's a goddess from above and that got me real upset," Rakim said in an interview later on. "Every time I heard it, I'd get real mad. I did not appreciate that one little bit." Rakim's response: "But now it's out of hand 'cause you told me you hate me / And then you ask what have I done lately." And then, later, and arguably better: "You scream I'm lazy, you must be crazy / Thought I was a donut, you tried to glaze me." It's couched as an insult but really it's a way of giving flowers. It was a record that sounded as good as hip-hop, which meant that it got taken personally.

As much as the song landed musically and lyrically, Rakim's rapping style was the true paradigm shift. Just as Run-D.M.C. banished outsize fashion, Rakim banished outsize vocalizing, either the radio boom or the B-boy yell. He was monotone and emotionless, almost surgical. He might say that he's angry but you have to listen to hear him say it. Rakim's technique, unprecedented and unparalleled, created the idea of flow. Run-D.M.C. had plenty of things, but flow was not one of them. They had punch. Rakim was like a snake sliding down an incline, except that he was sliding up it. (And it almost never happened. The rapper Freddie Foxxx was supposed to come over to Marley Marl's that day to record, but he didn't. Rakim stepped up. Marley Marl didn't quite hear it. Who was this monotone rapper with the charisma shortage? He handed over the reins to MC Shan and went into the other room to watch a game.)

More than maybe any other rapper from that era, Rakim attracted the attention of scholars. Adam Krims, the famed hip-hop musicologist (his name is also an anagram for "As Rakim, MD," which doesn't mean anything unless it means everything), has discussed at length the way that flow is one of the truest measures of development and evolution in hip-hop, and that changes in flow permit fans, both casual and die-hard, to separate one period from the period before it. By that standard, Rakim was a watershed, maybe the most influential single artist until . . . hard to say, in part because I'm too close to the river. Biggie? Eminem? (Dark horse candidate: Snoop.) Rakim had his own perceptive analysis of his style, explaining that he was drawing on the playing of John Coltrane, which he had heard often from his father's record collection (in fact, the young Rakim had played saxophone) and which had taught him to move around within a solo while still respecting the overall rhythm and melody. For years, Rakim topped lists of all-time MCs, in part because hearing that first album was like hearing the future. In fact, and this is a major flash-forward, the disdain that some people have for modern rap here in the 2020s—including Future—should at least acknowledge that all they are doing is picking up what Rakim put down and reupholstering it for a post-codeine-and-Percocet universe.

The single was so impressive that the group was immediately signed to 4th and B'way, part of Island Records, and went to work on a debut album at Power Play Studios in Manhattan. *Paid in Full*, which came out in the summer of 1986, included "Eric B. Is President," but also a number of other instant classics: the title track found the duo explaining their financial situation with documentary specificity, naming their agent, management company, record label, and more. The cover image showed them wearing heavy chains and Gucci knockoffs created by Dapper Dan (who called them "knockups," suggesting that the copy had something that even the originals did not).

In retrospect, Eric B. and Rakim, especially on that first album, are seen as James Brown–derived, and it's true that they were one of the first rap groups to make the most of the Godfather of Soul. "I Ain't No Joke," the second single, used the J.B.'s "Pass the Peas." "I Know You Got Soul," the third single, sampled the song of the same name by Brown's first lieutenant Bobby Byrd. (Interestingly, "I Know You Got Soul" is a masterpiece of unexpected reversals. It samples both James Brown and Funkadelic. If I told you that and then followed up with a quick quiz, you would think that the drums would come from the Brown camp and the guitars from the P-Funk camp, Stubblefield or Starks from the former and Hampton or Eddie Hazel from the latter. But this song was Bobby Byrd's guitar and

P-Funk drums.) The song "You'll Like It Too" is from *Connections & Disconnections*, the Funkadelic album that Fuzzy Haskins, Calvin Simon, and Grady Thomas made without George Clinton. It led to all kinds of claims and counterclaims, some in court, about who owned the group's name and spirit. In other words, how do you know who's got soul? Eric B. knew, and he knew that he knew.

1987

**BACK IS THE
INCREDIBLE**

1992

It becomes clear that hip-hop is talking not just to Black America, but to everyone in America, and that much of America is talking back.

"This is the dope jam," Chuck D says at the beginning of "Night of the Living Baseheads," which was tucked away on the second side of Public Enemy's landmark second album *It Takes a Nation of Millions to Hold Us Back*. No sooner has this dope jam started than it shifts into sociology: "Let's define the term called dope. / And you think it mean funky now, no. / Here is a true tale of the ones that deal are the ones that fail." Rather than offer up a party jam or even a small-scale portrait of the MC's best friend/girlfriend/mother/neighborhood bully, the song took an unflinching view of the crack epidemic that was in the process of gutting urban Black communities. What had caused these problems? How deeply rooted were they? Could they be solved? Why was it no longer possible to look away? When people called hip-hop, and especially groups like Public Enemy, the "Black CNN," this is the kind of song they were talking about. And "Night of the Living Baseheads" wasn't just an album track. They believed enough in the mission and the message to release it as a single, the album's fourth, after the unassailable first trio of "Rebel Without a Pause," "Bring the Noise," and "Don't Believe the Hype." The idea that the Black community was at risk from within was bracing, a powerful update of songs like "The Message." Public Enemy's broadside came at a time when there were various theories about how drugs arrived on corners and stoops. Was it years of PTSD and economic privation leading to a psychological prison and self-medication, or was it a more diabolical plot to cripple Black Americans by flooding their neighborhoods with a new form of enslavement? Public Enemy never got too far from a self-empowerment message, not even when describing social poisons—"Night of the Living Baseheads" opens with a sample of Dr. Khalid Muhammad, the so-called Truth Terrorist who represented both the Nation of Islam and the Black Panthers: "Have you forgotten that once we were brought here, we were robbed of our name, robbed of our language. We lost our religion, our culture, our God . . . and many of us, by the way we act, we even lost our minds." These snippets of dialogue were hardly accidental. The hip-hop stars of the late eighties weren't just witnesses to the plague that was gutting their communities. They were also the children of the SNCC and Black Panther activists of the sixties—sometimes the spiritual children and sometimes the actual children—and many were highly educated. Public Enemy, for example, came together in and around Adelphi University. The eighties might have been a crisis point for Black America, but it was also an opportunity point: there was upward movement along with the downward pull. This tension produced heightened art, both lyrically and sonically—in the search for new sonic palettes that could paint these more complex portraits. This isn't to say that hip-hop didn't get popularized during this period. It did. It isn't so that it didn't get watered down, too. It did. But the highest achievements of the genre got higher and higher. To some degree, this kept the focus on the East Coast. I think about jazz, and the ways in which East Coast jazz was generally considered to be dense and brilliant, while West Coast jazz mostly drew a shrug for its lighter approach. This is an instructive if reductive way to think about this period of hip-hop, in part because some of the East Coast innovators had close ties to jazz history—the jazz singer Ruth Brown was close to Rakim's family, and Nas (who would debut with his *Nasty Nas* mixtape in this period but come to maturity in the next frame) was the son of the jazz trumpeter Olu Dara. Jazz was about wrestling with difficulty and finding the beauty and power that could result. This was the footing, too, for hip-hop in this period. What was born from this bleakness was perhaps the greatest creative period for hip-hop. Artists were refining their approaches and consolidating the gains of earlier experiments. The genre was evolving at the speed of sound.

I n the summer of 1988, the Harlem rap duo of Rob Base and DJ E-Z
Rock released "It Takes Two," another hip-hop song powered by
a vintage James Brown sample. It featured not the funky drummer,
Clyde Stubblefield, but the other drummer, Jabo Starks, drumming
under vocal hook by Lyn Collins.

"It Takes Two" started out as a legitimate rap song that I heard
on Lady B's Friday-night show. That was the only place I heard it
at first. Then it was on *Yo! MTV Raps*, which was higher visibility
but still part of what you would call a subculture. Then, somehow,
Spin magazine named it as the top song of 1988. That gesture, which
I saw as a bit of clout chasing, somehow cemented it as a pop song.
Was it one?

There is no real consensus on what constitutes pop rap. I always
start with the idea that it's the rap that you are allowed to play in
front of your parents. This may be hard to fully understand from a
distance of decades, but in the early days of rap, the music was so
taboo that it was damn near like listening to Richard Pryor records.
In 1984, I remember having to sneak into an unpatrolled area of the
house to listen to UTFO's "The Real Roxanne," and the only cursing
in there was at the end of the song: "All you received was a kick in
the ass." When you hear the word "conservative" now, you think
of Fox News, flyover country, the white working class. To me, Black
people, especially born-again Christian Black people, were so much
more conservative than any of that. A group like Run-D.M.C., with

their big beats and forty-ounce bottles, was too much, even though the guys in the group came from stable middle-class families. There was a line and they stepped over it.

In the mideighties, hip-hop groups started to play around with the idea that there might be poses and styles that would not scare away Black families. The first big group that answered this question was Whodini. They came out of Brooklyn, had a relationship with UTFO, were managed by Russell Simmons, and were on the scene early, with the "Magic's Wand" single in 1982 (produced by British synth-pop pioneer Thomas Dolby). Their real breakthrough was not their self-titled debut, but their second record, *Escape*, in 1984. The singles started to appear immediately: "Friends," "Freaks Come Out at Night," "Big Mouth," "Escape (I Need a Break)."

But what was the group, exactly? Harry Allen, the minister of information for Public Enemy, once wondered if the Roots were hip-hop's softest group or R&B's hardest group. I can't answer that question, since it's about me, but I can say that the same question applies to Whodini. They came along at a time Jam and Lewis were making R&B edgy with beats for the S.O.S. Band and Alexander O'Neal and Cherrelle. "I Didn't Mean to Turn You On," which Cherrelle put out in 1984 and was later covered by Robert Palmer, is a perfect illustration of their style and technique of the time. Whodini, despite being categorized as rap, was quasi-interchangeable with those records. Even more to the point, Whodini took an everyman's perspective. "Freaks Come Out at Night" is not a novelty record, exactly, but it's a perfect portrait of nightlife by someone who's in it but not of it. There's bourgeois morality—look at those freaks— that is even more present on "Escape (I Need a Break)," which has a narrator who takes the train to work, gets coffee spilled on his shirt, and laments that his raise hasn't arrived after three years. There's a Rodney Dangerfield–crossed-with–*Office Space* vibe to it. And then there was the way the group dressed, which took them closer to a funk-pop band like the Gap Band than to the punky street style of early rappers. Subjects your parents can understand? Check. Clothes your parents can understand? Check.

Getting the sign-off from parents is part of the game. Another important part is reaching mainstream radio. Salt-N-Pepa's "Push It" might be the first authentic rap song that started on pop radio. You wouldn't have heard it played on Mr. Magic's Rap Attack or Lady B's Street Beat. It came out the box as a pop song, and stayed that way. All the girls at school with big hair that had *Slippery When Wet* stickers and were drawing hearts that ampersanded their names to Richie Sambora's, those were the girls who were singing "Push It." They didn't go deeper into the S&P portfolio. Salt-N-Pepa had another song, "Part II at Warp Speed," that was the B-side of "Beauty and the Beat." I heard that song on Black radio way more often than I heard "Push It." I was also, at the time, working at a record store, so I saw the effect in another way. I saw who came to the store and left carrying "Push It" under their arm.

"Push It" started a pop trend. Every group started putting at least one song on their record that seemed like they were reaching for that brass ring. Sometimes it worked, sometimes it didn't. I wasn't convinced by "You Had Too Much to Drink," which EPMD buried at the end of side two of *Unfinished Business*. Come on, dog. You got rock guitars. Just admit that you are trying for a pop move. You don't have to use PSA baffling to soften the blow.

That same year, 1986, marked the debut of another important early pop-rap group, though their early evolution is worth a closer look. And I had a closer look, since they came from Philadelphia, at DJ Jazzy Jeff and the Fresh Prince. DJ Jazzy Jeff (Jeff Townes) had met the Fresh Prince (Will Smith) at a party a few years before. They created their first song and put it out on a local label, Word Up Records. The rest wasn't quite history, but it was starting to be.

That song, "Girls Ain't Nothing but Trouble," featured an infectious sample from the *I Dream of Jeannie* theme. (Separate book idea: all the rap songs that sample TV themes. Right now in my head I am hearing Cam'ron used *Magnum P.I.* Doug E. Fresh and Slick Rick used *Inspector Gadget*. Outkast used *Police Woman*. Jay-Z used *The People's Court*. Busta Rhymes used *Knight Rider* [which got reused by Panjabi MC (which got reused by Jay-Z)]. Book will be out in 2028.)

From a narrative perspective, "Girls Ain't Nothing but Trouble" is a specific achievement. The year before, Slick Rick—performing at that point as MC Ricky D, over an instrumental by the beatboxer Doug E. Fresh—had released "La Di Da Di." It was a "this is my day" narrative, sort of a hip-hop take on the Beatles' "Day in the Life." Slick Rick told his tale in first person: he woke up, got out of bed, didn't drag a comb across his head but instead put some soap on his face and his hand on a cup. His style was perfect, loaded up with wit and cool. He sounded like he had total confidence that you would listen to the story until the end—and you did. (I have written about my "La Di Da Di" experience before. In 1985, I spent the summer in Los Angeles, visiting cousins, but I was also visiting my cousins' radio station, KDAY, which was playing hip-hop around the clock. That was a revelation, proof that this new genre was stepping up to the point where it could sustain not just an overnight or weekend slot, but an entire format. In LA that summer, one of the songs that was in heavy rotation was "Batterram," by Toddy Tee. "Batterram" was the unofficial name of the B-11, an armored LAPD vehicle with a battering ram mounted on front. If the cops wanted to get in, they were getting in. I had never heard of it before I heard the song, but after I heard the song dozens of time that summer, I was an expert. I brought news of the song, and the word, back to Philly, where I was greeted with blank faces. No one there knew what I was talking about. They had never heard of a batterram, or Toddy Tee, or the song that the latter made about the former. But the reason was interesting. "We don't know that song," one of my friends said, "because we know this song," and then they played me "La Di Da Di.")

As groundbreaking as "La Di Da Di" was, Slick Rick didn't capitalize on this break right away. He signed to Def Jam but his debut wouldn't come out until 1988. Space opened up and the Fresh Prince stepped into that space. And yet, when "Girls Ain't Nothing but Trouble" first came into my household, it was beyond taboo. I had to listen with the volume down. I might as well have been playing "Gangsta Gangsta" by N.W.A. In the original single, the Fresh Prince did more than borrow Slick Rick's story-of-my-day framework. He also took the slickness. He was still in high school, but he was the smoother-than-he-seemed kid who might stay behind for "extra help" and fuck the teacher. That's not part of the song, but there's sex in it, and a part where he's in a bar (repeat: he was still in high school). It was a borrowing, in a way, of the horniness of the other Prince, who released "Kiss" that year. (Interestingly, when the other Prince passed away in 2016—an event still so devastating that I have to put it in a parenthetical buffer—MTV aired a video marathon in tribute. Every song was a Prince song, obviously, except that this song somehow snuck in. It's probably just a simple matter of a mindless keyword search, but I like to believe that it was some kind of curation from beyond.)

The song also uncovered a winning formula, which is that your hero needed to take a pie in the face. It's not quite vulnerability, but it's something. No other rapper would do that. Rap was moving into romance in different ways—LL Cool J's "I Need Love" came out around the same time, but this was a specific take on the matter. The second song on that record, and the second single, "Just One of Those Days," solidified the formula. It sampled Taco's version of "Puttin' on the Ritz," but it was really a spirit remake of MC Breeze's "Discombobulator Bubalator." "Discombobulator Bubalator" was a huge hit in Philly, and a great record. But it had a third verse that was unfortunate, in that it had a scene where Breeze tried unsuccessfully to order Chinese takeout and mimicked the guy from the restaurant. We had a local newsperson, Loraine Ballard Morrill, who spoke up against the caricatures in the song. Jazzy Jeff and Fresh Prince picked up the baton. "Just One of Those Days" was another series of pies. The first verse was boilerplate: went to school, made a pass at a girl, got in trouble. In the second verse, he tried to get to work, couldn't start his car, stole a kid's bike, got in a crash, went to jail, only to realize that it was Saturday and he didn't have to be at work.

Will Smith's journey to superstardom has a long, winding history before it gets to *The Fresh Prince of Bel-Air*. That sitcom was inspired by the life of the producer Benny Medina, whose fortunes had changed in his teens when he went to live with a wealthy friend in Beverly Hills. Medina attracted the notice of Quincy Jones at around the same time that Smith attracted the attention of Medina. A deal was quickly put together with Smith, Jones, and the writer Andy Borowitz and his wife, Susan, who would be credited as co-creators of the show. *The Fresh Prince of Bel-Air* was fast-tracked, debuting in September of 1990.

As nineties sitcoms go, *Fresh Prince of Bel-Air* had some success mainstreaming rappers. Guest stars included Heavy D and Queen Latifah (though Jones's involvement meant that it also had mainstream music cameos from people like Al B. Sure, Don Cornelius, Boyz II Men, Branford Marsalis, and Jones himself). Two years after *Fresh Prince*, a sitcom came along with a stronger hip-hop sensibility: *Martin*, which starred two actors who had featured in supporting roles in *House Party*, Martin Lawrence and Tisha Campbell. In *Martin*, Lawrence starred as a radio personality, which gave the show the opportunity to cast a series of rappers as themselves, including the Notorious B.I.G., MC Hammer, and Snoop (then Doggy) Dogg. But the show also had a hip-hop sensibility to the point where actual roles were played by rappers, including Method Man and Yo-Yo.

Extended television digression over. Back to the albums. While "Nightmare on My Street" was the first track on *He's the DJ, I'm the Rapper*, and "Brand New Funk" was the first single, the most important song, historically, was "Parents Just Don't Understand." People may know it from *Fresh Prince*, where it was mentioned more than once, and where it seemed to be a kind of guiding subtext for the entire show, but it began life as yet another example of Smith's vivid post–Slick Rick storytelling. More to the point, it was storytelling that left off with the more mischievous aspects of "Girls Ain't Nothing but Trouble" and "Just One of Those Days," and instead went for a more mainstream (and teen-stream) approach. As a sheltered kid in Philly, I can say that the song rang true for me. I would go for that always. I wanted to shop at Urban Outfitters. My mom would be like, no, you have to go to JCPenney. It wasn't as cool as "Girls," but this was intentional. N.W.A., upon arriving, represented the first true danger element in rap. N.W.A., in crossing the line, created a lane, and DJ Jazzy Jeff and Fresh Prince drove fast to get there, and then drove fast in it. It was the we're-not-them lane.

It also helps that those two became the Buggles of hip-hop. Their video was the first one shown on *Yo! MTV Raps*, and it was in heavy rotation. I would run home from school just to catch it. Every repeat was an event.

It makes sense to start with pop, because this era for me is the opposite. It's when hip-hop truly elevated into art.

I always joke with Tariq that between us we hear hip-hop records in full, meaning each of us has ears—and the brains that connect to those ears—that hear them in half. He tends to focus on the lyrics and the meaning, while I tend to prioritize the sound and the rhythm. That division is clearer, and easier to respect, in the music we make together: division of labor. When we're actually cut loose in the world I'm sure that we both see both sides. The difference in emphasis, though, remains. In some ways, we are still back at that table in high school. He is still the kid who looked around the lunchroom, eyes on crosshair mode, collecting observations to load into his freestyle (that kid has one sneaker with a loose tongue, that guy's shirttail is hanging out strangely). And I am still the kid who ran from the high school cafeteria down eight flights to create a beat and then back up eight flights so that Tariq could rap over it. Old habits don't die, hard or otherwise.

The period of my life where that tendency was stronger, maybe, was the stretch between high school and when I officially entered the world as an artist. Meaning the late eighties and early nineties. Meaning what I still think of as a golden age of hip-hop, when innovative MCs and innovative DJs seemed to spring up every few months, and classic albums regularly sprouted on the vine. During that time, I made it my business to ferret out the finest, most innovative, most influential, and most visionary production styles.

The Bomb Squad was all of these. They emerged from Long

Island, from the scene that sprang up around Adelphi University in Garden City, New York, about an hour east of the city. Hank Boxley and his older brother Keith formed, with another local hip-hop enthusiast named Carlton Ridenhour—he's better known as Chuck D—a sound system named Spectrum City. That first incarnation of Spectrum City—which consisted of the two Boxleys/Shocklees, Chuck D, and a second rapper named Aaron Allan—cut a sole single, "Lies" / "Check Out the Radio." They also had an on-air presence on WBAU, the radio station at Adelphi, which put them in close contact with the station's program director, Bill Stephney, who soon joined the growing collective. Others in the circle included William Drayton, then going by MC DJ Flavor, later to go by Flavor Flav; Norman Rogers, more a DJ than an MC; Harry Allen, an aspiring journalist; and André Brown, the future Doctor Dré of *Yo! MTV Raps* fame, who started his medical/broadcasting career with a radio show called *The Operating Room*.

Spectrum City didn't hit the charts. They didn't become stars. They didn't even release a second single. Instead, they went back into the lab. When they came out the second time, it was as Public Enemy: Chuck and Flavor Flav (the former DJ Flavor) as the MCs, Rogers as the DJ under the name Terminator X. They were produced by the Bomb Squad (the Boxleys, now billed as Shocklees, along with Stephney and Eric "Vietnam" Sadler). Harry Allen came along as a self-styled minister of information.

They got to work reconstituting. The first Public Enemy record, *Yo! Bum Rush the Show*, was assembled and realized at Spectrum City Studios in Hempstead, about two miles from the Adelphi campus. It came out in February 1987. When I first got it, I was moderately skeptical. I have written about how MCs adopted Radio Voice. That was true of the early Chuck D, and then some. Add to that the fact that I didn't know their references. "Suckers to the side you know you hate my 98." What the hell is a 98? And "Sophisticated Bitch" was supposed to be edgy but it didn't come off that way. It was like your older brother was trying his hand at rap.

When I got to "Too Much Posse," my take on the record shifted.

It's the first track to foreground Flavor Flav. I fell for it hook, line, and sinker. Here's a comic rapper, and he has a solo feature. That song ended up in every mixtape I made. No one knew it because it was an album cut.

So there I was in the wake of the first album, neither thumbs-up nor thumbs-down. I was thumbs-waiting. It was the summer of 1987 when I heard "Rebel Without a Pause," the new Public Enemy single. It was like a thesaurus entry for "forceful": assertive, insistent, at times strident, but with too much wit and agility (and Flavor Flav) to fall into unpleasantness. The lyrics went all over the map, touching on Black radical thought, criticizing radio's timidity, promoting the Def Jam label (not to mention "Simple and plain, give me the lane / I'll throw it down your throat like Barkley," which seemed like it was tailor-made for Philadelphia). There were those Terminator X breakdowns. And then there were the samples, from various James Brown projects, from Jefferson Starship, from Joeski Love. It was almost as if they were so virtuosic that they just picked a narrow alphabetical window and worked within it. "Rebel Without a Pause" was followed by a song on the film *Less than Zero*, "Bring the Noise" (which laid out a radical theory of music/rhythm that connected PE to Sonny Bono, Yoko Ono, Run-D.M.C., Eric B. and Rakim, and Anthrax, exploding genres as it established them). And then that was followed by "Don't Believe the Hype" (on the one hand, even deeper and Blacker, on the other hand a nearly perfect pop song). That's a holy trinity.

Each of those songs hit. Some *were* hits ("Bring the Noise" almost went top fifty; "Don't Believe the Hype" cracked the top twenty). But then came the album, *It Takes a Nation of Millions to Hold Us Back*. The day it came out, I bought it on my way to my fast-food job. It changed the way I walked. It changed the way I thought. By the time I got to work, I was making excuses to sneak off and listen to it track by track. I took my lunch break to gobble up the back half of the record, and never came back.

A few years after that album, Bill Stephney gave someone a quote in an interview. It laid out his philosophy by reaching back to his first encounters with the genre. In his mind, hip-hop was primarily a sonic enterprise. "The point," he said, "wasn't rapping, it was rhythm, DJs cutting records left and right, taking the big drum break from Led Zeppelin's 'When the Levee Breaks,' mixing it together with 'Ring My Bell,' then with a Bob James Mardi Gras jazz record and some James Brown. You'd have 2,000 kids in any community center in New York, moving back and forth, back and forth, like some kind of tribal war dance, you might say. It was the rapper's role to match this intensity rhythmically. No one knew what he was saying. He was just rocking the mike."

Now, we can—and should—quibble with the idea of "just rocking the mike," especially by the time we had entered an era where the MCs "just rocking" included Run-D.M.C., LL, Rakim, and Stephney's colleague Chuck D. But I got it. Even though this quote wouldn't come along for a few years, Stephney and the Shocklees were thinking as composers. They had more samples than anyone and they made them sound like more. There was a density to the endeavor.

In part, what they were doing was replicating the sound of a city. They weren't the first. On MC Shan's "The Bridge," Marley Marl was trying to make the sound of a car. He took Magic Disco Machine's "Scratchin'," from 1975, took the horn stabs and spun them backward. That was the true pioneering moment. But the true pioneering moment sometimes gets buried in history.

That's what I heard in the Bomb Squad. They took the backward Magic Disco Machine aesthetic and pushed it further. They moved toward this strategy on the first record, perfected it on the second, and then continued on. While they worked with other artists—they produced half the songs on Slick Rick's debut, *The Great Adventures of Slick Rick*, and also did Doug E. Fresh's "Keep Risin' to the Top"— their best, most important, and most vital work continued to be with Public Enemy. They were lesser without PE and vice versa as well.

Public Enemy was on my mind all the time. They shared space, to some degree. The Beastie Boys were in the middle of a retrenchment period—the overwhelming success of *Licensed to Ill* set them back on their heels a bit, and they wouldn't release their follow-up until the summer of 1989. Other groups were still populating stores and airwaves. Run-D.M.C. was. Eric B. and Rakim was. But for a few years there, Public Enemy was top of mind for me. They were first thought, best thought, which is why I'll move through the rest of their arc before going to some of the others.

The group's third record, *Fear of a Black Planet*, was preceded by the epochal single "Fight the Power." It was a huge leap forward, in sound, in power, in philosophy. It was connected to Spike Lee's *Do the Right Thing*, which automatically elevated it, framing it as a Black justice anthem. (The movie was dedicated to various victims of violence, all recent at the time: Eleanor Bumpurs, Michael Griffith, Arthur Miller Jr., Edmund Perry, Yvonne Smallwood, and Michael Stewart.) But the song, in turn, elevated the movie. Much of it was Chuck D's doing. He went hard at everything. I remember listening to the song with my dad, never a hip-hop convert, and watching him light up when Chuck took down Elvis and John Wayne. It was one of those epiphanies when I actually put myself in my dad's shoes: here he was, an American man, having grown up in a time when the icons and role models were not only white, but white with ideas about color. It still didn't bring him around entirely to Public Enemy, but it moved the needle for one joyful nanosecond.

But much of it, too, came from the Bomb Squad. As dense and frenetic as they had been before, this upped the ante tenfold, with samples taken from the usual suspects but cut and positioned for maximum effectiveness (multiple pieces from the James Brown universe, Sly and the Family Stone, Rick James) to a museum's worth of hip-hop history (Kurtis Blow, West Street Mob, Spoonie Gee, Doctor Funnkenstein and DJ Cash Money, even Public Enemy themselves). The video showed the group at a racial justice rally in Brooklyn. People carried signs that carried the images of Muhammad Ali, Paul Robeson, Angela Davis, Frederick Douglass, and others. (Tawana Brawley was in the video, even.) "Fight the Power" was, for me, everything I had gotten from them up until that moment, and then some. It was also a testament to the group's ongoing power.

Those two singles were equally perfect examples of Bomb Squad production. "Welcome to the Terrordome" had a masonry of samples representing somewhere between twelve and twenty songs, including classics by the Temptations ("Psychedelic Shack" was one of the few pieces that your ears could pull out of the vortex), Kool and the Gang ("Jungle Boogie"), and James Brown (at least three songs), and rarities from groups like Funk Inc. (a cover of Kool and the Gang's "Kool Is Back"), Mikey Dread ("Operator's Choice"), and Thelonious Monk's son T. S. Monk (the aspirational disco anthem "Bon Bon Vie," which drew on the DNA of intelligently optimistic bands like Dr. Buzzard's Savannah Band and Chic). "911 Is a Joke" was a definitive Flavor Flav showcase, in part because it had real grit underneath it. And then there were the rest of the songs: the racial-consciousness anthem "Brothers Gonna Work It Out," the media critique "Burn Hollywood Burn," the self-sufficiency comedy "Can't Do Nuttin' For Ya Man," another definitive Flav performance. The album wasn't quite the achievement in songcraft that its predecessor had been, but it wasn't designed to be. It was conceived explicitly as a piece of political theory, with an eye toward creating a dense sonic document that would stand alongside monographs by Black scholars—the one that got mentioned most often was Frances Cress Welsing's "The Cress Theory of Color-Confrontation."

The tour that followed the release of *Fear of a Black Planet*—called, yes, Tour of a Black Planet—is legendary. Younger groups such as Digital Underground went along with Public Enemy as an opener, and their entourage included an aspiring rapper named Tupac Shakur, who was mostly working as a backup dancer and roadie. Chuck D has told a story about how eager Tupac was to establish his bona fides with the veterans. In Oklahoma City, someone stole some of the band's property from the backstage area. The culprit was apprehended and brought back around. Tupac immediately hit the man in the head. Chuck D stopped him. "It's just stuff," he said. But it wasn't just stuff to Tupac—it was stuff belonging to Public Enemy.

After that, a funny thing happened, which was that the Bomb Squad started to do top-drawer work with other artists. Take Ice Cube. I didn't just jump right on when N.W.A. appeared, as I'll explain. But Ice Cube's first album, *AmeriKKKa's Most Wanted*, was a revelation. For starters, I saw for the first time fully what an incredible writer he was. (I had a friend who called him the "New Dylan," and I laughed, but I didn't laugh that much.) The debut LP was produced not by some West Coast talent, though Sir Jinx (Dr. Dre's cousin) helped out, but by the Bomb Squad. When I touched down on the title track, I saw how they were expanding the idea of funk. They sampled from Funky George's drums, from Kool and the Gang's "Let the Music Take Your Mind," not just a break, but the whole solo with the hi-hat. I have said before that it's among the most violent drum sounds I have ever heard. They recognized it as pure sonic aggression and understood that it should remain intact.

The Bomb Squad also did half of Bell Biv Devoe's *Poison*, which wouldn't have been considered hip-hop proper, but it was a crown jewel of new jack swing, which was hip-hop adjacent. That was the genius of their genius, that it wasn't limited to East Coast, or to so-called politically aware hip-hop, or even to hip-hop. It could go west, go gangsta, go pop. All it needed was density, intensity, and a propensity for surprise.

These were visible albums that sold well and dented history. They have earned their classic status. But there were two surprising beneficiaries of this technique, both from 1991, that have not been admitted into the canon but illustrate the Bomb Squad's magic and mastery.

The first, *Bazerk Bazerk Bazerk*, was by Son of Bazerk, a Long Island group. The Bomb Squad treated them like little brothers, in the sense that they both gave them everything and beat them up a little. They loaded them up with almost more samples than an album could bear, and Son of Bazerk matched them with lyrics that themselves were dense allusions to soul and funk. Want a nod to the Ohio Players? The Bar-Kays? The Stylistics? How about Tavares, the Cape Cod funk group (sometimes Providence, Rhode Island, sometimes New Bedford, Massachusetts) best known for their disco hit "More Than a Woman"? Or—going deeper—how about Sir Joe Quarterman and Free Soul, a fairly obscure DC act who flourished as the capital evolved from funk to go-go? They're all in there, and in fact all in one song, "Change the Style," which was a high-concept project in every way, with a metal section giving way to a reggae section giving way to a straight soul section. The group matched the musical hyperactivity with lyrics that were just as interested in reference and meta-references. It's dizzying in a good way, like leaning back off a merry-go-round and watching the world go by. Elsewhere on the album, the band's lyrics dipped a notch but the music held firm: "What Could Be Better Bitch" was also on the soundtrack to *Juice*, "N-41" played like a Chuck D reboot, and "Are You Wit Me" made almost perfect use of a sample from Albert King's "Cold Feet." (In point of fact, it was a metasample. Rather than pulling from the original, they took it from another rap record that sampled King, Ultimate Force's "I'm Not Playin'." We get down on producers like Diddy for sampling recent rap songs, but the Bomb Squad doesn't get any flak for the same. When they did it—and this wasn't the only time—they were put-it-in-a-blender historians.)

The second was Young Black Teenagers, not Black, not teenagers, named by Chuck D. (It was also a joke about the shifting demographics of rap, which was making real inroads among white suburban kids for the first time, who carried with them the promise of a sustainable industry.) Also from Long Island—the Bomb Squad had their heart set on Strong Island supremacy—they had five rappers of competence, if not necessarily of note. But the Bomb Squad production turned every track into a borderline masterpiece, and sometimes even crossed the border. As diverse and dense as Son of Bazerk, this album pulled from the Rolling Stones, *Mary Poppins*, Otis Redding, and Rush. Even when the Bomb Squad dipped into breakbeats that had a history—they used "Chinese Chicken," by Duke Williams and the Extremes, which had also been used by De La Soul (on "Tread Water") and Ice Cube (on "The Bomb," the closing track of *AmeriKKKa's Most Wanted*, which they had also worked on and which also included samples from Parliament, the Commodores, Zapp, and Herbert Morrison)—they sharpened every edge. People like to call tracks "cuts." These earned the name.

Years later, I had the opportunity to talk to the Bomb Squad about those productions. I had always thought of them as a blender and then a pour, meaning that I assumed they mixed everything together and then figured out how to get it sounding perfect. When they came on the show, they told me that they were much more deliberate than that. They wrote out everything: which bar this sample entered, at what volume, how to then bury it later behind a new sample as counterpoint and callback. It was even more impressive than I had believed.

The Bomb Squad even helped me to understand records that came in from other corners. I was aware of the Beastie Boys from the start. *Licensed to Ill* was a massive mainstream success, the first rap record to sell more than a million. From a musical standpoint, they had pedigree—they were working on the same label as, and with the same producer as, LL Cool J. But could they survive? Could they sustain or improve? The jury was out. Then I heard that the Dust Brothers were working on it. I had heard them on Delicious Vinyl records, producing for artists like Tone-Loc and Young MC. I had a sense of their pop capacity and their love for obscure samples. I figured that was the fate for the Beasties: high-end novelty rap aimed squarely at the mostly white suburbs.

Then came Cherry Hill Mall. This was an occasional destination for my family. We went when there was special shopping to be done. This special shopping was connected to my high school graduation, which had happened the week before. As a present, I was getting a leather jacket, even though it was summer. (Pro tip: cheaper then.) I wandered into a bookstore and found the new *Rolling Stone*. Inside, there was a review of the new Beasties record, *Paul's Boutique*. Not just a review: a four-star review. At that time, that level of praise was unthinkable. This was a periodical that had to have their knives out for these snotty New York punks. Four stars felt more like getting five or six. I couldn't believe it. I had to have it.

The record was the surprise hit of that year. For me, it had an extra dimension. Prince had been tasked with providing the soundtrack for Tim Burton's *Batman*. The announcement had filled me with excitement. The actual album had filled me with qualified excitement. He had started to slip a bit, in my mind, on *Lovesexy* the year before— it was my first peaks-and-valleys Prince record—and *Batman* confirmed that. There were songs that soared and songs that just kind of sat there. That left a gap. What was going to fill it? The more I listened to *Paul's Boutique*, the more I saw that it was a kind of master class—specifically, it was a master class in a zone of sixties and seventies music that I hadn't quite conquered. It had samples from classic rock, like the various obscure (to me) Beatles samples that made up "Sounds of Science." It had samples from glam, the Sweet's "Ballroom Blitz," and specifically the "She thinks she's the passionate one" line that popped up in "Hey Ladies." There were songs that used Donovan samples ("Car Thief") and songs that used Mountain samples ("Looking Down the Barrel of a Gun"). Mountain? There was a band named Mountain? The album not only used these samples, but it used them in Bomb Squad–like ways, shifting the focus away from dense urban soundscapes to equally dense suburban ones.

The glory period for the Bomb Squad wound down after that. There were many reasons. One, of course, was the difficulty of clearing samples. A Bomb Squad song was like balancing everything as you come down a sharp flight of stairs, and you're going to ask me to account for everything as I try to keep track of the steps? It's too much! Bazerk alone was an unimaginable headache. The image that comes to mind is the *Sesame Street* cake-counting baker. You know him, right? He taught kids to count but also, as he did, he taught them to be afraid of gravity. He would come down a flight and then stumble and really come down. It's a trauma in my memory. Every time, I assume he had broken his neck. The voice in those short films was provided by Jim Henson, but the falls came courtesy of a guy named Alex Stevens. He's a footnote, but a fascinating one. He was a stunt performer (obviously) but also a stunt coordinator, and some of the films he headed up included *Shaft's Big Score* and *Super Fly*. That's right: he was a bakesploitation pioneer. *He taught kids the odds, he taught them the evens. | He fell down the stairs—he was Alex Stevens.*

I have traced the Bomb Squad's progress through the turn of the decade. Let's go back a few years. In the summer of 1987, I branched out in my media diet. I had been a longtime consumer of *Rolling Stone*, but I added *Billboard* to my regular reading list. Michael Jackson was the reason. I was an MJ fanatic, and *Bad*, his follow-up to *Thriller*, was in the process of being released. "I Just Can't Stop Loving You," the lead single, came out in late July, with the album following in late August. I wanted to track the record's progress. Michael Jackson was my way into *Billboard*, but once I got there, I stayed, absorbing everything else the magazine had to offer: all the charts, all the industry comings and goings, and all the advertisements. That's when I first encountered the Ruthless Records ads for N.W.A. and the Posse. I didn't like them. I probably had a bit of a bias, not pro–East Coast but at least a little anti–West Coast, left over from the summer of 1985, when I got all hyped up on "Batterram" only to learn that I was missing out on Slick Rick's "La Di Da Di." In the summer of 1987, the East Coast was dreaming into action, furnishing some of the most visionary acts I could ever want. (See above.) Why did I have to make room in my heart for this West Coast group with a less-than-progressive name and a Jheri-curled look that reminded me mostly of . . . oh, yeah, *Bad*-era Michael Jackson, which was the reason I was looking at this magazine in the first place?

I have talked about how Black Thought, my partner in the Roots, and I listen to records differently—he hears the lyrics first and I hear the arrangements first. There are other important distinctions. When we met in school, I was a nerd who hadn't seen or heard much of the world, where he was a kid who had seen too much of it. When rappers started to include more of the so-called real world in their music—more scenes of drugs (dealing and use both), more violence (gun-related but also emotional), more abject poverty, more overt suspicion of authority—I felt alienated and, at least to some degree, he felt seen. Or at least that was my thought when he came up to me one day at lunch, eyes wide, and asked me if I had heard *Straight Outta Compton*. I gave him wide eyes back. "What are you talking about?" I said.

"The N.W.A. album," he said.

"I know," I said. "But what are you talking about?"

"The album," he said again.

He kept hyping it and I kept scoffing, at least until he put it on his Walkman and gave me his headphones. I didn't know exactly what I expected, but it wasn't *this*. To me, they looked like half-assed electro-funk, but this was almost Bomb Squad–level production, with quick shifts, interesting dynamics, and breakbeats that might not have been as deep-in-the-crate as Public Enemy, but they were the next best thing—the smartest selects from the first few volumes of the *Ultimate Breaks and Beats* series. (Brief history: *Ultimate Breaks and Beats* was a twenty-five-album series that was released by Street Beat records in the Bronx, starting in the mideighties, continuing through the early nineties. A new volume would come out every few months, with a half dozen or so songs that featured breakbeats that the curator/compiler, Breakbeat Lou, born Lou Flores, thought would be useful for other hip-hop DJs. They were, and then some: you can track eras of hip-hop by observing when songs from *Ultimate Breaks and Beats* began to circulate through releases. This was era one.) On top of all that, there was the sheer audacity of the lyrics: violent, filled with guns, likening themselves to Charles Manson, "When I'm in your neighborhood you'd better duck / 'Cause Ice Cube is crazy as fuck." And that was just the first verse of the first song. I watched Tariq watching me. He saw that I was beginning to understand, and I saw him more clearly. He hadn't seen those *Billboard* ads. He had encountered the music out in the field. (That was one of the first times that I felt the obstructionist effect of having too much knowledge. Sometimes it was better not to know a thing, and just to feel what you felt.)

Even my shock didn't prepare me for the second song, "Fuck Tha Police." What the what? You could say that in a song? Groups like Public Enemy had been defiant, political, and hardcore, but they were powered more by ideas. This was just rage, barely contained. There inside the headphones, I gasped out loud—I could tell because Tariq's expression changed the way it would if you had given someone something that made them gasp out loud. When I heard *It Takes a Nation of Millions to Hold Us Back*, I walked away from my dead-end fast-food job. When I heard *Straight Outta Compton*, I cut class. Therein lies the album's undeniable power.

When I was able to get my breath back later that night, I applied a little analysis. I wanted cooler heads to prevail, and I wanted to be that cooler head. I knew what N.W.A. was building on. I remembered Schoolly D pioneering (if that's the right verb) the use of the word "nigga." But even his level of criminality rarely rose above mischief. *Saturday Night!—The Album* had some element of gangsterism, but how hardcore can you be when you go to the club or the bar and come home to the place you share with your mother? This was different, an angry scowl made even more menacing by the obvious talent at work: Ice Cube's writing, Dr. Dre's production, Eazy-E's overall vision. And while it wasn't political in the traditional sense—there were no policy papers or historical lessons—it was clearly capable of moving the crowd toward change. Public Enemy wasn't exactly Malcolm X, maybe, but they were at least that final year of Martin Luther King Jr.'s life, when his growing opposition to the Vietnam War made him more defiant and radical. PE had preacher energy. People saw N.W.A. as Black Panthers, but to me they also had street energy and fearlessness regarding message that put them closer to a comedian like Richard Pryor. In fact, "Gangsta Gangsta" sampled Pryor. What was so-called polite society supposed to do with this? It tried to push them out. In the spring, MTV banned the "Straight Outta Compton" video. Some record stores refused to sell the album.

All this did was boost the group's visibility and notoriety. But the best free promotion was yet to come.

The FBI, which had a long history of tracking any domestic organization considered a threat to orderly society—a category that seemed to include nearly every Black revolutionary group—put N.W.A. on its radar. They tracked the group through its tour and then, in August of 1989, wrote a letter to the band's label, Priority Records. That letter, penned by the agency's assistant director of the Office of Public Affairs, Milt Ahlerich, opened with a basic recap of "Fuck tha Police": "A song recorded by the rap group N.W.A. on their album entitled *Straight Outta Compton* encourages violence against and disrespect for the law enforcement officer and has been brought to my attention." No lies detected. "I understand your company recorded and distributed this album, and I am writing to share my thoughts and concerns with you," wrote Ahlerich, who went on to remind Priority that "advocating violence and assault is wrong" and that "violent crime, a major problem in our country, reached an unprecedented high in 1988. Seventy-eight law enforcement officers were feloniously slain in the line of duty during 1988, four more than in 1987." As nearly everyone, then and now, has noted, Ahlerich seemed unconcerned with the numbers of Black men who had been harmed by law enforcement officers. The conclusion of the letter, though, was the key: "Music plays a significant role in society, and I wanted you to be aware of the FBI's position relative to this song and its message. I believe my views reflect the opinion of the entire law enforcement community." N.W.A. proudly released the letter and claimed the "most dangerous band" title that had previously been held by everyone from the Kingsmen to the Sex Pistols. But if you want a group of young people, Black, white, or rainbow, to develop an interest in something, there's no quicker way to do it than to broadcast worry from the official corridors of power. Even though the band's third single, the Dr. Dre showcase "Express Yourself," was a full-on positivity anthem and anti-drug song (meaning anti-chronic, four years before *The Chronic*), the die had been cast. This was, in every way that mattered, an Officially Dangerous Group.

Soon after Public Enemy and N.W.A. changed the world, Ultramagnetic MCs changed it again. The question was who noticed. (I did, and I also noticed that there weren't lots of other people noticing.) But cult revolutions are still revolutions: they just have less bloodshed and more cachet.

Ultramagnetic MCs were from the Bronx, and in one configuration or another they had been on the scene since the mideighties, when they recorded a demo called "Space Groove" and put out their first single: "To Give You Love" backed with "Make You Shake." It came and went. Few people shook. That wasn't the case for their next single, "Ego Trippin'," which broke so much ground that construction on the site lasted for years.

Understanding that story means hopping in a time machine and traveling back to the early sixties, with a New Yorker named Herb Rooney. Rooney had started off his career as part of the Masters, a New York vocal group. The Masters had a sister group called the Masterettes. In the early sixties, Rooney hopped from the Masters to the Masterettes just in time to catch a break—a song called "Tell Him." A decade later, Rooney—or, if you believe the legend, his mother—made the acquaintance of an itinerant soul singer named Melvin McClelland, who would record under the name Melvin Bliss. Rooney gave him a song named "Reward." He intended it for a single, but that meant they would need a second song as well. Rooney cooked up something called "Synthetic Substitution," a song about how the future was bleak because machines might take over and strip away humanity. When they recorded the song, though, they had the good fortune of working with the drummer Bernard Purdie, already a legend for his work with James Brown and Aretha Franklin. Purdie gave "Synthetic Substitution" a rhythmic propulsion and complexity that turned it into a cult hit, which in turn meant that it was just sitting there, waiting to be discovered by an enter-prising hip-hop producer. Ced-Gee of Ultramagnetic MCs, who also helmed about half of Boogie Down Productions' *Criminal Minded*, was that producer.

Ced-Gee was also a rapper who liked dropping science in the form of references to frequencies, revolutions, and medical uten-sils. His partner in rhyme, Kool Keith, was less a scientist than a science-fiction-ist, a futurist obsessed with exposing the limits of the present. As left of center as Ultramagnetic MCs could feel, they were also a Bronx hip-hop group, which means that they were honor bound to go after Queens rappers. They took a swipe at Run-D.M.C. in "Ego Trippin'": "They use the simple back and forth, the same old rhythm / That a baby can pick up, and join, right with them / But their rhymes are pathetic, they think they copacetic / Using nursery terms, at least not poetic." "Nursery terms"? Was that a reference to "Peter Piper"? And would Run-D.M.C. even notice? The album, *Critical Beatdown*, came along in 1988 and didn't quite set the world on fire. It sold modestly, though it was beloved by the hip-hop-erati, especially Ced-Gee's production and Kool Keith's rapping. (And Run-D.M.C. did notice. There was a time in hip-hop, if you ever came into the presence of Run, you didn't know who you were going to get. There's no shortage of arrogant "Run hurt my feelings" stories from back them. He has evolved, atoned, but there are at least forty hilarious Arthur's fist memes where he made people furious by being dismissive or cold. In the late 1990s, during an interview on Hot 97, Run talked about how he didn't understand wordy rap groups like Kool Keith and . . . the Roots. We were just cresting with *Things Fall Apart*. What did we ever do to him? In a weird way, it made me feel like I was part of the group. When I fi-nally met Run, it was all water under the Queensbridge.)

Kool Keith was such a futurist, in fact, that it is worth moving into his future. After that first record, the group put out two more records, *Funk Your Head Up* in 1992 (which was heavily reworked by Mercury Records in the hopes of better sales, which did not ma-terialize) and *The Four Horsemen* in 1993 (a return to form critically and a continuation of form commercially). A breakup ensued, and Kool Keith went solo, or rather multiple—he started out by creating a persona called Dr. Octagon, releasing a record under that name in 1996, and then proceeded to inhabit a number of other pseudonyms and identities: Black Elvis, Dr. Dooom, Robbie Analog, Dr. Ultra, Matthew, and of course Mr. Gerbik, Dr. Octagon's 208-year-old uncle, half shark and half man but with alligator skin, who carries a dead walrus as he patrols Hollywood Boulevard.

Open parentheses: Kool Keith wasn't the first weirdo to emerge in hip-hop. The genre had room for genuine eccentrics. Biz Markie, for example. Biz first popped up on one of the Roxanne Wars songs, "The Def Fresh Crew," showing off his abilities as a virtuosic beatboxer. But he was a rapper, too, confidently comic, always hovering on the edge of novelty without slipping into minstrelsy. His first album, *Goin' Off*, produced a number of memorable songs, including "This Is Something for the Radio," "Pickin' Boogers," and "Vapors."

Open parentheses within parentheses: Many of the lyrics on Biz's first album were written by Antonio Hardy, another Juice Crew member who recorded as Big Daddy Kane. Big Daddy Kane was who you would invent if someone told you to invent an MC: he rapped rapidly over James Brown samples, wrote dense verses that relied heavily on internal rhymes, referred to himself frequently, including spelling out his own name midverse (a name inspired in part by martial arts movies—Kane stood for King Asiatic Nobody's Equal). He had no shortage of dexterity and cleverness and, at least in the beginning, on his debut *Long Live the Kane*, he had songs, too: "Set It Off" and "Raw" and especially "Ain't No Half-Stepping," which slowed down the beat, sampled the Emotions, and piled up lyrics attesting to his superior lyrical abilities. I liked it because it mentioned me, or at least I could pretend it did: there was a snippet, "a mere musketeer," that if I squinted my ears I could hear as "Ahmir musketeer." Thanks, Big Daddy. *Long Live the Kane* included "Just Rhymin' with Biz," which used Biz Markie the way that history intended: as a left-field hypeman, comic genius, and mouth-music maestro. (It also had a profanity redaction, a relative rarity for rap:

"Aw, fuck it, the Kane is invincible," Kane says, but the word is bleeped out, not just on a clean version, but on all versions.)

Open parentheses within parentheses within parentheses: In 1988, Dennis Hopper directed a film called *Colors*, a South Central gang-crime movie starring Sean Penn and Robert Duvall. The soundtrack included Ice-T's theme song of the same name and the immortal Coldcut remix of Eric B. and Rakim's "Paid in Full." Even though the movie was set in Los Angeles, the soundtrack was largely produced by Marley Marl, which meant that it leaned heavily on Juice Crew (and, in the case of Eric B. and Rakim, Juice Crew–adjacent) artists: Roxanne Shante was there with "Go on Girl," Kane with "Raw," and Kool G Rap with "Butcher Shop." Kool G Rap, born Nathaniel Thomas Wilson, was the third of the Juice Crew triumvirate. With a harder, more aggressive style than Big Daddy Kane and production masterminded by his childhood friend Eric B., the duo of Kool G Rap and DJ Polo painted portraits of street life that paved the way for future urban chroniclers and gangsta rappers (Nas, say, or Mobb Deep, or Biggie).

In 1992, Kool G Rap and DJ Polo put out their third record, *Live and Let Die*. It marked a break from Eric B. and was a kind of coastal crossover: a concept album about East Coast gangster living produced by Sir Jinx, a West Coast producer. The record had a cover photo of the pair robbing a bank and lyrical content rough enough that Cold Chillin's parent company, Warner Bros., eventually backed away from the album. G Rap broke from Polo and went solo, a sentence that could be a lyric. Close parentheses.

Big Daddy Kane put out a follow-up, *It's a Big Daddy Thing*, the year after *Long Live the Kane*, and while it was respectable enough, with plenty of the raw spirit of the first record, the cover gave me a sense of what was to come. Kane moved into smoother sounds, a lower vocal register, and romantic raps, and released records with diminishing returns across the nineties. (Which isn't to say that there was anything wrong with that persona. In fact, it was probably more authentic than *Long Live*. That second record was a *Scooby-Doo* reveal of the hot-tub rapper with champagne and a Barry White baritone.) Still, he remained a giant and pioneer on the basis of that first album alone. The Roots would later work with him on a song called "Boom!" which was written to fit his style and performed live at the concert that became *Dave Chappelle's Block Party*. There's a longer story here that I'll hold for later. Close parentheses.

Biz took a half step away from the Juice Crew for his second record, using Cool V (his cousin) and Paul C (Paul McKasty, a New York kid—well, early twenties—who was one of the most innovative producers of his day). It worked, wondrously, producing one massive hit, the awesomely goofy "Just a Friend." It's the song that Biz will always be remembered for, unless he's remembered for "Alone Again," from his 1991 *I Need a Haircut*, which used an uncleared sample from Gilbert O'Sullivan's 1972 soft-rock hit "Alone Again (Naturally)." It was an O'Sullivan sample, but it was more so a tribute to the Cold Crush Brothers and their interpolation of O'Sullivan's song in a 1980 routine. (Black latchkey kids of the 1970s and 1980s were fed mainstream TV and music, and turned it into art. I'll get back to this later when I talk about the Wu-Tang Clan.) Other groups were doing routines like this. But O'Sullivan did what other artists didn't: he sued and won, securing a judgment that would change the way that hip-hop artists were able to dip into the musical past. Biz became a comic martyr—his next album was called *All Samples Cleared!* He continued to appear on other people's records and popped up as an occasional actor. Close parentheses.

Ultramagnetic MCs were mad scientists: forward thinking, prone to experiment, entirely content with being poorly understood at first. I have thought for years about what that makes EPMD. I'll be thinking about it until the end of this section.

EPMD was Erick Sermon and Parrish Smith, a pair of friends from Brentwood, Long Island. The name, eventually, stood for Erick and Parrish Making Dollars. I say "eventually" because that wasn't how things started. They started as EEPMD, when Erick Sermon was Easy Erick and Parrish Smith was Parish the Microphone Doctor. It's a little unwieldy, though it could have been worse—Parrish could have been "Parish the Microphone M.D.," and then you'd have EEPMMD. They looked around and saw that there was already an Easy Eric, sort of: N.W.A.'s Eric Wright, doing business as Eazy-E. Dropping that other *E* was easy enough.

EPMD grew up in Brentwood. Not O. J. Simpson's Los Angeles Brentwood. This one is on Long Island, also the home of Craig Mack, who came up at around the same time and had a long professional relationship with them. Back in the nineteenth century, the city was the site of the Utopian community of Modern Times, which was founded on the ideas of Josiah Warren, a socialist and anarchist. It was a fascinating community, inspired by the failed Utopia of New Harmony, Indiana. It was based on labor-for-labor. It didn't work. The work within the community wasn't enough to sustain the community, which led to the end of the experiment. A little more than a century later, the community—now Brentwood—was the site of another kind of Utopia. Erick and Parrish were both raised there. They started MCing and DJing, with a third member, DJ K La Boss, who thankfully didn't make it into the name (EEPMDDJKLAB?).

The group's first record, *Strictly Business*, came out in 1988. On the face of it, it seemed like the polar opposite of the Bomb Squad. Where they were the natural evolution of Grandmaster Flash, adventuring on wheels of whatever is stronger than steel, EPMD was the natural evolution of the Sugarhill Gang. They would take a single memorable song, one that's in the recesses of your mind, and loop it. They wouldn't just let it sit statically on the record, the way that some other acts did. They would manage the loop, slicing it, making an idiosyncratic entrance and exit, but the songs still depended on one prominent, dominant sample.

That album opens with the title track, which uses the chorus of Eric Clapton's "I Shot the Sheriff." (Here, too, they had Sugarhill echoes. We called the EPMD song "I Shot the Sheriff" because of its chorus. It was like hearing "Rapper's Delight" and fixating on the first two words, "hip-hop." The title meant less than what meant more.) The next song, "I'm Housin'," uses the main riff of Aretha

Franklin's "Rock Steady." It's a specific technique. If you're a Black American human who spends time at family barbeques, you know that there are songs that are certain to surface. Those are the uncle songs, brought to you courtesy of your older relative who was cool in his day and still retains a trace of that. He wants the people his age to hear them because they're reminders of that former cool. He wants the people younger than him to hear them because he's teaching. And he wants to hear them for all those reasons: nostalgia, ego, pure pleasure. EPMD brought that to genius levels.

EPMD also had a genius vocal approach. They took Rakim's understated deadpan delivery and brought it up (or is that down?) a notch. That (along with Erick Sermon's lisp) made them menacing in a whole other way. If you are out in the street and you hear a voice talking to you, the tone that should frighten you is the cool monotone. That's the voice that's coming for you.

The best moment on that opening album, in my opinion, was "You Gots to Chill." It has an underlying sample of Kool and the Gang's "Jungle Boogie," which is also on *Strictly Business* (that's one of the rules of barbecue songs—there's no shame in recycling them—they're original green). The main sample in "You Gots to Chill" is from Zapp's "More Bounce to the Ounce" (easy to loop, since it's already an eight-bar loop).

Again, the rep is that it's somehow simple. But if you really listen to that first album, you hear Bomb Squad sophistication. Sermon wasn't just looping a song. He was layering it. He used his source material perfectly and with such a specific energy. To me, this is the seed that got planted that later on made a tree grow in LA, specifically the tree of G-funk. Even though Digital Underground gets the credit for making the most of George Clinton's body of work, Erick Sermon's early production is a direct precursor to G-funk.

EPMD was amazing to me. And yet, they don't get mentioned in the same breath as the other major stars of the era. Why? Well, when you play Monopoly you could do some damage with the mustards and the yellows. You only truly pay attention to the purple with an eye to the blue. They have made a masterful career. Even when you say their name what comes into mind is something more solid. Swanson, not Eleven Madison Park.

Eventually, Erick Sermon branched out beyond the group. His productions continued to be incredible. I think of an achievement like the first Redman record, *Whut? Thee Album*. To me, it's the last album of the crack era. That was the last of the chaotic cram-every-sample on top of each other, the last one to really demonstrate the Bomb Squad level of production. The finest examples are probably the singles, "Blow Your Mind" and "Time 4 Sum Aksion." Everything stuck to his arrangements. Even more so: it stuck to me. Erick Sermon, in a direct sense, birthed the idea of the Soulquarians sound. There's a remix that he did of Redman's "Rockafella" in 1994. It froze me to my core. Dilla agreed. "He's a motherfucker," he said. (Sermon also shifted his vocal approach. Redman rubbed off on him and he became a more energetic MC, which cost him some of his deadpan genius and cool points.)

Let's go back to the scientist question. Dilla's answer would suggest Freud. But I would say Pavlov. He had an almost perfect sense of stimulus and response. As they said on their second record, "Knick knack paddy wack give a dog a bone."

Over the years, hip-hop producers took the reins, more and more. We'll talk later about producer tags. Many had trademarks. Erick didn't have a trademark in that way. Or rather, his trademark was the absence of one. His first solo record wouldn't appear until 1993. It was called *No Pressure*. The second single, and the best song on the record, was "Stay Real." There was nothing really notable about it save its incredible consistency. Sometimes you need consistency and safety to ground you and to show you how crazy risk-takers are by comparison. The Erick Sermons are your anchors, your basslines, a lesson in ongoing excellence.

And finally we arrive at the Native Tongues. Welcome. Take a seat.

As I said, I had absorbed Public Enemy and though I admired them beyond compare, I also knew that wasn't exactly me. I had absorbed Ultramagnetic MCs and EPMD and a million other groups, too, but I also knew they weren't exactly me. When I heard De La Soul's *3 Feet High and Rising*, I heard myself. I was that weird-shaped kid.

The Jungle Brothers preceded them, importantly. They had been active for a while by the time they released *Straight Out the Jungle* in 1988. Even though they were named JBs like James Brown's group, they had a more interesting set of samples at a time when James Brown samples were already getting tired. I liked the song "Black Is Black," which featured a rapper I didn't know (he had an oddly smooth, conversational style) introducing himself as part of something called A Tribe Called Quest (was that what he was saying?). But I didn't sense that it was seismic. It turned out that other artists were even more drawn to it than I was. They were playing the same tour circuit and discovered a common sensibility.

The collective included the Jungle Brothers, A Tribe Called Quest (the rapper I didn't know was named Q-Tip), and De La Soul. They borrowed the phrase "Native Tongues" from an old Motown-adjacent group, New Birth. (New Birth arose out of the ashes of the Nite-Liters. Harvey Fuqua mentored them, which meant that they were in touch with the original trunk of American soul—he was married to Gwen Gordy, sang with Etta James, helped set up Marvin Gaye. His granddaughter, Tina Farris, has been my tour manager for the last quarter century.) Eventually there would be other acts as well: Queen Latifah, Monie Love, Black Sheep—whose incredible "The Choice Is Yours (Revisited)," probably the best remix/remake in hip-hop history, sampled its drums from New Birth's "Keep On Doin' It."

Jungle Brothers were first. The album that brought me to a . . . well, a new birth . . . was De La Soul's *3 Feet High and Rising*. It came out in 1989, and cemented everything I was coming to understand about Native Tongues. It summed up my inner state and proved to me that it was mirrored and echoed in the world.

Remember that story about how Public Enemy's *It Takes a Nation of Millions to Hold Us Back* put steel in my spine as I walked to my fast-food job, to the point where I listened to it all morning and quit in the afternoon? You should. It's only a few pages ago. That record made me feel that I was in full control of every thought and every decision. Warrior for clarity and justice. But not every day was like that. The fact was that I was a teenager moving through Philadelphia, through the minefield of high school and the more dangerous minefield of the streets that led to and from high school. We had bullies in our neighborhood. They were twins, like you might see in a movie. They were even named like movie characters, Chauncey and Charles. They had a third bully to complete their corporation, Reggie, a cousin. They had been around forever. When I think of those idyllic afternoons spent watching MTV, waiting for a new Michael Jackson video, some of the sense of safety came from where I *wasn't*: out in the street, walking from one place to another, worried that CC&R were going to appear without warning and take whatever small amount of money I had. As we got older, they acquired more lieutenants, and the stakes heightened. Now it wouldn't just be taking spare change, or horning in on your game at the video arcade. Now it might be something meaner, actual violence and malice.

One day around this time in 1989, could be February, could be May—I'm usually good with dates but trauma can blur the memory—I was walking from one place to another, either home from school or out to Wawa or the library or from a different place to another different one (trauma can blur), and I saw them on the corner. They were a gang of six by now.

I was fully into the Native Tongues ethos now, so I was also fully into the style. Bold colors, big prints, baggy pants. They have discussed this in various interviews, how they moved away from the Kangol, from the leather, from the gold chains, from sneaker chic, from paramilitary muscle. Out there on Long Island, Pos and Dave would raid their father's closet for square-looking pants with square-looking patterns, plaid or something, and then put them on and pull them up high.

"Yo," I heard. This was Charles, yelling. "Yo!" I didn't turn. I tried not to even pause in my stride. "You look like one of those De La Soul niggas!"

They had marked me as one of the faithful. I didn't care what was coming. I would take the beatdown. I needed to stand up for my beliefs. I needed to justify my core. "That's my favorite group," I said.

"That's my shit," he said. "That Buddy shit." "Buddy" was the new single from *3 Feet High and Rising*, following a string that included "Plug Tunin'," "Potholes in My Lawn," and "Me Myself and I." Each single went a step further in introducing mainstream America to alternative Blackness and dissolving the monolith. By the time "Buddy" was out, there were enough videos not only to calm down bullies but to make me the fashion leader of my neighborhood. "Buddy" was near the back of the record. But it was more than just a single. It was a statement of purpose for the whole Native Tongues collective. De La Soul was the artist of record, but the Jungle Brothers and Q-Tip joined in. The "Buddy" single contained more than one important song, but it also contained more than one important "Buddy." The album version, five minutes long, was subdued and sedate. The extended single, subtitled "Native Tongue Decision," not only had the JBs and Tip, but also Monie Love and Queen Latifah. And it sounded different. The album version sampled the Commodores, the Five Stairsteps, Bo Diddley, and the Invitations. The longer version kept some of this, like the Stairsteps, but it was mainly powered by a sample from "Heartbeat," a hit by the disco/ boogie singer Taana Gardner. "Heartbeat" had been used before, by the Treacherous Three back in 1981, but it would really blow up in the late eighties and 1990s (you may know it from Ini Kamoze's "Here Comes the Hotstepper").

Those were the first thunderclaps of this new thing. Soon enough other bands joined up and joined in. A Tribe Called Quest was the third to come along but in some ways the most complete. They were led by Q-Tip, born Jonathan Davis, named (eventually) Kamaal Ibn John Fareed. Q-Tip had appeared on the Jungle Brothers' debut, which is where I first heard him, and also sat in on much of the *3 Feet High and Rising* sessions. That's what a collective gets you: experience. In April of 1990, two years on from Jungle Brothers, one year on from De La Soul, Q-Tip and his bandmates—Phife Dawg, Jarobi White, and the DJ and multi-instrumentalist Ali Shaheed Muhammad—stepped into their own light with their debut *People's Instinctive Travels and the Paths of Rhythm*. They had a lyricism that was slightly different than the others: not a party vibe, exactly, and not as playful, but intelligent as the day was long. Which isn't to say they weren't also playful. The album had four singles, starting with "Description of a Fool," before the record, and continuing with "I Left My Wallet in El Segundo" and "Bonita Applebum" before ending with "Can I Kick It?" (Many of them were leftovers from Q-Tip's high school years. In fact, I knew the inspiration for "Bonita Applebum." The pretty apple-shaped derriere belonged to a woman named Grace Harry, who we worked with later at Universal. Sometimes it would embarrass her but it's like being a hip-hop *Mona Lisa*.)

The record was an instant critical hit. *The Source* gave it five mics. Five! There aren't any more mics than that. It was the first to get that coveted honor. The second? Eric B. and Rakim's third record, *Let the Rhythm Hit 'Em*, which is connected to one of hip-hop's landmark true-crime stories. It was slated for production by Paul C, Paul McKasty, but soon after the record started, McKasty was murdered. Many of the artists he worked with were questioned as suspects, which was a more complicated matter than it seems, since Paul C was white and they were, well, not. In some cases, suspicion derailed their careers. The murder has never been solved.

The second De La album also trafficked in matters of life and death. By the time *De La Soul Is Dead* appeared, it felt like a whole generation of Native Tongues releases had already been born, been raised, grown to size, and moved out of the house. The release date was May 1991 but I didn't have to wait that long. There was an advance copy, a bootleg of some type, making the rounds a few months early. A friend of mine had it, which meant that I had to have it, but he wouldn't give it to me, so I at least had to hear it. I have a vivid memory of a February Sunday that started with Sunday school and then continued with church, except that my Sunday didn't continue with church. It continued with me and my friend sneaking out to the parking lot to sit in his Chrysler and listen to *De La Soul Is Dead*. I was hooked from the first song, but not in the traditional way, as a series of hammer blows: great sample, great lyric, great single. There was all of that but something else I hadn't experienced before. I was hooked because I was listening to a completely realized work of art. I even liked the pair of James Brown samples, "Funky Drummer" on "Oodles of O's" and "For Goodness Sakes, Look at Those Cakes" on "Afro Connection at Hi 5." (I liked them not because they were innovative in any traditional sense—if James Brown samples had been tired before, now they were exhausted—but because they were perfectly calibrated ironies. The first was a played-out staple. The second was a bizarre post–golden age oddity. It was used for a diss track whose backstory I know but cannot reveal. Wait for the De La Soul book.) The album achieved a perfect sequence and a perfect build. It was like listening to a tapestry. I knew that I would have to commit it to memory until May, because my friend was scrupulous about not making a copy for me, so I tried to absorb everything.

That got five mics also.

Later that year, A Tribe Called Quest released *The Low End Theory*, which might not have upped the ante, but it kept the ante at least where it was and injected a different kind of energy into it. You heard the songs, you loved the songs, you admired their artistry and intelligence, but there was an additional element, which was that you found yourself thinking about them later. One of the songs I like to think about later was "What." It's just questions by Q-Tip on a Quest record, which is redundant or alliterative or something. Before the last verse, there's a break and a line: "Chill for a minute; Doug E. Fresh said silence." James Brown said don't be a dropout, but that's what the song did, for four seconds. The song stopped but time stopped, too, or at least stretched. I tried to remember all the questions that the song had asked up until that point. What was weird was that I heard them not in his voice but in my own. All around those questions were answers, specifically in the way the group's sound had shifted even more consciously away from Bomb Squad hard funk into a jazzier bottom.

That got five mics also.

As Native Tongues groups rose, as I became more comfortable in that space, I was interested—and even a little pleased—to see that some of the alternatives were losing steam. N.W.A. had spent the late eighties not only as a cultural lightning rod but as a bona fide great hip-hop group. But like many groups who rise that quick, there was a fall-off to be reckoned with. Ice Cube, the group's strongest writer, left for a solo career. The rest of the band soldiered on, first with an EP, *100 Miles and Runnin'*, in 1990. Their second LP, *Niggaz4Life* (stylized in reverse as *Efil4zaggin*, to hide the slur), came out in May of 1991. The thinking behind it seemed to be this: the more extreme we go, the more we scare, the more dangerous we look, the more records we'll sell. It was packed with violence and misogyny, and wit seemed to be in short supply. A song like "Findum, Fuckum & Flee" wouldn't have made the cut for *Straight Outta Compton*. What was missing wasn't only skillful execution, but also authenticity. This was some kind of minstrelsy, looking extra-dangerous so that the suburban kids would rush to buy the record. And it worked: on June 22, the album hit number one on the new, SoundScan-derived *Billboard* Top 200.

N.W.A. had established the rules for gangsta rap and then turned into a cartoon. But not all was lost. A month or so after *Niggaz4Life*, the Houston-based rap group Geto Boys released their third record, *We Can't Be Stopped*. The record was preceded by its lead single, "Mind Playing Tricks on Me." Whereas N.W.A. was playing with a kind of gangsta triumphalism, the Geto Boys painted a portrait of isolation and paranoia, self-deception and self-doubt. The bleak, almost hopeless verses glided by atop a sample from Isaac Hayes's "Hung Up on My Baby," a song from the soundtrack of the 1974 blaxploitation-adjacent movie *Three Tough Guys*. Largely written by the group's de facto leader, Scarface, and originally earmarked for his solo album, the song was redirected to the group by its label, Rap-A-Lot, and the label's founder, J Prince. Scarface remained at the center, rapping the first and the third verse and handing off the others to Willie D and—most memorably—Bushwick Bill, the group's three-foot-eight, Jamaica-born MC, who was one of the most singular figures of nineties hip-hop. Three tough guys. A few weeks before the album's release, Bill, high on PCP and Everclear and in the midst of an argument with his girlfriend, shot himself in the face, costing himself his right eye in the process. Bill's verse, which dealt explicitly with mental health issues (including hallucinations and self-harm), leapt out of the rest of the song, especially after the video, which included a scene of two EMTs (one white, one Black) loading a distraught Bill onto a stretcher. It was an incredible scene in an incredible video for an incredible song that did its part in counterweighting the pandering that had befallen N.W.A.

We started this chapter with pop, so it makes sense to end it the same way. (It's a palindrome, after all.) People like to talk of this period as the true birth of gun-for-the-charts, style-over-substance rap. Their Exhibit A is always "U Can't Touch This," which came out in January of 1990, and their Exhibit B is always "Ice Ice Baby," which came out in August of that same year. Let's start with A, eh? There was a regular radio feature in Philly called "Make It or Break It" where the station played a record and asked the audience to weigh in on it. Thumbs-up or thumbs . . . well, the other way? Usually "Make It or Break It" happened in the evening, which is why I thought it was strange one day when I was finishing up breakfast, getting ready for work, and heard an announcement of a new competition. Strange, but I did what I always did, which was to listen dutifully and think about the record. The record, in this case, was "U Can't Touch This" by MC Hammer. I was definitely aware of his second album, *Let's Get It Started*, which sent a few singles to the chart, from the title track to "Turn This Mutha Out." (Hammer was also a forerunner of the coming coastal wars, in surprising ways. The "Turn This Mutha Out" video showed him coming to New York to beat up the East Coast, and included a parody of Run-D.M.C.)

The first time I heard "U Can't Touch This," I loved the silly loop of the chorus. It stuck to my brain immediately, like a perfect pop song. But the qualities that made it work—its repetitiveness, its simplicity—also made it, after a little while, not work at all. By the third week or so, I was no longer interested in hearing about how I could not touch it.

Soon enough, it became obvious that I was not the only one. At a time when the West Coast was trying hard to be hard, Hammer was a problem. He was a clean rapper, for starters, which placed him outside the cylinder of cool. He was arguably more dancer than rapper: see above. Maybe the biggest sin was the way he used samples. Rather than transform them the way that a brilliant artist might—see Boogie Down Productions, see Eric B. and Rakim, see EPMD—he just let the original song do his work for him. It worked. "U Can't Touch This" was a massive hit, topping the R&B chart and going top ten on the main chart, the Hot 100. (It wasn't the only song to be pushing boundaries. Digital Underground's "The Humpty Dance," which came out a week after Hammer's single, also went top ten or near it, and it even took a swipe at their Oakland neighbor: "People say 'You look like MC Hammer on crack, Humpty!'" Side note: while the humor and general P-Funk spirit of the Digital Underground song was great, what made it work for me was the drum part, taken from both Sly and the Family Stone and Parliament, which became one of the most resampled loops in hip-hop history, used by everyone from Public Enemy to Ice Cube to Redman to LL Cool J.)

A pop-rapper like Hammer wasn't entirely unprecedented, but what was unprecedented was the backlash. It wasn't just Digital Underground lightly mocking a member of their rising class. 3rd Bass's "The Gas Face," which was structured as a general diss song—the gas face is the face you make when someone else passes it and stinks up a room—took a swipe at Hammer even before "U Can't Touch

This," with Pete Nice's plea "Hammer, shut the fuck up!" Ice Cube's "True to the Game" video portrayed Hammer as a willful sellout, changing his look to appeal to the mainstream. And "To da Break of Dawn," which LL Cool J placed on the *House Party* soundtrack before including it on *Mama Said Knock You Out*, numbered Hammer among the various rappers LL dissed. "That amateur, swingin' a hammer from a body bag, so run and get your camera" and "You swing a hammer, but you couldn't break a glass" were among the insults, but LL held the most savage for the end of the verse: "My old gym teacher ain't supposed to rap."

LL kicked off the verse after that with more choice words: "How dare you stand beside me? / I'm Cool, I freeze I-C-E." This diss was directed at Ice-T, but there was also another Ice on the scene: Vanilla Ice. A white kid who had been born Robbie Van Winkle in Dallas, Vanilla Ice moved to Miami as a child, and aspired to rap stardom at an early age—practicing both beatboxing and breakdancing—before moving off into motocross racing, where he competed successfully, winning a number of championships. An ankle injury kept him off the bike, and he directed his energies back to performing, becoming a key member of a troupe that would open for acts (everyone from Public Enemy to N.W.A.) in a Dallas nightclub called City Lights. In 1987, he was stabbed outside of City Lights and, during that recuperation, started to put together music of his own. His first single, released by the Atlanta indie label Ichiban—which also put out his debut album, *Hooked*—was a rap cover of Wild Cherry's "Play That Funky Music." The B-side, called "Ice Ice Baby," used the bassline of Queen's "Under Pressure."

Ethical questions aside, the song was catchy enough to get more attention than the A, which happens sometimes. It started to climb. Partly Van Winkle had the benefit of *Video Music Box*, a video show where underground pop-rap songs could surface. A few years before, this populist technology had benefitted the Miami bass group 2 Live Crew and their song "Me So Horny." Now it helped Vanilla Ice. In November of 1990 "Ice Ice Baby" became the first *Billboard* Hot 100 number one for any rap song.

The tide turned for Vanilla Ice. No one was going to call him out just for being white or being wack. And yet, there were issues. The main lyrical hook bore more than a passing resemblance to Alpha Phi Alpha's "Ice Cold" chant. (You can see it in Spike Lee's *School Daze*, from 1988: they come out to step and recite their slogan—"Ice ice baby / The black and gold / Ice ice baby / Too cold too cold.") Conversations about cultural appropriation in hip-hop, white taking from Black, are not always appropriate. Earlier we talked about how the Beastie Boys came by their New York downtown cred honestly. Later we'll talk about Eminem's legitimacy. For that matter, 3rd Bass was white, and one of the most authentic groups around. Art is inherently a site of vibrant combination. But occasionally there are more overt examples of borrowing that require a discussion. As "Ice Ice Baby" went up the charts, Vanilla Ice started to make the rounds as a talk show guest, and one of his stops was *The Arsenio Hall Show*. Arsenio wasn't always a hard-hitting interviewer, but that day he felt compelled to ask Vanilla Ice about his place in the hip-hop world. Vanilla Ice didn't answer especially well. He deflected. And at one point he deflected in an especially problematic way, which was to bring up Flavor Flav from the audience for smiling and hugging and photo-op-style look-at-the-two-of-us-together-type stuff. It seemed like one of those moments where a politician on the hot seat suddenly produces a Black friend from the wings, and Arsenio said so.

Grand claims are made for 1991 and I am one of the people who has made them.

It's the year that gave us "Summertime," the first single from DJ Jazzy Jeff and the Fresh Prince's fourth record, *Homebase*. Will came on more confident. There was more age in his voice, more patience, more gravity. He was also clearly aware that he was reentering a history in (rapid) progress. "Just a little something to break the monotony / Of all that hardcore dance that has gotten to be." Was he pushing against new pop songs? Against his own pop past? Whatever it was, he was doing it rooted in place, in Philly, where "we be out in the park / A place called the Plateau is where everybody goes." (The Plateau is now our home for the Roots Picnic.)

It's the year that gave us Tim Dog's "Fuck Compton." Gruff and thrilling, with a style that was almost like proto–New Orleans bounce, Tim Dog made a show of going after N.W.A., both generally ("You think you're cool with your curls and your shades") and then by name (he vowed to "crush Ice Cube"). If you are trying to locate the Ground Zero of the East-West problem, this is a good place to start.

It's the year that gave us Naughty by Nature's "O.P.P." As pop-rap hybrids go, this is among the best-executed. Treach had a point to make, and the Jackson 5 sample was letter-perfect.

With so much birth, you need some death. Is that melodramatic? Or rather: with so much new, you need to feel that some of what used to be new is now old. That happened for me in the fall of 1991, when my two North Stars, Public Enemy and Prince, put out new albums. In fact, *Apocalypse 91 . . . The Enemy Strikes Black* and *Diamonds and Pearls* were released on the same day, October 1. Both were . . . underwhelming. Something was wrong. I'd never thought that my two pillars would teeter. But teetering became a cue to find a new way to hold things up, at least on the hip-hop side. The second single from *Apocalypse 91*, "Shut 'Em Down," was released both in its album version and in a radical remix by Pete Rock (born Peter Phillips to Jamaican American parents who moved from New York City to Mount Vernon, another island influencer). It was a literal changing of the guard: the strongest song on the first PE album not to fully turn my head had been handed off to a newcomer who was ready to usher in the next chapter of the genre. With its floating horns and its overall re-creation of the song's energy—the feel wasn't Bomb Squad aggression anymore, but something looser and tighter simultaneously that felt like a quantum leap forward—I would say that it's the greatest rethink except that we live in a universe that also contains Black Sheep's "The Choice Is Yours (Revisited)."

I was interviewing Pete Rock once and asked him about it. I

expected a complex story about balancing coasts and genres and historical periods (sort of like the one in the last paragraph). Pete Rock gave me a different story, which was that he had the session booked, slept late, swept a bunch of records into his bag as he headed out the door, and made what he made. He knew he had to do the work so they didn't move on to the next young producer on the list. Sometimes history is inadvertent.

The "Shut 'Em Down" remix left a mark on hip-hop, not just because it elevated Pete Rock. It solidified the idea of a producer tag. Here it was aural. Later, it could be verbal, like with Lil Jon and the *Gangsta Grillz* series (more on that later) or Metro Boomin here in the present. Producers announcing themselves is like Minnie Pearl leaving the price on her hat on *Hee Haw*, or is it? It's like Alfred Hitchcock wandering through his own movie, or is it? It's like a guy standing by the front door of his party, forcing you to acknowledge him as you head into the place, or is it? What it is, definitely, is a shift in the power from artist to producer: while producers had always starred, here they were asking for name above the title.

1992

WHILE I GET MY PROPER SWERVE ON

1997

The conversation shifts West, the art shifts with it, the East holds on stubbornly so as not to lose what it had, and in the ensuing struggle everyone loses.

No matter how you slice it, this is the chronic era, in large part because it is the *Chronic* era. In May 1992, at a presidential candidates' forum, the Arkansas governor Bill Clinton declared that he, while in England, "experimented with marijuana a time or two." You probably remember the rest of that quote: "I didn't like it. I didn't inhale it, and never tried it again." There was plenty of smoke in America no matter what Bill admitted. Some of it came from blunts lit and lifted (Dre's album title carries those tiny torches, as does his first and most important protégé, Snoop Dogg). But some of the smoke came from other sources, including the unrest in Los Angeles that broke out in the wake of the Rodney King beating. King, an African American motorist, was pulled over for driving while intoxicated on the I-210 and brutally beaten by four LAPD officers. The officers were arrested, tried, and then, in April 1992, acquitted, a decision that did not sit well with the city's Black community. The result was six days of violence, more than eighty deaths, nearly a billion dollars in property damage, and limitless material for West Coast rappers. Ice Cube, Dre's former N.W.A. bandmate, became a superstar in the wake of the unrest, in large part because he gave voice to the rage of Black Los Angeles. The focus of America, which had been on the end of the Cold War during the Reagan and Bush years, was returned to domestic issues, especially those around race and social justice. Clinton was a player here, too, a governor from a Southern state who came into office with a commitment to diversifying the federal government. And then there was the O. J. Simpson saga, which also consumed the national interest and exposed racial divisions in perceptions of justice. But equally important in this equation is the California factor. Ten years earlier, Run-D.M.C. had built their music on the sounds and sights of their Queens neighborhood. LA hip-hop not only sounded different, but it was sourced differently, a product of car culture rather than stoop culture, urban reality offset by the vistas of the nearby coast. G-funk ran more smoothly than Bomb Squad production, but it was no less compelling. For the first time, if you stopped a person on the street and asked them to identify the epicenter of the hip-hop, you'd get not one answer, but two at once, both coasts contributing. But they were competitive rather than cooperative forces, on a collision course, and the growing tensions would end with not one but two tragedies that would forever change the complexion of the genre.

O nce again, hip-hop was making strides, and once again I was listening to everything I could. These were different destinations than back in the eighties, new frontiers and horizons.

Set course for "They Reminisce Over You (T.R.O.Y.)."

We ended the last chapter with Pete Rock. Let's Rock on. He had his own project, with the rapper CL Smooth (from New Rochelle, on the other side of Pelham from Mount Vernon), and released an EP in 1991 and then an album, *Mecca and the Soul Brother*, the following year. The album had a standout track, a memorial song dedicated to Troy Dixon, also known as Trouble T Roy. Dixon was a dancer with Heavy D and the Boys, who was on tour with them in Indianapolis in July 1990, when he was walking down an exit ramp outside Market Square Arena. He wasn't just walking. He was clowning around, and someone else who was clowning around overturned a trash can, which started rolling down the ramp. Dixon jumped up on a ledge to avoid the can but lost his balance and fell to the street. He died the next day. Heavy D dedicated *Peaceful Journey* to him the next year, but T Roy's true legacy was this Pete Rock and CL Smooth track, their debut album's debut single. The song comes in both clamorous and heavenly and then pulls back out to its jazzy background. In 1992, as we'll see in a minute, rap made a sharp turn toward certain kinds of samples, which meant that whatever wasn't those kinds of samples got raided. That meant that producers who were proud of their sound had to go out and find other kinds of artists. That's what came to be called "jazzy." In reality, it was what some people thought of as second-tier jazz artists, not icons but groove masters: Monty Alexander's piano, Vic Juris's guitar, Tom Scott's saxophone. Rock's "Shut 'Em Down" remix had sampled Tom Scott and the California Dreamers' "Never My Love." This used another Scott/Dreamers track, "Today," which Large Professor had used for a Slick Rick remix the year before. "They Reminisce Over You" is maybe the high point of a certain kind of hip-hop, which is ground-level neighborhood portraiture, and there's a line in it that the Roots' manager, Rich Nichols, used to always cite to prove that rap once truly measured the reality and most importantly the warmth of the Black community and then, as time went on, failed to do so. "After ten years without no spouse," CL Smooth raps, "Momma's getting married in the house." In the final verse, there's a straightforward, almost sentimental moment: "T to the R the O-Y, how did you and I meet? / In front of Big Lou's, fighting in the street / But only you saw what took many time to see / I dedicate this to you for believing in me."

Set course for "DWYCK."

Gang Starr was based in Brooklyn, but their roots were more diverse. DJ Premier (born Christopher Martin), the musical brains behind the duo, was from Houston, and Guru (Keith Elam), the rapper, was from Boston. Gang Starr, the name, had started life as a Morehouse College rap collective, but various personnel changes forced dissolution, reconstitution, and collaboration with Premier. The duo bent toward jazz—not exclusively, but enough so that it became their establishing shot, especially when Spike Lee heard a song called "Jazz Music" from their debut record and asked them to rethink it for the soundtrack of his new movie *Mo' Better Blues*. That track, "Jazz Music," featured Branford Marsalis and launched Gang Starr as a forward-thinking (if sometimes retro-sampling) enterprise. Their sophomore album, *Step in the Arena* in 1990, was considered by some to be the best hip-hop album ever, and I mean no disrespect by saying that it's not quite that but still a stone-cold classic. Guru's delivery was Rakim-adjacent, in the sense that he didn't get exercised unnecessarily, and he had a journalist's eye for street scenes. *Daily Opera-*

tion, two years later, was only a slight step down, and *Hard to Earn*, their fourth record, was an expansion of mission. Gang Starr widened their scope to showcase the Gang Starr Foundation, a collective that included other rappers like Jeru the Damaja, Big Shug, and the duo Group Home. It also included a collaboration with Nice and Smooth, a Bronx duo who had appeared on records by Big Daddy Kane and others. That collaboration was "DWYCK," a straight-on smooth boast classic with an immortal couplet that predicted (and maybe created) other great left-field rap jokes by Lil Wayne and others: "Lemonade was a popular drink and it still is / I get more props and stunts than Bruce Willis." It also has the rhinoceros/esophagus rhyme that would be surfaced later by Flight of the Conchords.

Set course for "They Want EFX."

Two kids, one from Jersey, one from Brooklyn, meet at Virginia State University. Is that the setup to a joke? Not really, but the result was an effective punch line: Das EFX, a rap group that teetered on the edge of novelty. "Das" combined their two names, Dray and Skoob. EFX was their unique style, which they called "sewage" and which involved rapid rapping that rolled additional syllables into words. (These kinds of vernacular variations had existed forever—think of Frankie Smith's Izz Latin or the shizzle variation popularized by Snoop Dogg later.) They pulled everything together and filtered it through underground rap. Everyone took it and chewed it up. Das EFX's debut record, *Dead Serious*—the title alone tells you that it was affiliated with the EPMD camp—came out in April 1992, preceded slightly by a debut single, "They Want EFX," which went to number one on the rap chart and almost went top twenty pop. They had follow-ups, including the hit "Mic Checka" and a very effective appearance on Ice Cube's "Check Yo Self" remix, but the shelf was short and so was the shelf life.

All of these songs, bright spots, were soon in the shadows, thanks to a massive object that slid into the hip-hop sky in late 1992.

The Chronic, the debut LP by former World Class Wreckin' Cru and N.W.A. member Dr. Dre, had no advance singles. The album appeared in late 1992 and did only one thing, which was to change everything. In trying to describe the power of the record, future analysts said that it made white fans want to turn away from being white. I think there's something to that. As we will see later on, hip-hop ended up fully embracing an aspirational and then materialistic ethic. This is the first real twinge of that. It was aided by the fact that white America's rock hero of the moment, Kurt Cobain, genuinely seemed to understand the notion of privilege, and seemed to want to interrogate and even reject it. Dr. Dre's smooth machine, built mostly on the chassis of G-funk and California soul, sailed along, seeing the sights. There were scenes of inner-city life and violence, but they were engineered to go down smooth. Snoop Dogg emerged here as an MC, delivering his raps in the most distinctive tone since . . . Slick Rick (Rakim? Guru? Q-Tip? Hard to say precisely, but Snoop was distinctive), and that did part of that work, but the production did the rest. The production did everything.

Dre had been a producer before, of course, for years. He had produced N.W.A. and all the acts within their orbit, from Eazy-E to J. J. Fad to Michel'le. His most definitive production before *The Chronic* was the work he did on the D.O.C.'s *No One Can Do It Better* in 1989. The D.O.C. (Tracy Curry) started out in the Fila Fresh Crew, where he honed his writing, and his debut was one of the strongest releases from the N.W.A. camp. Songs like "The Formula," "Mind Blowin'," and "Whirlwind Pyramid" were sharply conceived and funky, with samples from the Sylvers, Heatwave, and Marvin Gaye, and the skits between and around the songs held their own. (My favorite was the one at the end of "Portrait of a Masterpiece," where Dre and the D.O.C. argue over whether the D.O.C. needs a break from Dre's relentless rhythms.) The D.O.C. was one of hip-hop's brightest success stories until he was one of hip-hop's saddest tragedies: just a few months after the album came out, he was in a car accident that nearly killed him and mostly robbed him of his voice. He continued to write and even managed to record a few more albums, but his career as a performer was effectively over.

As funky and persuasive as *No One Can Do It Better* was, *The Chronic* was a quantum leap forward. The Bomb Squad had layered sample upon sample upon sample, like a display rack at a carpet store. Dr. Dre just put down carpet and let you walk on it. Songs were built on a few samples, or a single sample. But he polished them until you could see the light reflecting off them from a mile away: or, in my case, 2,700 miles away.

I resisted the record at first. I couldn't entirely turn my back on the first single, "Nuthin' but a 'G' Thang," because one of its samples (the hook) was taken from Congress Alley, a 1970s band started by two people named my parents. (That's right: my dad had started out as a doo-wop singer with Lee Andrews and the Hearts, gotten married, gotten older, and gotten back into the game with a soul/funk band with my mom and aunt. A hipper 5th Dimension. They put out a self-titled album, and the first track was "Are You Looking," written by Billy Jackson and Eva Darby, recorded by my family. Dr. Dre was looking, or at least listening. The song had a history after *The Chronic*, turning up in songs by Jay-Z, Killer Mike, and the GZA, but this was its first appearance.)

The Chronic was a hit immediately. Its three singles—not just "Nuthin' but a 'G' Thang," but also "Dre Day" and "Let Me Ride"—all made it to the *Billboard* Top Ten, and the record sold three million copies that year, securing Dre a place in the year's top ten bestselling artists, the only rapper in a group that also included Garth Brooks, Kenny G, Pearl Jam, Eric Clapton, Janet Jackson, Billy Ray Cyrus, Reba McEntire, the Spin Doctors, and Michael Bolton. The people had spoken. A kajillion *Chronic* fans couldn't be wrong. Or could they? I tried to appreciate the record but something got in my way. There were qualities it represented that were off-putting to me. It was too well-oiled, almost too successful in its aims. It sounded too . . . what's the word? I'll think of it. What I could see immediately was that *The Chronic* was bringing about a number of major shifts in hip-hop. For starters, there was the shift from East to West. Up until now, hip-hop had been definitively oriented on the right side of the map. We all knew Too $hort. We knew Ice-T. We had followed N.W.A.

and the solo careers that rose from its ashes, first Ice Cube, then Dre himself. But *The Chronic* was a new level of world-building, adding Snoop Doggy Dogg, Nate Dogg, Kurupt, and more. It also quashed the bad blood within N.W.A. that had led to the group's breakup and songs like "No Vaseline." And so one of the signal moments for me was Ice Cube's cameo in the "Let Me Ride" video, when he came out of a bathroom and said "Damn right, it was a good day." So was there no more bad blood between Cube and the other members of N.W.A.? If there was a unified front on the West Coast, what did that mean for the future of hip-hop geopolitics?

But it wasn't a Utopia, either. There was a pinched quality to the lyrics. Hip-hop had always had plenty of room for the rough stuff, and I wasn't a prude by any stretch. Street violence and a certain amount of retrograde sexual politics were all over the music, just like they were all over rock and roll. Even so, I expected a certain level of creativity. I wasn't sure what to do with lines like "Hop back as I pop my top, you trip" or "Well, I'm peepin' and I'm creepin' and I'm creepin'" other than downvote them. And the cruder lines from songs like "Dre Day" were beyond the pale. Equally important was the sonic shift, away from the jackhammer intensity of the East Coast sound, which had influenced N.W.A. and its Bomb Squad–like production—and which had brought Ice Cube and the Bomb Squad together for the kickoff of his solo career—and toward something that was unquestionably California in feel, about getting yours, about hanging out all afternoon with a blunt and a girl, about rolling through the streets with your posse. The music had a breeze to it. It also had different musical forbears than the James Brown samples that had backboned the Golden Age. The other cameo in the "Let Me Ride" video was archival footage showing George Clinton and the P-Funk Mothership. P-Funk had been in the air and on wax before. Digital Underground had made a meal of them. But this was a different use, a fuller embrace that served notice not only that Dr. Dre was trying to assume the musical mantle of Dr. Funkenstein through sampling but that he was attempting the same kind of free-wheeling sensibility. This was high-level, professional, expensive cultural production. Expensive: that was the word I was looking for. Through this book, I have divided eras by their dominant drug, and the *Chronic* era was the chronic era. But it was also the money era. Suddenly, hip-hop wasn't a type of folk music. Mama wasn't getting married in the house. It was high-end in every way, almost merciless.

The Chronic took me more than a decade to fully absorb, understand, and endorse. Other rap revolutions came up on me more quickly. Wu-Tang, for example. The story of my time with the record starts in a time before the record, in a big van, fifteen-passenger capacity. Back then, the Roots had musicians. We had songs. What we didn't have was a record deal. We had put out an independent record, *Organix*, in May 1993, and then gone in search of a record deal with a major. We had played for executives and talent scouts. We had shown up at showcases. But as of yet, no one could see clearly to a world where we were an act on their roster. Unsigned, I considered the possibility that I might have to resign myself to that fate. The gospel backing gig surfaced and I couldn't say no. It was music and it was money, two of the things that moved energy through the world. But from the road we regularly checked in with our people back east: with management, with families, with the other proto-Roots. One day on the telephone, Tariq told me that he had some news. I think the van was in Northwest Kansas, miles from anywhere that made sense to me. I wasn't getting along with the gospel group, though I wouldn't say I was feuding with them exactly. Some of them would sneak away to get high. Was that godly behavior? We were on the outside looking out. I needed another look.

"Tell me the news," I said to Tariq, and he told me: we had a record deal.

I couldn't believe it. I made him repeat himself, maybe more than once. Then I quit on the spot. I got my things from the place I was staying—the basement of the house of a pastor affiliated with the church where the gospel group was playing—and that was that. I was on my own, in one sense, but in another sense I was more connected than ever. The phone call was a massive punctuation mark in the sentence of that year. Before Tariq hung up, we had a moment that we had in many of our discussions: the record recommendation portion of the call. Depending on where we were, one or the other of us would tell the other to hurry to the record store and pick up the newest records. In this case, I was out of pocket, and he was in the city, which meant that he had access to better stores, which meant that he was up to speed on what was new. He had two specific recommendations. The first was that I needed to buy A Tribe Called Quest's *Midnight Marauders*. The second was that I needed to buy Wu-Tang Clan's debut, *Enter the Wu-Tang (36 Chambers)*.

As I have explained, A Tribe Called Quest was right in the sweet spot for me. We had been inspired by the Native Tongues groups since the start. We were on board with their philosophy, their sound, their lyrical approach. That was a ship I was willing to ride all the way home. The Wu-Tang was a trip to a less familiar place. I knew a bit of their background. It had started with a trip of cousins working together, as Force of the Imperial Master, as the All In Together Now Crew, tried to get signed, went down the same roads that the Roots had gone down, auditions, showcases, no one could see clearly to getting them across the line. To survive, they splintered. One of the cousins went to Tommy Boy Records as Prince Rakeem (one of his aliases—he had also operated as the Scientist) and released a solo record, *Ooh I Love You Rakeem*, that was pretty much just an extended single with various mixes of two or three songs. It was a coproduction with Easy Mo Bee, who had been and would continue to be an underrated shadow presence for years. (His most interesting chapter would come in the midnineties, when he bridged the East Coast–West Coast gap, producing significant amounts of both Biggie's *Ready to Die* and 2Pac's "Runnin' from tha Police," which was earmarked for *Me Against the World* but ended upon on the *One Million Strong* compilation.) Easy Mo Bee also worked with a second cousin, who went by the Genius, for *Words from the*

Genius, which was released on Cold Chillin' records. Those two albums came out in 1991 and disappeared, more or less, in 1991. The two cousins retooled their alter egos—they were now the RZA and the GZA—and met up again with the third one, now going by Ol' Dirty Bastard, and a fourth member, a Staten Island rapper named Ghostface Killah.

As the group came together, a sonic and lyrical aesthetic began to develop around certain pop-culture touchstones: comic books, cartoons, kung fu movies, and more. The foursome kept growing, adding Method Man, Raekwon, Masta Killah, U-God, and Inspectah Deck. Right toward the end of 1992, there was a single, "Protect Ya Neck," that made a sizable splash. The group was now signable, but there was a catch; the collective wanted to keep sprawling, to allow each individual member to pursue a solo career at the same time that the group moved forward. Eventually Loud/RCA agreed to terms, the group signed, and the debut album, *Enter the Wu-Tang (36 Chambers)* came out on the same day as *Midnight Marauders*: November 9, 1993.

(This is the rough story. If you want the full soap opera, you may want to skip ahead to the Hulu series *Wu-Tang: An American Saga*, which takes the group's founding and early years and blows it up into brighter colors and sharper conflicts, keeping certain parts of reality while discarding others. The RZA has called it "historical fiction." In cases like this, it's possible that less is more, and that historical fact is better.)

In retrospect, I can understand the importance of that day as one of the last great days (if not the last great day) of hip-hop releases. But at the time, my reaction was a little bit different. I played *Midnight Marauders* first. It was everything I hoped that it would be. It included the single I had already heard, "Award Tour" with Trugoy the Dove from De La Soul. It was "Oh My God" with Busta Rhymes and a Kool and the Gang sample. It was "Electric Relaxation" (powered by a sample from the jazz organist Ronnie Foster [the song, "Mystic Brew," was toward the back of his album *Two Headed Freap* (which was recorded on January 20, 1972, a date that was noteworthy because it was, among other things, my first birthday)]). That entire record was right in the pocket of the music that was already inspiring me. It was a glove that fit.

Wu-Tang was something else, at least at first. People talk about the way that they remade group size, how they came in as a large collective when hip-hop was dominated by duos and trios. That's true, but it's not entirely true. When I saw the size they were, I flashed back to groups like Boo-Yaa T.R.I.B.E. and Lifers Group. They were sprawling. How was this going to be different? When I heard how, it didn't necessarily work to their advantage. What I remember most about listening to that cassette on the drive back up to New York and Philly was that this was a group using lots of old breakbeats. In my mind, at the time, I took off points for people who covered ground that had been covered already. On the very first song, "Bring da Ruckus," the group used a sample of "Synthetic Substitution" by the soul singer Melvin Bliss, which had in its time been a nothing B-side but was already making a name for itself as a heavily trafficked hip-hop sample. It had been on Ultramagnetic MCs' "Ego Trippin'" and Public Enemy's "Don't Believe the Hype" and N.W.A.'s "Alwayz into Somethin'" and Naughty by Nature's "O.P.P." and that's just the tip of the iceberg. (The Iceberg used it, too—Ice-T sampled it for "O.G. Original Gangster.") To hear a sample that was, by 1993, already everywhere was not an auspicious beginning. The second song, "Shame on a Nigga," at first had the feel of a raid on *Ultimate Breaks and Beats*, since it used Syl Johnson's "Different Strokes," which was on the fourth compilation. But it didn't take the Captain Obvious part of the song, the first minute. It went deeper. I was coming around. But the third song, "Clan in the Front," used "Synthetic Substitution" *again*. In the van, heading east, I saw it as a step backward. When it comes to the use and misuse of samples, there are different ideas about the best and worst ways to interact with the history of recorded music. Some producers and artists have an archaeological mindset, though it's not even that academic. They are down in the ground trying for truffles. It's hard to do, but when you manage to find one, whoo! What a payoff.

Not everyone is that dogged (or piggish, if you're still thinking truffles). Others are just making music for the moment. They aren't saddled with all the pressures of the whoo-what-a-payoff. They aren't racking their brains to decide if this record is rare enough, if this exact section of it has been properly framed, if maybe this next song on this old soul record that no one really knows might make for an even better sample. There's nothing particularly villainous about what they are doing. Let's say that they are calibrating their efforts. There's a third group that in my mind stands behind the other two: the Johnny Come Latelys (Johnnys Come Lately?). The reason that people get on Puff—see also: Puffy/P. Diddy/Diddy/Love(?!)—for his method of sampling is that it can sound like it's aimed at beginners, at kindergarteners when there are graduate students in the vicinity. You want samples that, like lyrics, respect the intelligence of audiences. Structuring an entire song simply on a Diana Ross song or a David Bowie song, to the point of interpolation, doesn't necessarily do that. So that's the box where I put the RZA when I first heard Wu-Tang. I have written elsewhere about how there's a certain persistent strain of fronting in hip-hop, affecting expertise where it does not in fact exist—this is the tendency to pretend that you know an old soul song even though you have just heard it for the first time in sample form, and it's the tendency to overdramatize the search for samples. I don't remember specific interviews where the RZA made high drama out of his search for his samples. But I know there weren't any where he confirmed the picture I had in my mind's eye, which was him, in his basement, surrounded by the *Ultimate Breaks and Beats* and the *Complete Stax/Volt Singles* box set (released in 1991), mining these motherlodes for a good chunk of his album. I am tempted to believe that he bought the Stax box set with his Tommy Boy advance. It times out right, not to mention that there are some songs (like the Charmels' "As Long as I've Got You," which forms the spine of "C.R.E.A.M.") that were not readily available outside of that set. But that's just (informed) speculation.

What's not speculation but rather recollection is my belief, at the time, that it came up short. Tribe would never do something this pedestrian, I told myself. I may even have said it out loud. And I had proof. "Mystic Brew," though it ended up being used by other artists like Madlib and J. Cole, made its first hip-hop appearance on "Electric Relaxation." Tribe unearthed it. Tribe put it in place. Tribe earned pride of place. Main Source would never do something this pedestrian. Premier would never do something this pedestrian. This sounded like it was made in the basement I imagined, half-baked in a rudimentary kitchen. And so, through November, I stood on that rock. We went back to New York, where we signed with DGC records, a division of Geffen. We set about making our next record, our first major-label release, which would be called *Do You Want More?!!!??!* (original title: *Home Grown*).

Then it was December, and we were mixing our song "Mellow My Man" at Battery Studios with Bob Power, engineer extraordinaire. Bob had worked on a million Native Tongue projects but the one that was maybe most important to us was A Tribe Called Quest's second record, *The Low End Theory*. Bob has called it "the *Sgt. Pepper's* of hip-hop," and in a sense I know what he means. It refashioned and reshaped people's brains with regard to sampling and structure. It was exactly everything that truffle-hunters valued. So there I was at Battery Studios, mixing, and Q-Tip dropped by to visit Bob. All he was talking about was how dope Wu-Tang was. With Q-Tip's cosign, I let my guard down. I was able to see it through his eyes. Most importantly, I was able to get past my own intellectual resistance, to understand that sometimes the mathletes and the jocks can find common ground. Soon after that, the record earned a 4.5-mics review in *The Source*. The review didn't talk about the samples very much. Instead, it focused on the way that the group's worldview was a throwback to the mideighties state of the art, "when rap was filled with honesty, greatness, and skill." Elsewhere it hailed "furious freestyles that sting as the Clan lyrically combinate." The record was on everyone's mind all of a sudden. Fifty thousand Elvis fans couldn't be wrong, right? I returned to it for further study and began to develop a deeper appreciation for some of the MCs. Other people were going crazy for Raekwon or Ghostface. To me, at that time, they looked like street hoods, post–Kool G Rap, nothing special. My views would evolve. But in those early months I was drawn to Method Man because he sounded like my uncle Willie, and to Ol' Dirty Bastard because he was indisputably entertaining. You didn't hear deliveries and tones like that in most hip-hop. I also started to understand the songs better. One thing that hit me hard was how pop the record was. I would almost put it next to "He's the DJ, I'm the Rapper," which sounds far-fetched, but all you have to do is listen. For that matter, think about the group's second LP, *Wu-Tang Forever*, which came out in 1997 after the first wave of solo projects. That pop sense is the one thing that's missing.

36 Chambers' pop wasn't just in the songs, not just in the hooky choruses and the immediately accessible (in part because they flirted with predictability) melodies. It was also woven into the entire zeitgeist of the record. The more I listened to the record, the more I saw it not as a forward-thinking manifesto about kung fu community, but as a historical document of being a latchkey Black kid in the late seventies and early eighties. When you were that kid, it meant that the TV was always on, which meant that you were delivered an immense amount not just of old kung fu movies, but of variety shows like *Hee Haw* and *Donny & Marie*, which featured all the top pop songs of the day, not to mention almost any cartoon.

That aesthetic wasn't just in Wu-Tang. Other groups may have been less glued to the boob tube, but they had a similar attachment to straight-up-the-middle American pop culture. Take the Cold Crush Brothers, who were part of hip-hop from near the start— Big Bank Hank, who managed Grandmaster Caz, one of the group's members, was discovered by Sugar Hill Records rapping over a Cold Crush Brothers tape. (Hank was then brought in as a member of the label's new group, the Sugarhill Gang. In fact, Hank took some of Caz's rhymes without credit and used them on a little song called "Rapper's Delight," down to the point where he introduced himself as the Casanova Fly. But that's a different story. We've been there already.) This story goes back to Cold Crush Brothers' old music, damn near all of which touched on mainstream (white) radio. You could hear snippets of Glen Campbell's "Rhinestone Cowboy" or Starland Vocal Band's "Afternoon Delight." It was like an update of the Billy Joel bite from Boogie Down Productions' "The Bridge Is Over." Wu-Tang had a kind of brilliant trash aesthetic. You had to use what was available to you.

That stayed part of the way they did business. In the wake of the debut album, the Wu-Tang members did what they had planned on doing from the start, and began to emerge as solo artists. That let all the fans pick their standard-bearers and favorites. As I have said, there was a big Ghostface contingent, and a big Raekown contingent. I wasn't against them. At certain times later on in my listening evolution I would be all for them. In those early days, though, I gravitated toward ODB and especially Method Man. His official showcase on the record, "Method Man," was a perfect illustration of this principle. It drew on "Method of Modern Love," a Hall & Oates song from 1985 that pre–name checked him, not to mention "Chim Chim Cheree," from *Mary Poppins*, and *Fat Albert*, and *Looney Tunes*, and Bootsy Collins, and Dr. Seuss, and Kool and the Gang. That knocked me back. Who was this? What if Big Daddy Kane had done that? He couldn't have. This was a pretty impressive curation of both the Black and white culture that had leaked into everyone's brains when the television was on.

When Method Man's first solo album, *Tical*, came out, it confirmed my suspicions. *Tical* wasn't the most beloved of those early solo Wu records, though it sold the best based on his star power—in those early videos, you could see that he was a charismatic performer, and he later proved it when he started to act in shows like *Oz* and *The Wire* and movies like *Soul Plane* and even *Garden State*.

But it wasn't just about a charisma check. In "Bring the Pain," the first single from that album and an instant classic, he samples a relatively obscure soul song: Jerry Butler's "I'm Your Mechanical Man." It wasn't overexposed or overused. It wasn't on *Ultimate Breaks and Beats*. But he quotes Annie. By Annie, I don't mean the one from Michael Jackson's "Smooth Criminal," though I hope she's okay. I mean Little Orphan Annie, the 1920s cartoon character who became famous all over again in the late 1970s and early eighties because of the Broadway musical, cast album, and Hollywood movie. Method Man arrives at Annie, or at least *Annie*, twice: in "Bring the Pain" ("Coming from a vet on some old Vietnam shit / Nigga, you can bet your bottom dollar, hey, I bomb shit") and in "Wu-Tang Clan Ain't Nuthing ta Fuck Wit" ("the Meth will come out tomorrow").

This was, for me, one of the most clear-cut examples of this never-mind-the-truffles-here's-the-mainstream approach. When I was a kid, we all saw the movie. Most Black people won't claim that they know Geoffrey Holder from Eddie Murphy's *Boomerang*. Some might reach back into history for a blaxploitation movie and cite *Live and Let Die*. But the truth is that they know him because he played Punjab in *Annie*. Annie wasn't the must-see movie event of 1982. In fact, it was panned somewhat. But it was seen widely. And for Black kids like me, it was seen as a way of bridging into mainstream culture. Wu-Tang and its members, in casting the net this wide, stumbled upon a kind of genius. De La Soul did something similar, but they had an inclusive pose, a D.A.I.S.Y. age mentality, that made it make sense for them to push Steely Dan up against the Mad Lads. Wu-Tang was hailed as the return of street cred, as gritty exemplars. "This record is harsh," said *The Source*, awarding them 4.5 mics, "but so is the world that we live in." Method Man chose to illustrate this harshness with . . . Annie. Though she did say in no uncertain terms that it was a hard-knock life. (I apologize for the not-great joke, but it's also a serious point and a point of departure for the use of the little orphan in hip-hop and hip-hop-adjacent properties. Jay-Z would come back to Annie, and the hard-knockness of life, five years later for a huge hit, and he was on board as a producer along with Will Smith for the 2014 "Black *Annie*" starring Quvenzhané Wallis and Jamie Foxx.)

For what it's worth, I don't believe that RZA had a strategy of conscious cultural inclusion. He didn't sit in a conference room with a white board and plan out which samples would bring in which constituencies. I believe that it reflects what I sketched out above, which is that these samples and references are ways of being in the world. I come from a generation that learned that you had to know your yacht rock better than you knew your funk. I didn't know every Little River Band hit because I liked the band, though I might like the band. I knew them so that I could survive socially at school. People were impressed that I knew every last lyric of Ambrosia's "How Much I Feel," but it's hard to say whether it was by choice or by force. It was survival. You get down or you lay down. Wu-Tang got down with all of it. I didn't quite understand that the first time that I heard *Enter the Wu-Tang (36 Chambers)*, and I might not have gotten it fully when Q-Tip turned me back against my initial truffle-minded snobbery, but I got there and stayed there.

One final note about the Wu-Tang Clan and the way that they shifted the way that I listened to hip-hop. I have spoken about my theory of innovators and first followers back when I talked about Bomb Squad production, and how it evolved from innovations by producers like Marley Marl. They seemed too good to emulate. What they were selling struck Steven Van Zandt as unattainable. The other shoe didn't drop until a few months later, when the Rolling Stones appeared on *The Hollywood Palace*, a variety show that was hosted by Dean Martin. Mick Jagger didn't smile, which seemed to irritate Martin, who believed that show business was about projecting your appreciation for your audience. The Stones struck a rebel pose but more importantly they closed the distance between the idea of a rock and roll career and the kids watching from home. Less attractive than the Beatles, less fashionable, less clean, less perfect, the Stones offered Van Zandt a foothold into this new way of thinking and being. Garage bands, he argues, sprang up after the Stones with more fervor than after the Beatles.

This is, for me, part of the secret of that first Wu-Tang album. A year and a half before, when *The Chronic* came out, I understood that it was ascending to a new level of achievement. It was engineered better than anything I had ever heard. It was unfair in its polish. Wu-Tang, willfully lo-fi, delivered a Stones message in the wake of *The Chronic*'s Beatles achievement, and the combination of those two records cracked open my sense of what hip-hop could be. Before that, all my hip-hop meals had to have a Michelin star. Afterward I understood that the best restaurant in the world might be located in a strip mall. You had to hear what was there and where it came from, not just where it was leading you.

In 1995, the Roots put out our debut. More on that later. Less on that now, because we had actually put out our debut in 1993. That album, *Organix*, was made independently and sold in Europe, where we lived and worked at the time. It was intended to attract the attention of major labels. (I won't keep you in suspense. It did. Which ones? I'll keep you in suspense.)

An album that came out in 1993 meant a band that was refining its sound in 1992, and that meant a band that was writing songs, experimenting with production styles, and touring. It also means a band that is paying attention to other bands. I was already paying attention to the Native Tongues groups and Public Enemy and EPMD, sometimes to the point of obsession. In 1992, I added to that list the Pharcyde. They were an LA group that had started off as a dance crew, signed to Delicious Vinyl, that started to put out singles that didn't grab me immediately, especially "Ya Mama," the first one I heard. I was dismissive. It was yet another "Synthetic Substitution" song, for starters, and it also used the "Brothers and sisters" vocal tag from Jesse Jackson's intro to the Soul Children's performance at Wattstax. Maybe that's inside baseball, but it struck out with me, and the song built around that music wasn't . . . kind enough? Clever enough? I'm not sure. It's hard to say exactly why but it missed my mind. I voiced my displeasure, and other people, some older, some wiser, came back at me with a warning, which was that I could think whatever I wanted to about the single but I shouldn't sell the album short. The album was called *Bizarre Ride II the Pharcyde*, and even that threw me at first—why have the *II*, which suggested sequel, in the title of your debut? But when I listened to it around

Thanksgiving of 1992, I realized with a start that I had been wrong and they had been right. The album was excellent. I was taken with "Passin' Me By," which was the second single, and especially taken with the third, "4 Better or 4 Worse." The vocal performances and perspectives were sharper, but I really went in for the music. It had a sound in it, a Fender Rhodes, that reminded me of a certain reverb-and-tremolo sonic property in late-seventies Parliament, and specifically the animated commercials, sort of videos but not quite, that promoted *Motor Booty Affair*. It turned out this music was being played live by J-Swift. I remember watching them on TV and when the music arrived at that underwater undulation (it was in keeping with the theme of the album), the cartoon picture also rippled. Hearing that used so well on "4 Better or 4 Worse" was like an electric shock, and an underwater one, which is even more powerful. It stayed with me across the decade, to the point where I retooled the Roots sound to accommodate it, bringing in Scott Storch. Eventually I would point directly back to the Pharcyde by constructing a similar sonic feel for "Star," the leadoff track on *The Tipping Point*. But that was more than a decade away. At the end of 1992, all I knew was that I had found another hip-hop act to populate my personal pantheon.

We went on through the next few years connected to the Pharcyde by a kind of umbilical cord. We were taking nutrition from them. But the way that we were nourished changed. *Organix* brought us to the attention of labels. We were wined and dined and orange-juiced—at one meeting someone opened a refrigerator and told us to take whatever we wanted, even fresh-squeezed juice, which seemed like heaven's gates opening. Eventually we signed to DGC. It had been originally distributed by Warner Bros. and moved over to MCA. When we came aboard in late 1993, we were hot to record and release our debut. Titled *Do You Want More?!!!??!*, it incorporated everything we had learned up until then, which means that it was rooted in the recent past. In fact, it was a little more past than people even knew. We were eager to get done, then mostly done, then done. However, as a result of a variety of circumstances beyond our control, inclement weather you might say, the release of the record was slightly delayed.

I can (should?) briefly recap what happened, though it's not really a hip-hop story so much as it is a story about how other genres and markets could choke out hip-hop. Our parent label, Geffen, was riding high because of its big rock acts, especially Guns N' Roses, Aerosmith, and Nirvana. Guns N' Roses had been massive for them in the late eighties with *Appetite for Destruction* and *GNR Lies*. Their follow-up, the two-volume *Use Your Illusion*, was also huge, but felt a little worrisome to them. It was bloated in a way that meant either a band at the absolute peak of its powers, unwilling to edit itself, or a band teetering on the edge. Turned out to be the edge. They would put out a stopgap record of punk covers in 1993 and then . . . nothing . . . for fifteen years. Aerosmith had self-destructed in the early eighties on Columbia and been revived by Geffen, who steered them through a four-album cycle that returned them to megastardom, especially on *Pump* and *Get a Grip*, both of which were multi-multi-platinum. But after *Get a Grip* in 1993, Aerosmith left Geffen and went back to Columbia. The label's third major rock act and in some ways their most promising, Nirvana, had come up on Sub Pop and come over to Geffen for 1991's *Nevermind*, which cemented grunge as a commercial force, eventually selling more than ten million copies in the US and thirty million internationally. The band's follow-up, *In Utero*, was released in 1993. It was weaker by half in terms of sales, but that still meant that it was one of the top-selling rock records of the year. And then Kurt Cobain killed himself. Our manager, Rich Nichols, called me and told me that a storm was coming. That was the inclement weather. With three massive earners gone, what would the label do?

Rock digression over.

We took off for England. While we were living there, I tried to keep track of American hip-hop, but inside I was going crazy. We had no internet back then, and to get a *VIBE* or a *Source* every two weeks was both a godsend and a reminder of the pain I felt without them. I bought records when I could, though it was an economic consideration. I distinctly remember the fall of 1994, when musically all we had to hold us down were a quartet of records: *Tical* by Method Man, *The Main Ingredient* by Pete Rock and CL Smooth, and *Everything Is Everything* by Brand Nubian. That's three. The fourth record was Redman's *Dare Iz a Darkside*. If I say that if your album cover is better than your record, that's problematic. And *Dare Iz a Darkside* had a great cover, an update of Funkadelic's *Maggot Brain*, and two sides of music that were . . . well, Redman had hit higher heights, though maybe not higher states. (He has talked himself about how drugged up he was during the making of the record, and how he has a hard time listening back to it.) But I listened, and I learned, particularly from the remix of the album's lead single, "Rockafella." Erick Sermon produced the remix, and something about it awakened what I would come to recognize as my Soulquarian chakras. It was light in the ass, which was a state that had been enabled by *The Chronic*, this mellow thing that set it against the hardcore crack era that had preceded it. I listened. I learned.

Flash forward. We finally came back home in January 1995 for our record release. Some of the label's stunned paralysis had lessened. To celebrate the release of that album, we played a show at Irving Plaza in New York City. It was truly a celebration, in that we were being inducted into a kind of fraternity of bands with major-label records. The audience was filled with others: Brand Nubian, the Wu-Tang Clan, Mad Skillz, and the Pharcyde. I remember talking to them after the show. I remember thinking about altitudes and attitudes. Just a few years before, I had listened to a single, dismissed it, listened to an album, absorbed it. We weren't signed yet so there was a bright line separating us from them. Now we were on the same side of that line. We were conversing as colleagues. They started telling me about their upcoming music. Their first album had been produced largely by J-Swift, a Spain-to-LA producer who also worked with the Jazzyfatnastees, a female quartet who would join the Roots orbit. But the relationship between group and producer had curdled and so their second album would be something different, a change in creative direction. They had their eye on a collaboration with Q-Tip. I started to hear heavenly angels. A group as talented as the Pharcyde working with a legend like Tip, well, how could that be anything but amazing? I left the show on a cloud. A month or so later, I got word that Q-Tip had pulled out of the project. He didn't have music for them, or music that he thought was a good fit for them. He had directed them to a guy named Jay Dee, a producer out of Detroit. I must have shrugged. It was the only reaction available to me: slight disappointment that the dream pairing hadn't happened, professional pessimism (and maybe a bit of snobbery) that a young guy I had never heard of would be able to get anything other than the minimum out of the Pharcyde.

Flash forward again to the Roots on the road. We were the opening act. The Pharcyde was headlining. The distance that I had imagined back in 1992 that had disappeared backstage at Irving Plaza was back to some degree. One night, we were done playing, packed up, getting ready for postshow interviews. I went out to the parking lot, to the van, to get a jacket. While I was out there, I heard the Pharcyde starting its set. The sound wasn't crystal clear but I could hear the beat, which meant that I could hear the weird shape of the beat, which was a kick drum wobbling like it had just been pulled over by the cops after a night out at a bar and was trying (and failing) to walk the line. The song I was hearing was "Bullshit," which would end up being the first song from their upcoming second record, *Labcabincalifornia*, and the effect had been produced by their new producer, this Jay Dee person who was a complete cipher to me. The kick drum sound was revolutionary. What do you do with a revolution? What I always do is stand in place, staring straight ahead, a kind of empty look in my eyes because all the energy I have is being expended thinking through what I have just encountered. If I was in America in 1776 or France in 1789, I would have worn that same expression. I wore it when I first heard the Wu-Tang Clan, when I first heard *The Chronic*. And I was wearing it again as I stood in the club and listened to the kick drum in "Bullshit." There are a number of other flash-forwards built into that moment. There's a time about a year later, when this Jay Dee produced a record for his Detroit hip-hop band, Slum Village. There's a time even later than that, when Jay Dee shifted his name to avoid confusion with Jermaine Dupri, who also went by J.D., and reemerged as J Dilla. Dilla became one of my most important creative inspirations and one of my closest friends. What he was doing during those years ranked up there with the innovations and brilliance of any producer in hip-hop history. And just because I didn't understand it immediately, standing in that club with my eyes vacant, didn't mean that I wouldn't understand it eventually. What he was doing, mainly, was returning humanity to hip-hop rhythm. Up until then, I had believed, devoutly, that the point of hip-hop drumming was to approach the precision of a machine. This was a relic, maybe, of the earliest days of the genre, when producers would invite drummers in to re-create breakbeats rather than sample them. Human drumming had to be machine-perfect to preserve the illusion. That's how I had been raised. That's how my mind had been shaped. Jay Dee reshaped it. Suddenly I understood that the point was to emphasize imperfection. If you take the most meaningful, moving, and powerful songs in history, whether from rock or soul or funk, and you submit their percussion to a click-track test, you'll see that they are nothing like machine beats. They fall short of it—or maybe it's more accurate to say that they transcend it. So much clicked into place for me when I experienced that epiphany. For starters, I understood why musicians like Stevie Wonder, who is not really thought of as a drummer, was one of my favorite players. It was because of his limitations, his idiosyncrasy, his personality. It also counterweighted some of the unease I was still feeling with regard to *The Chronic*. That album was polished and perfect, like a robot. It was undeniable in its relentless power. But what if it was only one possibility? What if this was another one, and what if it was in some ways more powerful? I have written about this realization before, most extensively in *Creative Quest*, because it illustrates such a fundamental lesson about trying to find a creative path that reflects your specific, individualistic abilities and limits. You will do the most when you are the most you.

Just as we were finding a new sound, the landscape was changing in other ways.

Hip-hop is history, as this fifty-year celebration—and also the title of the book you are holding—attests, but hip-hop also has a history. We've been through some of it, from the first stirrings in James Brown and Brown-adjacent funk to the development of turntablist and toasting cultures to the formalization of basic rules and the release of foundational records. By the midnineties, by the time that I became a recording artist, all of that history was in the past. (Is that redundant, history in the past? Maybe not. There is plenty of history in the future. We just aren't there yet.) But it also meant that I had a ringside seat to the history that was in process at the time, the kind of history you don't need to read about because you're experiencing it in real time.

The 1995 Source Awards was one of those moments. You don't have to take my word for it. You can listen to Dave Mays, one of the founders of *The Source* ("How the 1995 Source Awards Changed Rap Forever"). You can listen to *Slate*, or the *New York Post*, or dozens of blogs, or hundreds of people who were there that night. I'm not the only one who sees that moment as a hip-hop version of Gettysburg. But I'm one. It's such an influential moment that I have discussed it before, on stages, in pages, in countless conversations. And it's such an influential moment that it's worth discussing over and over again.

We're talking August 3, a Thursday, in the evening. That's what you have to circle on the calendar. We're talking New York City, Madison Square Garden, Paramount Theater. That's how the camera would get there through a series of aerial shots, increasingly close-up. I was there with the rest of the Roots because we were nominees. Since the beginning of the year, we had been out on the road, a real touring band trying to put across our major-label debut,

Do You Want More?!!!??! People were noticing us, to the extent that they had nominated us.

In a normal movie, the close-ups would stop at the roof of the Paramount Theater. That night, though, they would have to go deeper than that, into the theater, to show that the crowd was already divided up. The hip-hop world was composed of regional families, label-based cliques, stylistic affinities, but that night was the first time that the divisions were so starkly apparent. There was a section dominated by Bad Boy Records, the company that Sean "Puffy" Combs had started in 1993 after being bounced from Uptown by Andre Harrell. They had made a splash right off the bat with Craig Mack's "Flava in Ya Ear." In retrospect, the single was considered a death knell for the underground. But at the time the underground loved it. Easy Mo Bee made the instrumental for "Flava in Ya Ear." It was earmarked for Apache, from the Flavor Unit, but he was on tour and it went to Mack. It's an underground producer track. The remix of "Flava in Ya Ear" featured many other artists, including a young Brooklyn rapper named Christopher Wallace, better known as the Notorious B.I.G. Biggie had been tapped as a future talent in *The Source*'s Unsigned Hype column back in 1992, the same year that he had appeared on the remix of Neneh Cherry's "Buddy X." In August 1994, he had a big single, "Juicy."

(Oh, there was at least one more single released in the summer of 1994, which I know because I released it: It was our debut single, "Distortion to Static." I specifically remember hearing the news from our manager, Rich Nichols, and I remember the next week, too, when he came back with more news: when you ran all the numbers—adds at college stations, adds at commercial stations—our single was actually outperforming Craig Mack and Biggie. What we didn't fully understand was that their adds were early leaks and only two days of reporting. They'd blow by us the next week. Still I hold on to that victory, even if in parentheses.)

Biggie's single was followed by his debut album, *Ready to Die*, which marked him as a major artist. More singles followed: "Big Poppa" in December (that song was rereleased a few months later with a historically significant B-side, which we'll get to soon), and "One More Chance" the next June (the single version was cleaned up for pop, and scored, going platinum). Not released as singles: several songs that anchored the record and have become street classics over time, from "Things Done Changed" to "Gimme the Loot" to "Machine Gun Funk." In the summer of 1995, Biggie had also appeared on "This Time Around" from Michael Jackson's *HIStory*, and he was about to release the debut album by Junior M.A.F.I.A., which he had executive produced and which would expand his empire further.

That's part of the life story, which intersected with my story when I walked into the theater and saw the Bad Boy contingent sitting together on one side. On another side was the Death Row section. While Puffy (Harlem) and Biggie (Brooklyn) were New Yorkers through and through, Death Row were visiting from LA, or more specifically Compton. Death Row had started as a partnership between Dr. Dre and Suge Knight, a former bodyguard, promoter, and manager. They had helped Dre and other artists, including the D.O.C., exit their relationship with Ruthless Records. Some said that their tactics were coercive. With what seemed like alarming speed, at least from an East Coast perspective, they started turning out hit after hit—first *The Chronic*, then Snoop Dogg's *Doggystyle*. Dre, Suge, and Snoop were all there. Tupac Shakur, a young rapper who was being courted by the label, was not, for reasons that were disturbing at the least. The previous November, Tupac had been in New York for a sexual assault trial—the incident had occurred almost exactly a year before that, and Tupac faced up to twenty-five years in prison if convicted. After a day of jury deliberations, Tupac went to the Manhattan apartment of Ron G, a DJ and an aspiring rapper. Tupac helped him out by adding some vocals to a track (called "Representin' 4 Ron G," or sometimes "The Heat"). He could have called it a night, but another call came in asking Tupac to head to Times Square to record with the up-and-coming producer and rapper Little Shawn. The session had been arranged by Little Shawn's manager, Jimmy "Henchman" Rosemond, and there was some negotiation over whether Tupac would get paid. When he was getting paid, he was in. When he wasn't, he was out. They went back and forth, and finally Tupac was satisfied about the fee and went to Quad Studios, where another rapper, Lil' Cease, was sent downstairs to bring him up. Before Tupac could get into the building, he was ambushed, mugged, robbed, and shot. He survived, but as he reconstructed the evening, he developed a belief that he had been set up by Puffy, Biggie, and Jimmy Henchman, in part because they were angry that he was passing Bad Boy over for Death Row. Of course, these events were decades ago, blurry now, and everyone has their own take on what happened. This is merely one version of those events. The next day, as Tupac recuperated, he received word that he had been convicted in his trial—not on the most serious sodomy charges, but on two counts of forcible touching. He went to jail. (While he was in there, he heard a reissue of Biggie's "Big Poppa" with a new B-side, "Who Shot Ya," that seemed to be making light of what had happened to him, even though it had been finished for more than a year at that point.)

So those were the two opposing armies in the Paramount that night, and then there were the rest of us. That's where I sat, along with various other rappers and producers who were not directly involved in the growing animosity between Bad Boy and Death Row. Who was in that section? Mobb Deep, one of the sharpest New York duos, was there, fresh off of releasing their second (and arguably best) record, *The Infamous*. Outkast, one of the bright lights of Southern rap, was there, a year and half removed from their debut album, *Southernplayalisticadillacmuzik*. Much of the Wu-Tang Clan was there. Busta Rhymes was there. And Nas was there.

Nas, of course, was Nasir Jones, a New York city native and son of the jazz cornet player Olu Dara, who had played with everyone from Henry Threadgill to James Blood Ulmer to Don Pullen. Nas had started off as "Kid Wave" (a whole book could be written about unfortunate early rap nicknames), moved on to "Nasty Nas," came to the attention of Large Professor and Main Source, featured on the song "Live at the Barbecue" on their classic 1991 debut *Break-*

ing *Atoms*, put a solo song called "Halftime" on the soundtrack to *Zebrahead* (an early hip-hop movie), and then started work with a number of producers (mostly Large Professor and DJ Premier, along with single songs with Q-Tip and Pete Rock) on his first record. (Whew. They don't call them capsule histories because they are easy to swallow.) Nas's debut, *Illmatic*, came out in April 1994 (a week before Outkast's debut, in fact) and quickly became recognized as a classic of East Coast rap, filled with street-level storytelling from Nas's childhood in the Queensbridge projects and brilliant emotional introspection. The record scored a coveted five-mic review from *The Source*, and it was easy to see why. It was lyrically sharp throughout and musically diverse. "Life's a Bitch" featured Nas's dad and the first guest verse from AZ. "One Love" was structured as a series of letters from Nas to friends in jail, including fellow rappers like Cormega. And while "N.Y. State of Mind" actually folded in a little Philly (the sample came from "Mind Rain," from Joe Chambers, the legendary drummer and pianist), it contained an entire dictionary's worth of street vocabulary (steelo, cee-lo, baseheads, G-packs, Mac-10s, Moët).

Illmatic was the first major hip-hop album to let the listener direct the experience: it was buffet, not omakase. *Illmatic* wasn't just a triumph of execution. It was also a triumph of positioning. Beginning with its first track, "The Genesis" framed itself as an authentic artwork that resisted a growing tide of commercialism (on the one hand) and gangster posturing (on the other). In one sense, it succeeded completely—over the years, it became possibly the most written-about album in the history of the genre, fully acknowledged as a landmark and a classic. But at the Source Awards that night, its achievement was seen in a more equivocal light.

Nas's street style had been note-perfect on the record. That night, it was slightly off. He arrived in a Tommy Hilfiger shirt that he was swimming in a little. Later on, it came to light that he'd had to borrow money to buy it. (This wasn't solely because he was a street-level rapper with an artistic conscience. It was also because he spent too much money, not an uncommon situation for a young artist.) While the seating arrangement was a visual metaphor for the tension between Bad Boy and Death Row, Nas was also up against Bad Boy, though in a completely different sense. *Illmatic* was up for most of the major awards of the night, and its main competition was Biggie's *Ready to Die* (4.5 from *The Source*). Everything that Nas seemed to be warning the hip-hop community about was perfectly represented by Biggie's record. It was artistically brilliant, but it was also an aggressively commercial proposition, with its street songs as outliers. And it was doing what it set out to do, trouncing Nas commercially.

But awards were different, right? They rewarded pure creative achievement, right? Wrong. Over and over again that night, nominees were read, nominees held their breaths, winners were read, and everyone except winners exhaled in disappointment. Nas exhaled in disappointment repeatedly that night. Minute by minute his shirt got bigger.

People remember that night for the way it accelerated East-West animosity, and that's fair. Suge Knight insulted Puffy in the form of recruiting for the Death Row roster: "Anyone out there who wanna be a recording artist and wanna stay a star, and don't have to worry about the executive producer trying to be all in the videos, all on the records, dancing, come to Death Row." The New York crowd booed. Snoop, taking the stage a little later, reflected on the negative reception: "The East Coast ain't got no love for Dr. Dre and Snoop Dogg and Death Row? Y'all don't love us?" And Puff, though he made remarks that hinted at mutual respect, started his performance with a manifesto of division: "I live in the East, and I'm gonna die in the East." (The back-and-forth was so dominant that it swamped representatives of other regions. André 3000 was booed, tried to quiet the crowd by saying, "We just want y'all to know the South's got something to say," failed to do so, and then put that audio on their next record, *Aquemini*.) It wasn't just awards-show talking, either. Within a few months, Tupac would officially join Death Row after Suge Knight bailed him out of jail. The West Coast artists Tha Dogg Pound—a Snoop spinoff with Kurupt and Daz Dillinger that also backed Death Row's least likely signing, MC Hammer—released "New York, New York," which questioned East Coast supremacy and had a video that showed them stomping Manhattan buildings, Godzilla-style. (There was an answer record, "L.A., L.A.," by Capone-N-Noreaga, featuring fellow East Coast artists Mobb Deep and Tragedy Khadafi.) Things escalated until . . . well, everyone knows what the "until" was. The escalation that wiped out two of the genre's brightest stars and, in some people's minds, cemented the idea that hip-hop was a violent scourge was a historical disaster. But in a sense, the creative massacre that night was even worse. Nas left the awards and changed his entire outlook and his approach—his follow-up, *It Was Written*, tried for Biggie-style success, and largely succeeded. But it also marked the birth of a self-mythologizing Nas, foregrounding his mafia persona, Nas Escobar, and employing slicker production that resembled West Coast G-funk. If the most promising street poet could be flipped, what did that mean for everyone else? What it meant was that everything had changed, and that it was now left to us to come to terms with that.

1997

DARE ME TO DRIVE?

2002

Hard realities—life and death, time and space—become all too real for a genre not yet out of its adolescence, and growing pains turn into labor pains for a new generation.

This period is filled with agony and ecstasy. Agony because hip-hop was emerging from its most painful period yet, one that saw coastal rivalries escalate, that witnessed the deaths of two superstars, and one that also established an underlying political and ethical structure that was, depending on where you stood, either triumphalist or endlessly destructive. The *Chronic* era had begun to shift hip-hop away from its DIY origins, but it was still very much an album rooted in street poetry (though the West Coast variety differed significantly from what had come before). By the time this next half decade rolled around, much of that was gone, and then there was a further shift, toward a brand of hip-hop explicitly concerned with window dressing, suits, champagne, cars, boats, and more. That's the ecstasy. If you could create a situation that got the girls dancing, you were more than halfway home. Everyone was going to get paid and popular. Everyone was going to get loaded in every sense of the word. These movements are linked, of course—the pain and the sadness of losing some of the genre's brightest talents touched off a countermovement that was about pleasure and escapism. But it was very much about succession, about the search for the next star who would be a standard-bearer for hip-hop. The temporary vacuum created by the violent erasure of Biggie and Tupac let people look beyond the two-coast model, and stars that had been bubbling under in Houston, Atlanta, or Virginia started to boil over. Before this period, I was dismissive of other coasts, simply because the East Coast–West Coast narrative was so dominant. I knew about Jermaine Dupri and his body of work. How could you not? But I told myself that it was pop-adjacent, not to minimize it, but to locate it. I knew about Miami bass as a subgenre, but that felt like it was a soundtrack for the strip clubs as much as it was a way of keeping a finger on the pulse of the broader culture. By 1997, I was receptive to the idea that the genre had put roots down all over the country, and that the music we were hearing from Outkast, say, was a unique post-*Chronic* variant rather than the same music reflected back at us. Which isn't to say that it didn't take some getting used to—the jazz footing that connected to the intellectual content that was so present the previous half decade gave way to what sounded initially to me like random musicians playing a groove. Like so much of hip-hop innovation, I had to catch up to it, to understand how to appreciate it. I did.

To tell the story of this half decade, we have to step back a bit. We'll be moving through time but talking about place.

Hip-hop had always had pride of place. Where you were mattered. We talked about KRS-One battling with MC Shan, "The Bridge" set against "The Bridge Is Over." But that was borough rivalry, KRS-One repping the Bronx against the Juice Crew's Queens. That idea that your hip-hop meant more than the other guy's accelerated and intensified, especially when it came to New York and LA. Remember Tim Dog's "Fuck Compton"? No one in Compton forgot it. By the time of the 1995 Source Awards (that should be easy to remember—it was just a chapter ago), battle lines were drawn. At least two types of battle lines: there was the one that separated storytelling rap from materialistic rap, Nas from Biggie, but those were both New York MCs. The deeper and more troubling divide was the East against the West, Bad Boy versus Death Row. Each of these labels had a clear superstar: Bad Boy's, again, was Biggie, and Death Row's was Tupac. (This division only sort of made sense. Biggie was all Brooklyn, born and raised, but Tupac had been born in Harlem and raised in Baltimore. In fact, his first rap name was MC New York, which he took in Baltimore and carried with him when he moved to California in his teens.)

Guns entered the picture. One gun in particular: the one that shot Tupac outside of Quad Studios in November 1994. Following that, Tupac went to prison on a sexual assault charge, where he stayed for much of 1995. He missed the release of his third record, *Me Against the World*, which debuted at number one and produced singles like "Dear Mama" (an unflinching and heartfelt tribute to Tupac's mother, Afeni Shakur, that followed her through her Black Panther activism and her crack addiction, and that went Top Ten) and "So Many Tears" (produced by Shock G of Digital Underground, and featuring a prominent sample from Stevie Wonder's "That Girl"). He missed the 1995 Source Awards. While he was missing all those things, Tupac began to believe that he had been set up by Bad Boy, specifically by Sean "Puffy" Combs. Tupac spoke about his suspicions in interviews, but his anger didn't pick up until the release of "Who Shot Ya?" The single, a Biggie B-side, seemed to openly taunt Tupac for his shooting. "Clip to TEC, respect, I demand it / Slip and break the Eleventh Commandment / Thou shalt not fuck with nor see Poppa / Feel a thousand deaths when I drop ya." In the summer of 1996, his jail sentence over, Tupac fired back with an answer song, "Hit 'Em Up." Now, there was no question about the subject: he openly called out Puffy, Biggie, Lil' Kim, Junior M.A.F.I.A., and more.

Now it's September. The seventh. Saturday. Tupac traveled to Vegas for a birthday party and a boxing match: Mike Tyson fighting Bruce Seldon. Tupac went with Suge Knight, big event at the MGM Grand. The fight was a bust, with accusations that Seldon took a dive: punches that barely brushed his face somehow knocked him down, and he was out by the end of the first round. Accusations of throwing the fight would never leave him, and he would retire within weeks. Did the crowd feel they had gotten their money's worth? Maybe that's what Tupac and his friends were discussing in the hotel lobby afterward when they saw Baby Lane. Baby Lane was the street name of Orlando Anderson, a Compton Crip who had tried to take a chain owned by a member of Tupac's entourage. Not just a chain: a chain with a Death Row medallion on it. Tupac and his boys stomped Baby Lane as punishment.

Up to the hotel room, down to the car, out to the street, off to the club, Knight's place, Club 662. Knight (driving) and Tupac (passenger seat) were in the car, a black BMW 750iL, worth nearly a hundred thousand dollars. On the way they were pulled over by cops. "You have no plates," they said. "And you have to turn down the radio." The license plates were retrieved from the trunk and affixed. The music was turned down. And that was that. Knight and Tupac continued toward Club 662. Fifteen minutes later, going east on Flamingo Road, they stopped at a red light at Koval Lane. A car pulled up alongside them, a white Cadillac next to their black BMW. Shots were fired, many. Knight caught shrapnel. Tupac took four bullets: one in his thigh, one in his arm, and two in his chest. He was rushed to the University Medical Center of Southern Nevada, injuries severe, life support. He died the following Friday afternoon. There was no public funeral. He was cremated. His mother spread his ashes in various locations: at least in Los Angeles, and then, depending on the version of the story, either in Stone Mountain, Georgia, or in Soweto.

Tupac's death was a final punctuation, as final as it could ever be, at least for him, and everyone else was left to reckon with the finality, to mourn and remember. There was a third type of reckoning as well: theorizing. Almost immediately, the speculation started up like popcorn. Has Tupac been taken out by Bad Boy? By someone who believed that he was acting on Bad Boy's behalf? By gangs? The feds? Had he faked his own death? Each of these theories, including the absurd final one, had legs. You heard all about all of them for a while. One of the chief suspects was Baby Lane, the Crip who had been beaten in the lobby of the hotel. That made sense, in an Occam's razor way—guy gets beaten, guy comes back looking for revenge. Anderson ended up in court with Death Row and the Shakur family, seeking money for injuries suffered during the beating, and Afeni Shakur countersued. Anderson himself died in 1998 after a shooting, but he remained at the top of the list for many people. A reporter named Chuck Philips published a piece in the *Los Angeles Times* in 2002 (since retracted due to credibility concerns) that claimed to be backed by interviews and documents, and that also claimed to link Anderson to the Bad Boy camp, and in 2011 a former LAPD detective named Greg Kading added his voice to this chorus, alleging that Puffy had contacted Anderson's uncle, Duane "Keefe D" Davis, a known Crip (and longtime friend of Eazy-E), and contracted either Davis or Anderson or both to shoot Shakur and Knight. Combs strongly denies any involvement. The case has never been formally solved. (After I finished writing this book, while we were well into edits, Las Vegas police arrested Davis and charged him with the murder.)

All of this is a tragic story, but it is also getting ahead of the story, because Tupac's murder was the first of two shoes to drop. Exactly six months later, the Soul Train Music Awards were held in the Shrine Auditorium in Los Angeles. I was not there—the Roots were touring Europe at the time, dates in Switzerland, Belgium, France. The hosts were Brandy, Gladys Knight, and LL Cool J. Performers included Blackstreet (who played their undeniable monster hit "No Diggity"), the Fugees ("Killing Me Softly with His Song"), and Mary J. Blige ("Love Is All We Need"). Award recipients included Blackstreet ("No Diggity," of course, named Best R&B/Soul Single by a Group or Duo), Maxwell (Best New R&B or Rap Artist and also Best Male Single, for "Ascension"), and Tony Rich (Best Male R&B/Rap Album for *Words*). But that was all overshadowed by the night's most emotional moment, which was Tupac's posthumous Best R&B Album award for *All Eyez on Me*.

The most contentious moment came during Best R&B/Soul Single, Female. The presenter for the award was Biggie, who had been in LA for a little while, mainly to promote his second record, *Life After Death*, which was due out in a matter of weeks, and to film a video for the lead single, "Hypnotize." He stuck around for the awards—big industry event—but the Shrine crowd didn't want to see him. They booed loudly, which seemed to faze him only a little. "What's up, Cali?" he said.

Biggie got through the nominees, presented the award to Toni Braxton for the double A-side "You're Making Me High" / "Let It Flow," and got offstage. The next day, he was supposed to fly to England. Instead, he went to Museum Row on Wilshire Boulevard, and specifically to the Petersen Automotive Museum, where Kidada Jones, Quincy Jones's daughter, had organized a kind of after-party for the Soul Train Awards. Plenty of stars were there, from rappers (Goodie Mob, Missy Elliott) to singers (Biggie's estranged wife Faith Evans, Aaliyah) to comedians (Chris Tucker, the Wayans brothers) to industry figures (Irv Gotti, Russell Simmons), but there was also a gang presence, with both Crips and Bloods represented. The party got shut down soon after midnight—too many people in too small a space. Biggie went back to his hotel. He was in a GMC Suburban, in the front passenger seat (sound familiar?), though in this case his label head wasn't with him in the car but in another Suburban. Just up the street, at the corner of Fairfax Avenue, Biggie's car stopped at a red light (sound familiar?). Another car, a black Chevy Impala, pulled up alongside (sound familiar?), and the driver fired repeatedly from a 9-millimeter pistol. Four shots hit Biggie (sound familiar?) and he was rushed to Cedars-Sinai, where he died despite emergency surgery. Sounds familiar.

Nine days later, mourners crowded the Frank E. Campbell Funeral Chapel at Eighty-First and Madison: Run-D.M.C., Flavor Flav, Busta Rhymes, Lil' Kim, Foxy Brown. Jay-Z was famously not in attendance. The former mayor David Dinkins was there as well. Biggie, in death, was dressed in a white suit and hat. Faith Evans sang. Puffy gave a eulogy. Then Biggie's body went on tour: his coffin was loaded into a hearse, which joined a motorcade of Cadillacs and drove through Brooklyn, through Bed-Stuy, through Fort Greene. Following that, his body was transported to Fresh Pond Crematory in Queens, where it was returned to ashes.

Biggie's death, too, was followed by a wave of conspiracy theories. Fingers pointed at Suge Knight, obviously, and specifically at alleged collusion between Knight and an LAPD detective.

Biggie's death felt faraway, not entirely real, and close to home. I was in a rap band, but we weren't the kind of band to have beef, at least not of the guns-drawn variety. And yet, we were intertwined with the Biggie story. Remember the story about our "Distortion to Static" single, and how it got out ahead of "Juicy" for a moment? Well, that had been the first song released from our second album—the first on a major label—*Do You Want More?!!!??!*. Our next record, *Illadelph Halflife*, came out in September 1996, preceded by a lead single of its own, "Clones." *The Source* liked it. After lamenting that talent didn't always equal success, they surmised that maybe the second album would be the charm: "They rip through this first single and leave a pointed mission statement on the brain: we are fucking dope MCs."

That pointed mission statement was amplified by the "Clones" video. Rappers were starting to make videos that showed them getting off their private jets and taking limousines to their mansions, where they would change clothes and be driven by limousine to their speedboats. In quieter moments, they were surrounded by women and bottles of champagne. This kind of high-gloss presentation had been gateway-drugged by *The Chronic*, and then Biggie and Puffy, in collaboration with the video director Hype Williams, started really moving weight. That haves/have-nots tension had been palpable at the 1995 Source Awards. We decided to go the other way, to perform our song out on a street corner in lo-fi black-and-white (along with cutaways that showed that the band was actually filming its own video). Even though I understood that this was part of the point, I wasn't entirely thrilled with how we looked—a little raggedy for my tastes. When we made our video for "What They Do," we upscaled: there was a mansion and there were fancy cars and there were women and there was champagne.

Cut to Paris, in early March 1997. The Roots were in the City of Lights to perform when the phone rang. It was Selwyn Hinds from the *Source* asking me to respond to Biggie's remarks. "What are you talking about?" I said.

He explained. Evidently, on his publicity tour for *Life After Death*, Biggie had brought up the Roots, and specifically the "What They Do" video. Up until that moment, Biggie had been cool with us. He had liked the Roots, to the point where he mentioned us in interviews. But the "What They Do" video rubbed him the wrong way. He saw it as a parody of his videos. He had explained that he had always been in our corner, but that he was stepping out of it. "It hurt my feelings," he said. "They were one of my favorite groups," he said. "Why did Thought go and shit on me?" *Were* we one of his favorite groups? And we had been demoted because of a video? I have said several times, in interviews, in my own head, that mocking Biggie was not our intent. I didn't think it or feel it on the set of the video. I knew that we were generally reframing the conversation around materialism in hip-hop, and beyond that I didn't think or feel much, to be honest—I was just trying to make it work and suffering through the endless downtime. Even when I saw the finished product, I did not fully understand that it seemed like a direct hit on Biggie's work with Hype Williams. But then dream hampton pointed out to me that we were outright dissing them, and my blind spot turned to denial turned to the *Source* reporter relaying Biggie's remarks to me.

I called Rich and Tariq and we set about crafting a response. Silence was not an option, and neither was obliviousness. We were, in fact, interrogating a set of issues, and we felt that the interrogation was important. Someone needed to say something and that someone was us. Rich wrote some. I wrote some. We came back to it. We revised. Finally, we had a statement that was ready for release. I called *The Source* to get their fax number. That's how you delivered a manifesto back then: a phone call, a symphony of screeching and beeping, and words out the other end. "What?" said the voice on the other end. I explained: Questlove here, sending in response to Biggie, need fax number.

"You didn't hear?" said the *Source* voice.

"Didn't hear what?"

"He's dead."

I never got the fax number.

Biggie going away after Tupac had was beyond tragic and beyond operatic. With fearful symmetry, two of the brightest lights in hip-hop had been cut down. But what did it all mean? In some ways, it was symbolic. Everyone knew *Life After Death* was going to be huge, but it was clear—even before the murder—that it was wrapping up an era. "Ten Crack Commandments" was many things, but it wasn't a guide to a world that we were entering. It was a guide to a world that we had (and he had) just left.

I remember having a conversation with a few other rappers after Biggie was shot. We understood that his death, following so closely after Tupac's, would leave room for someone else to step into the center spot and assume the mantle of hip-hop superiority. We were talking about it like there was a golden ticket to go visit Willy Wonka. Who would it be? These were reasoned arguments, with exhibits—this particular rapper has a good sense of X and Y, but let's not forget about this other rapper who has recently demonstrated a surplus of Z. Some of the people I knew thought that they might be coronated. Others demonstrated a command of recent history, working analytically through the narratives of meteoric rise that had just preceded the two murders.

I had a story, too, one that I witnessed up close and personal. Back in 1993, when the Roots first signed with Geffen and started work on *Do You Want More?!!!??!*, I was working at Ruffhouse Records in Philadelphia. I loved the place and loved the job but a record deal was everything I had been working toward, so I went to the label and gave notice. Chris Schwartz, who had cofounded the label with Joe Nicolo, took it in stride. He had followed my journey from the beginning. He told me that he already had someone in mind to replace me and asked if I could show her around the place. That was fine with me. (My replacement was a woman named Santi White, later Santigold.) During that tour, a woman named Davida Garr at the label congratulated me on the signing. I told her that there was a party coming up for us. She congratulated me again, and then asked me something: Ruffhouse had a new group that seemed to her to be cut from the same cloth as the Roots. Was there any way I could lean on the people who were planning the party and get this group a short set? I leaned and it panned out, and the night of our show, a van brought this group to the show. Well, it brought people to the show. Some of them were not from the group, though I recognized them: there was an actor named Abdul Hassan Sharif, who had been in *Zebrahead*. Then another actor came out of the van. She was familiar to me from her role on a soap opera, *As the World Turns*, where she had played a homeless girl. I racked my brain for her name. Lauren something? It turned out to be Lauryn Hill, and it also turned out that she was not an actress anymore, or at least not only one, but that she was one of the MCs for the group that the woman from the label had pitched to me for the party. The group Lauryn Hill was with was the Fugees. They played that night and put out their debut, *Blunted on Reality*, within a few months. Their follow-up, *The Score*, also on Ruffhouse—by now distributed by Columbia—came out in 1996, seven months or so before our next record, *Illadelph Halflife*. Our record did pretty well. Their record did almost unprecedented business, with four big singles ("Fuu-Gee-La," "Killing Me Softly," "Ready or Not," and "No Woman, No Cry"), international acclaim, and six million copies sold. We were right there, ringside, in part because we toured with them, and saw clearly what it meant to be capturing the public imagination (and the public dollar). Many interviews focused on them and left us as an afterthought. A worthy afterthought, but an afterthought nonetheless. Watching the Fugees pick up steam and blow right past us—at least in market terms—taught me not to put too much stock in predictability. Sometimes you had no idea where the next star was coming from. (The Fugees, of course, would break up after *The Score* and produce hip-hop's next solo superstar in Lauryn herself. Her solo record, *The Miseducation of Lauryn Hill*, put her in the pantheon. A divisive live record taken from her *MTV Unplugged* session almost took her out of it, depending on who you ask, and after that, well, there wasn't really an after that. She released a handful of singles, popped up in a handful of other people's songs, but nothing more. She maintained her near-divine status on the strength of just that one album.)

I turned out to be right: I knew enough to know that I didn't know anything. When Biggie was in California during the lead-up to *Life After Death*, he was already telling reporters that he was going to executive produce Puff's record. We all laughed. Diddy didn't seem like a plausible superstar on his own. Two months after Biggie's death, Puff and Faith Evans and 112 released "I'll Be Missing You," a memorial single based (heavily) on the Police's "Every Breath You Take." I couldn't get behind the way the song was built and delivered, but I couldn't put it behind me, either. You know that scene in *The Untouchables*, where Al Capone is holding a girl hostage in the train station as the feds shoot at him? They stop shooting. That one time, they cut him a break. That was the vibe around "I'll Be Missing You." Your friend died, a sentimental song, this is about him. We'll put the guns down. Any other day we would have all roasted the shit out of him for daring to think he could use that sample.

But then Puff kept winning and winning. Every week it seemed that he was just flaunting it, and no one could give him a pass anymore. I don't want to revisit my own feelings about that time unless they're overlaid with analytical distance, and with that distance I'll just say that he had a one-in-a-trillion winning lottery ticket. Or rather, he took full advantage of what was happening to him and demonstrated an almost unbelievable talent for Teflon life. Think about when he fell on the motorcycle in the "Missing You" video. That was real, but Hype Williams kept the camera rolling. The result was an endearing moment, a rare humanity that he would not have shown otherwise. But then came "Mo Money Mo Problems," which became Biggie's second posthumous number one and kept the train rolling for Puffy, and then "Been Around the World," where he not only had Quincy Jones in the video but also showed off his new girlfriend, J.Lo. We held our tongues but were called haters.

Even if we didn't see Puffy coming, we did see someone coming. That was Jay-Z. He had come out of Brooklyn, a kid who had grown up in the Marcy Houses in Bed-Stuy, experienced some rough living along the way (at age twelve, he shot his brother in the shoulder for stealing his jewelry) and some taste of hip-hop culture (he had attended George Westinghouse tech school with Biggie and Busta Rhymes, though he was a few years older). He attained . . . visibility (is that the word? Audibility?) in the midnineties, popping up on songs by Jaz-O (his mentor, and the source of his name) and Big Daddy Kane, and attracting the attention of Irv Gotti, a DJ and producer who was looking for the next big thing. Gotti tried to put Jay-Z together with two other up-and-comers he had scouted, Ja Rule (from Hollis, Queens) and DMX (from Yonkers), in a planned supergroup called Murder Inc. It didn't quite take, but all three of them started to get traction. Ja Rule stayed with Gotti and the Murder Inc. label. DMX released singles (started on Ruffhouse, moved to Def Jam) and began to establish his own identity, gruff and hyper-macho, which would flourish over the next half decade, bringing him five number one albums in five years. And Jay-Z sold a single called "In My Lifetime," produced by Ski, from the trunk of Damon Dash's car. (See? Billionaire rappers: just like us!) A year after that, he had an independent record, *Reasonable Doubt*, on his own in-dependent label, Roc-a-Fella, which was in business with Priority, which had been in the rap business since the mideighties, and had distributed, with Ruthless, West Coast gangsta classics by N.W.A., Ice Cube, MC Ren, and others.

On the strength of that first record, everyone understood that Jay was going to be . . . something. He had a dope single, "Ain't No Nigga," a relationship-leverage back-and-forth with a teenage female rapper named Foxy Brown that looped "Seven Minutes of Funk," by the Whole Darn Family. We felt Jay-Z's lyrical dexterity and his will to win. But we still weren't fully open to the idea of more from him. I firmly believe that people know from the first whether they're going to be open to something or not. I was not open to the idea of Jay-Z as anything larger than a talented artist who was going to make some great records.

And yet, he pierced my defenses by degrees. His second album, *In My Lifetime . . . Vol. 1*, was mostly handled by Puff's production team. To me, it's his *Pinkerton*, the record most beloved by so-called Jay-Z insiders. We all swear that we're unique. "Imaginary Players" became my go-to for years. On the track, Jay described his new tri-umphant lifestyle, materialist to the core. He talked about alcohol brands and fashion and jewelry and jets and cars. The outro of the song, which focused on the two kinds of Range Rovers, stuck with me: "Ask me some stupid shit like, 'Yo, yo dog, what's the difference between a 4.0 and a 4.6?' Like thirty to forty grand, cocksucker, beat it!" I vowed to myself that I would never be one of those people who didn't know the difference.

But I didn't want to be one of the people who knew all the differences, either. As I was processing my thoughts about these new stars, I dreamed every day of a moment when the tide of hip-hop would reverse, when a Mos Def and a Black Thought would wear the crown, and there would be a full reckoning of what was dope versus what was manufactured. But that reckoning would have ruined what was, in fact, a more interesting dynamic. Dominant things make margins. The do-or-die atmosphere that solidified around stars like Jay-Z and Puffy was like a Monopoly game with only Boardwalk. But that's not how the game is played. While people were staring at the dark blue properties, I understood full well that I could hook some shit up on the yellow, Marvin Gardens or Ventnor. It was beneath-the-underdog thinking, and if I had it, that meant that other people understood it, too. As a result, 1998 was a revelation. The year before had felt like a dull thud, in large part because *Wu-Tang Forever* had come out to healthy sales but underwhelming reviews. I had waited a half decade for Wu-Tang to get back together and get it done, and what did we get? An overblown, bloated double album that would have worked perfectly well as a single album but lost steam at its larger size. (Don't believe me? How many times have you come back to this record in the last two decades compared to the group's debut? I rest my case.) But then came 1998, and Gang Starr's *Moment of Truth*, Big Pun's *Capital Punishment*, Slum Village's *Fan-Tas-Tic, Vol. 1*, and new Southern classics like Goodie Mob's *Still Standing* and especially Outkast's *Aquemini*, a brilliantly new take on funk both lyrically and musically. Ten years earlier, every other record I heard changed my life. The numbers weren't quite that high in 1998, but it was the last year I truly believed in hip-hop. So in a sense, I thank Puffy for that. As that first phase of Puff Takeover waned—Puffy released a lackluster follow-up record, *Forever*, in 1999—some of those groups that had made 1998 a watershed year picked up steam and confidence, and some of the groups that had been silent for a few years capitalized on the momentum. We were among them. At the start of 1999, the Roots released *Things Fall Apart*, which would become our most acclaimed album. It was a report on the state of the world at a time when the world wasn't holding together. We didn't know how right we would end up being.

Things were coming apart but you had to pretend they were still together. And though shots ruined this era, they also made it. There is a famous photo that many Americans have seen, shot by Art Kane for *Esquire* magazine in 1958, more than a half century before now, more than a decade before I was born. The point of the photo was to pay tribute to jazz, a uniquely American and largely African American art form that sprang up new in the New World in the twentieth century. Sound familiar? Kane and the *Esquire* editors made a wish list of subjects and most of their wishes came true. They got everyone from giants of the genre (Roy Eldridge, Dizzy Gillespie, Coleman Hawkins, Thelonious Monk, Gerry Mulligan, Sonny Rollins, Horace Silver, Mary Lou Williams, and Lester Young) to lesser-known artists (most casual jazz fans don't know Zutty Singleton or Bill Crump except for their appearance in the photo). Fifty-seven people in all showed up at 17 East 126th Street on August 12, a Tuesday, so Kane could set up and record the group portrait that came to be known as *A Great Day in Harlem*. There is so much backstory to the photo, from how he invited the musicians (it was nothing formal—he just sent out word along the grapevine) to how the location was selected (Harlem had been the epicenter of jazz at one point in time, but by the late fifties the scene had moved down to midtown, with Fifty-Second Street as the genre's main artery). Still, the picture became iconic over time for the way it brought together so many inspiring artists.

Hip-hop was entirely different than jazz, of course, but it shared some important qualities. It was predominantly African American.

It was not always accepted by the dominant culture, in part because it sometimes explicitly set itself against the dominant, turning art into a form of protest, and that lack of acceptance sometimes took the form of demeaning the music as unskilled, made for a brute body rather than a refined mind. It wasn't true for jazz in its time, of course, and it wasn't true for hip-hop later, but people in positions of cultural power can be stubborn.

Hip-hop, sharing some important qualities with jazz, evolved to the point where it seemed to call for its own group portrait. This was in 1998, forty years after *A Great Day in Harlem*. Art Kane had died in 1995, and it's not clear that he would have been the best man for the job anyway. Sheena Lester at *XXL* magazine, then in its infancy, came up with the idea. She hired Gordon Parks, a pioneering photographer in his own right. Parks had already followed in Kane's footsteps. The same year that Kane died, Parks returned to the Harlem brownstone for a group portrait of the players who were still alive. There were a dozen survivors at that point. He got ten, as two were unavailable due to travel or touring commitments. In the time since, all but two, Sonny Rollins and Benny Golson, have also passed away. That was age. That was history. Three years later, on September 29, 1998—a Tuesday again—it was youth and it was history again. Parks put out the call for hip-hop stars and they responded in force. Hip-hop more than tripled the original jazz head count, with 177 artists showing up for the photo shoot. The Metropolitan Community Methodist Church served as a kind of greenroom, which meant that whoever came to be photographed was also able to rub elbows, say hello to familiar artists, meet unfamiliar ones. Depending on when you marked the birth, this was a celebration of at least two decades of hip-hop. If you accepted the Kool Herc back-to-school party as the genesis of the art form, it was almost exactly twenty-five years.

I have a special connection to that photograph, because I was in it. The Roots were, at that point, heavily on the upswing. Our second major-label album, *Illadelph Halflife*, had come out in 1996. It had not only impressed critics but solidified the idea that we were at the center of a community: guests on that album, friends of ours, included D'Angelo, Raphael Saadiq, Cassandra Wilson, Steve Coleman, and Amel Larrieux. *Illadelph Halflife* earned us 4.5 mics from *The Source*, which highlighted our collaborative chops and also pointed to the way we were trying to break the male stranglehold on hip-hop by bringing in different kinds of female artists: vocals groups like the Jazzyfatnastees, poets like Ursula Rucker. I mention that album only (mostly) because the Parks shoot was scheduled on the same day that we were finishing up *Things Fall Apart*. You never know for sure when you are making something how it may rise and where it may land, but we felt pretty good about the new record. Even as a natural progression from *Illadelph Halflife*, it had the potential to be something special. I spent the morning putting final touches on the record and then hightailed it out the door to make it to Metropolitan Community Methodist Church, and the photo to follow.

That day was a celebration simply on the basis of who was there. So many artists who had meant so much to the genre showed up: Kool Herc, who had kicked it off, Grandmaster Flash, Marley Marl, Kool Keith, Fab Five Freddy, Wyclef Jean, Busta Rhymes, EPMD, the Wu-Tang Clan, Rakim, E-40, Fat Joe. There were moments of sentimentality, of pride, even of humor—I have talked about how two-thirds of Run-D.M.C. was in place but Run came running down the street just before Parks snapped the shot. The entire convocation was something to behold, not to mention something I couldn't quite process. It was in the back of my mind when it wasn't in the front of my mind from that day on, right up until I tried in February 2023 to do an awards-show, poetry-in-motion version of it for the Grammys.

The photo was an artifact, but it wouldn't have meant much unless all the people in it knew how to make records: records that moved the needle and moved the crowd, that paved over what had come before and paved the way for what would come later. It's important to note that the photo was taken on a Tuesday not just because it echoed the scheduling of Kane's original photo, but also because Tuesday was record release day back then, the day of the week when new albums appeared in stores. What came out that Tuesday? For starters, A Tribe Called Quest's *The Love Movement*, which was at the time the last will and testament of what was for me maybe the most important hip-hop group; they had announced their breakup at the end of the summer, and would not reunite until 2016's *We Got It From Here . . . Thank You 4 Your Service*. It was also the day for *Mos Def and Talib Kweli Are Black Star*, a landmark of new conscious hip-hop; for Outkast's *Aquemini*, an Afrofuturist manifesto that pushed forward with songs like "SpottieOttieDopaliscious" and looked back with appearances from Raekwon and even George Clinton; and Jay-Z's mega-selling third album and early high-water mark *Vol. 2 . . . Hard Knock Life*, which would earn Jay a Grammy for Best Rap Album and earn the Grammys a boycott from Jay, who felt that the ceremony was only giving lip service to hip-hop, only trying to understand it in terms of a few artists ("If it's got a gun everybody knows about it; but if we go on a world tour, no one knows").

A little more than four months later, on February 23, 1999 (a Tuesday, of course), the album I was finishing up the day of the photo, *Things Fall Apart*, would come out and more than pay off the hope we had in it. It would become, in some ways, the Roots' defining record, certainly the one that brought us to the attention of the most people and laid out most clearly our range and depth. *Mojo* magazine went straight for the aspects of it that made me proudest, the questions that had been on my mind for a decade or so: "in a hip-hop world dominated by well-worn pop samples and rap rewrites of eighties chart hits, such risk-taking should be cherished." That was gratifying, but what was more gratifying was to think not just about what the shape of our particular piece was, but how we fit into the overall puzzle. It had been a great day for hip-hop, but hip-hop was great enough to contain many days of equal importance.

Things Fall Apart was a banner release for us. We got nominated for a Grammy for Best Rap Album, alongside Busta Rhymes' *E.L.E. (Extinction Level Event): The Final World Front*, Nas's *I Am . . .* , Missy Elliott's *Da Real World*, and the album that beat us all: Eminem's *The Slim Shady LP*. Eminem, born Marshall Mathers in Missouri, raised in the suburbs of Detroit from the age of twelve, initially an aspiring comics artist, after that a young and very verbose rapper, had put out an album (*Infinite*) and an EP (*Slim Shady*, which introduced a psychopathic alter ego) on a small Detroit indie called WEB Entertainment run by Mark and Jeff Bass. They did what indie releases normally do, which was not much. Mathers went to Los Angeles to participate in a freestyle competition, came in second, and managed to get a copy of his EP to Jimmy Iovine at Interscope, who in turn managed to get it to Dr. Dre. Dre was amazed. He sent for Eminem. The result was a working relationship between the two of them and the Bass Brothers, and the result of that was *The Slim Shady LP*, which came out in February 1999—February 23, in fact, the same exact day as *Things Fall Apart*. We got acclaim throughout the year, and one of the songs from our record, "You Got Me," charted internationally and won a Grammy. (It featured vocals by Erykah Badu, who rerecorded the original vocals by Jill Scott after the label expressed a strong desire for a better-known female collaborator. I have spoken plenty before about the awkwardness of telling Jill that she was off the single. I won't go into it again. But trust me: no fun.) At the same time, *The Slim Shady LP* was going haywire. The lead single, "My Name Is," charted, but more than that, the whole album did massive business from the start, bowing at number two on the *Billboard* 200 and selling all year long.

Eminem was a white rapper in a mostly Black genre, and here he was beating sales records left and right. What did it say about America? Was it Elvis all over again? They had asked the same questions of Vanilla Ice, but the answers here were different. Dre had been right to be amazed. No one could dispute Eminem's technical abilities. I was in a band with one of the best technical MCs in the game, and I heard Eminem's talent coming through clearly. I sat with the record and went through the lyrics just to see if I could follow what he was doing. It wasn't easy. And whereas I had balked at other rappers for foregrounding the money they made or would make, this was different: Eminem was deep inside a lyrical world of his own. There were legitimate questions about the violent fantasies on the record, which sounded satirical to me but were also delivered in a way that I understood would be misunderstood. Would Eminem collapse under the weight of his debut? Would the backlash mount? Would his narrative perspective hit a dead end?

Soon, none of these questions mattered, or they mattered only if you were writing history. *The Marshall Mathers LP*, released the following year, upped the ante and then some, with another huge pop hit ("The Real Slim Shady"), a stalker anthem that played like a movie ("Stan"), and "The Way I Am," which directly confronted the downside of the fame the first record had brought. And his third album, *The Eminem Show*, not only produced his third pop anthem, "Without Me," but led into his starring role in *8 Mile*, a semibiographical film directed by Curtis Hanson whose soundtrack included "Lose Yourself," not only Eminem's first number one, not only a number one that held that spot for twelve weeks and also got there in twenty countries, but a dominant, international number one that earned him the two highest honors in show business, an Oscar and a parody version by "Weird Al" Yankovic. It was also our moment in the Eminem business—he had us back him when he played the song at the 2003 Grammy Awards.

The juggernaut, unstoppable, slowed down a little bit after that. *Encore*, in 2004, wasn't as successful, and Eminem took a hiatus after that to work with other artists and beat a prescription pill addiction. The long wait ended with *Relapse*, in 2009, a divisive record filled with puzzling performances (many songs featured accents that seemed to suggest that he had been born on the border between Jamaica and Ireland) that even Eminem disavowed on *Recovery* in 2010. A direct sequel to his breakthrough debut, *The Marshall Mathers LP 2*, was hailed as a comeback in 2013 (and won him a Grammy), after which he became a consistently proficient, sometimes prolific elder statesman, maybe with nothing to say anymore, but with quite a talent for saying it. The reason this may feel like an encyclopedia entry is that Eminem belongs there. He changed so many things about hip-hop from the outside looking in—the demographics of the genre, the monumental sales figures, the unprecedented penetration into mainstream media—that his legacy will always mention them before they mention his prodigious talent or his deep commitment to the genre. He'll persist as a symbol longer than as an artist. That's the Elvis connection.

As big as Eminem's story was, I still thought small. Not small talents, but those small stories that illustrated what hip-hop had once been. For years, I had run a kind of loose fan community called Okayplayer, and toward the end of the twentieth century, it went online. Online? That was a new place that knit people from all over the world together via their computers. The people in the community started to put me onto new music. I listened to their recommendations and then I listened to the songs. Blackalicious's "Deception (Don't Let Money Change Ya)" was one of those songs. I liked the recommendations and I liked it, too, because it was a cautionary tale in the vein of (and the downstream of) Slick Rick's "A Children's Story." Those kinds of narratives were correctives to triumphalist rap songs; they told stories of people who had too much money, or too little, and made wrong choices as a result.

The community also turned up another name: J-Live. I knew of J-Live. Back in 1995, there was a song called "Braggin' Writes" where he played the turntable, using an Annette Peacock break, and rhymed at the same time. It got him into *The Source*'s Unsigned Hype column, which got him noticed by all of us. J-Live was too early to be viral. If he had put that clip up ten years later on YouTube, he would have been the biggest thing ever. But there was no YouTube back then, and J-Live, not the biggest thing ever, just put his head down and made his debut record. It was called *The Best Part*, and it had a Murderers' Row of producers—Pete Rock, DJ Premier, Prince Paul, not to mention Grap Luva (Pete Rock's younger brother), 88 Keys, DJ Spinna, and J-Live himself. It was scheduled to come out in 1999, the same year that J-Live appeared on Prince Paul and Dan the Automator's conceptual satire record *Handsome Boy Modeling School*, duetting on "The Truth" with the Irish singer

Róisín Murphy. But when J-Live's label, Raw Shack, tanked, he moved *The Best Part* to Payday Records, which also tanked. J-Live started teaching English at a middle school in Brooklyn, a job that I am entirely certain he did extremely well. His industry purgatory lasted for months stretching into years, and the record finally emerged on Triple Threat in 2001.

"Them That's Not," one of its highlights, was yet another cautionary tale, which meant that I was predisposed to like it. But I also genuinely liked the way the verses moved ("Once upon a time there was a brother named Castro / Had a little problem with his cash flow, word / More than once upon a time he had a dream to clock mad dough / Only at the time it all seemed mad absurd") and the depth of the samples ("All but Blind," a 1974 track by the Pittsburgh-to-Detroit jazz keyboardist Eddie Russ). The song was backpack rap before it existed. If he had been able to post the record on Bandcamp or Soundcloud, he would have fully reached his potential audience. But there was no Bandcamp or SoundCloud back then, and J-Live, not fully reaching his potential audience, just put his head down and made more records: an equally strong sophomore release, *All of the Above*, in 2002; *The Hear After* in 2005; *Then What Happened?* in 2008; *S.P.T.A. (Said Person of This Ability)* in 2011; and so on. The praise continued for 2014's *Around the Sun* ("he's just so good at making golden era rap music that its appeal is self-evident"). J-Live never hit it big, exactly, but he hit the mark time and time again, and more importantly he remained an example of what hip-hop could be but too rarely was—a showcase for talented artists working in a verbal and musical medium and working out their narrative, spiritual, political, and ethical concerns in innovative and gratifying ways that aspire to but don't serve at the pleasure of the market. It's too simple to call J-Live the anti-Eminem, or the anti-Puff, or the anti-anybody. He's a pro.

Big legacies, little legacies. Big statements, small statements. By this point, hip-hop was old enough that it was taking stock of itself, which meant taking stock of its own past. And when you take stock, there's a market. There are lots of critics in lots of publications in the world, but there are only a few true gold standards when it comes to album ratings. There are the five-star *Rolling Stone* reviews from the days before Mick Jagger inflation (lots of Beatles, James Brown's *Live at the Apollo*, Otis Redding's *Otis Blue*). There are Robert Christgau A+ grades (Al Green's *Call Me*, Neil Young's *Rust Never Sleeps*, Sly and the Family Stone's *There's a Riot Goin' On*). There are the rare *Pitchfork* 10.0 ratings (Radiohead's *OK Computer* and *Kid A*, the Flaming Lips' *The Soft Bulletin*, Fiona Apple's *Fetch the Bolt Cutters*, plus plenty of archival reissues). In hip-hop, there are *Source* five-mic ratings. Only sixteen albums have been awarded the rating since the magazine started publishing in 1988. Here are the original sixteen, in chronological order:

- A Tribe Called Quest, *People's Instinctive Travels and the Paths of Rhythm* (1990)
- Eric B. and Rakim, *Let the Rhythm Hit 'Em* (1990)
- Boogie Down Productions, *Edutainment* (1990)
- Ice Cube, *AmeriKKKa's Most Wanted* (1990)
- Brand Nubian, *One for All* (1990)
- De La Soul, *De La Soul Is Dead* (1991)
- A Tribe Called Quest, *The Low End Theory* (1991)
- Nas, *Illmatic* (1994)
- The Notorious B.I.G., *Life After Death* (1997)
- Outkast, *Aquemini* (1998)
- Jay-Z, *The Blueprint* (2001)
- Nas, *Stillmatic* (2001)
- Scarface, *The Fix* (2002)
- Lil' Kim, *The Naked Truth* (2005)
- Bun B, *Trill OG* (2010)
- Kanye West, *My Beautiful Dark Twisted Fantasy* (2010)

I present this debate so that hip-hop fans across the world can discuss and argue among themselves. Which albums are indisputably deserving of the honor? (For me, the De La Soul and Tribe records, definitely.) Which ones might have been the result of irrational enthusiasm on the part of editors? (*Stillmatic? Naked Truth?*) But wait! Revisionism is part of hip-hop, remember, and *The Source* has taken several opportunities to adjust its original thought. In 2002, the editors of the magazine went back into its own archives and bumped a number of albums up to the five-mic tier. There were three groups awarded this privilege.

The first was made up of albums that were not rated the first time around, whether it was because they predated the practice of awarding ratings or because the magazine skipped them for one reason or another. There were sixteen of those, doubling the original class. As a historian, I am obligated to list the upgrades, though I feel a certain way about it.

- Run-D.M.C., *Run-D.M.C.* (1984)
- LL Cool J, *Radio* (1985)
- Beastie Boys, *Licensed to Ill* (1986)
- Run-D.M.C., *Raising Hell* (1986)
- Boogie Down Productions, *Criminal Minded* (1987)
- Eric B. and Rakim, *Paid in Full* (1987)
- Boogie Down Productions, *By All Means Necessary* (1988)
- Public Enemy, *It Takes a Nation of Millions to Hold Us Back* (1988)
- Big Daddy Kane, *Long Live the Kane* (1988)
- Ultramagnetic MCs, *Critical Beatdown* (1988)
- Jungle Brothers, *Straight Out the Jungle* (1988)
- EPMD, *Strictly Business* (1988)
- Slick Rick, *The Great Adventures of Slick Rick* (1988)
- N.W.A., *Straight Outta Compton* (1988)
- The D.O.C., *No One Can Do It Better* (1989)
- 2Pac, *All Eyez on Me* (1996)

From there, we tunnel into deeper revisionism. In that same 2002 package, the magazine decided that some original ratings were too low. They explained that the historical importance of an album is not always clear at the time of release, and that original rankings should be adjusted upward. This, I feel even worse about. The original rating is part of history. You can't change it just because you feel differently later. On top of that, I believe that the 4.5-mic rating is superior, often because it identifies albums that are immensely powerful but imperfect, which in some strange way increases their power. Still, here are the albums that were bumped up from 4.5 mics to five. (There are eight more of the half-mic bump beneficiaries, bringing the total pantheon to forty.)

- Main Source, *Breaking Atoms* (1991)
- Ice Cube, *Death Certificate* (1991)
- Dr. Dre, *The Chronic* (1992)
- Wu-Tang Clan, *Enter the Wu-Tang (36 Chambers)* (1993)
- The Notorious B.I.G., *Ready to Die* (1994)
- Mobb Deep, *The Infamous* (1995)
- Raekwon, *Only Built 4 Cuban Linx . . .* (1995)
- Dr. Dre, *2001* (1999)

But wait, there's more! The magazine also gave a glow-up to six albums that were originally awarded four mics. Adding the extra mic brought the entire set to forty-five albums.

- Geto Boys, *Grip It! On That Other Level* (1989)
- Snoop Doggy Dogg, *Doggystyle* (1993)
- Scarface, *The Diary* (1994)
- 2Pac, *Me Against the World* (1995)
- The Fugees, *The Score* (1996)
- Jay-Z, *Reasonable Doubt* (1996)

No albums were demoted in the remaking of this ever-expanding list.

2002

EXCUSE ME, MISS, I FORGOT YOUR NAME

2007

Hip-hop learns that to keep producing, it must keep producing. Superstar producers and their trademark technologies rise as high as—if not higher than—individual artists.

The last period, when new superstars rose into view, also ended with the World Trade Center falling. That set everything back. There were narrow consequences, like the pulling of the original cover image of the Coup's *Pick a Bigger Weapon*, which showed Boots Riley detonating an explosive at the base of the Twin Towers. But there were larger consequences as well. September 11 led to a new sense of government power and police power, which led to a new sense of suspicion on the part of hip-hop artists. This had been part of hip-hop since the midnineties, to some degree—there was illuminati thinking, for example—but it became anchored in this new reality. You couldn't have a Patriot Act and not touch off the frustration of Black American men, some of whom expressed it in lyrical form. The other consequence of 9/11 was regional. At first, all eyes were on New York. New York represented American pride, strength, and resilience, some of which flowed through its hip-hop stars. But there was also national pride, and that helped to motivate and grow other scenes, sometimes with New York's blessing. For me, it's about remembering the first seed that was planted when Biggie rhymed in double time to Bone Thugs-N-Harmony on "Notorious Thugs," his crossover single from 1997. Biggie recognized that the Midwest and the South were more than potential markets for New York hip-hop. Regional cooperation could double your outreach and consequently your money. Once the Northeast recognized that the Southeast (give or take) could be given accommodation and even cooperative partnerships, the whole map was redrawn. When people said East Coast, they meant the whole thing. This became especially true for Virginia. In the years leading into this period, there were various creative forces that emerged out of Old Dominion and established new dominance: the Neptunes and Timbaland were the top names in production, but the artists ranged from D'Angelo (who was my own personal connection to the entire scene, since he existed as a central figure in the Soulquarians) to the Clipse to Missy Elliott to Chris Brown. Finally, this was also a period marked by a certain liberation. Let's think of a more recent memory, which is a flash-forward in terms of this period: COVID. Remember how, as the pandemic ended, people started talking about how we were about to enter a new period of ceaseless partying, the Roaring Twenties all over again? The restrictive policies and forced patriotism of the period had a certain oppressive feeling, and toward 2003 or so people started moving back toward a hedonistic footing. We saw that in the culture in general, and we saw it more specifically in hip-hop, where overt political statements went to the back and sex and drugs came up front. These things are cycles, but they are motivated cycles, and there was plenty of motivation in this period.

In 2003, a reporter asked me who I was listening to, and who I thought might be coming up in the world. I talked about the North Carolina trio Little Brother (we'll get back to them soon) and also 50 Cent. Born Curtis Jackson, 50 Cent was from Queens, had had a rough upbringing, had been a boxer, had been a dealer, had been arrested. He had also, at that point, been around for a bit as a rapper. He had apprenticed with Queens legend Jam Master Jay, who signed 50 Cent to his label, Jam Master, and developed him as a writer of both lyrics and hooks. He graduated from Jam Master to Columbia in the last years of the previous century and put out a single called "How to Rob," a song that bounced along on a flip of George McCrae's "I Get Lifted" and detailed how 50 Cent was going to catch and bring down every other music star around. He started by paying homage to Biggie and Tupac and then listed all of the people he was coming for, a nearly endless list that included Puff, Mase, OBD, Jay, Slick Rick, Big Pun, Master P, DMX, Canibus, Heavy D, Busta Rhymes, Missy Elliott, Mariah Carey, Blackstreet, Boyz II Men, various Wu-Tang members, and many more. The song was mean, but it was also tremendously energetic, more than a little funny, and fascinating. We couldn't tell if he was serious, releasing a record like this so soon after violent conflict had torn apart the hip-hop world.

"How to Rob" was intended as the first song from his upcoming debut album, *The Power of the Dollar*. A second song, "Ghetto Qu'ran (Forgive Me)," in which 50 Cent discussed various drug dealers from his neighborhood by name, was leaked in early 2000. Then, in May 2000, 50 Cent was in a car outside of his grandmother's house in South Jamaica when another car pulled up alongside him and shot into his car. He was hit nine times, almost killed, had to walk with a walker for months, eventually recovered. But he didn't recover his career, at least not right away. He was dropped by Columbia when they learned of the shooting and more or less blacklisted by the entire record industry.

He regrouped and started to release mixtapes. Lots of them: four in 2002, including the scrape-up-the-ends-of-Columbia *Guess Who's Back?* and then a trio credited to him and his group, G-Unit: *50 Cent Is the Future*; *No Mercy, No Fear*; and *God's Plan*. The first was the best, but I liked them all. He stayed funny in a way I hadn't seen by a gangsta rapper—it wasn't that he was a gifted comedian, necessarily, but his sense of humor was never far away, and he didn't seem to have any fear. He was also rethinking the way that hiphop worked, not only repossessing other rap songs but also rapping over R&B songs (like Raphael Saadiq's "Be Here") and turning them into something risky and gritty. He was mixing elements in a way I hadn't seen before, messing with these superlyrical motherfuckers, staying in that gangsta spot. And his charisma carried over to other members of G-Unit, whether Lloyd Banks or Tony Yayo. Soon enough, he was through his mixtape phase and signed to Shady Records, Eminem's label. His first single with the label was "Wanksta," a swipe at other gangsta rappers for being broke posers that was on the *8 Mile* soundtrack. (The next day, Jam Master Jay was assassinated in a Queens studio. Some people blamed the release of the single, or Jay's association with 50 Cent. Others said the killing was the result of an unpaid debt. Arrests in the case weren't made for two decades—not until August 2022 and May 2023, when a total of three men, including Jay's godson, were arrested and charged with the murder in connection with a cocaine deal gone wrong. The trial began in January 2024 and ended in the conviction of two of the defendants in February 2024. [Appeals may follow, of course.])

"Wanksta" was a bonus track on 50 Cent's Shady debut LP, *Get*

Rich or Die Tryin'. That album came out right around Grammy time in 2003. That year, the Roots backed up Eminem for his performance of "Lose Yourself" during the ceremony. The show was at Madison Square Garden. We were all working, rehearsing, at S.I.R. Recording Studios. Eminem had the new 50 Cent record with him and he was playing the songs, not in order, jumping from one to the next. When he got to "Heat," I was immediately taken by it: Dr. Dre programmed the snare drum so that instead of hearing a drumbeat, you heard a gun going off. I was obsessed with the production, but not so much that I didn't notice that Rich had a strange look on his face. "What?" I said.

"This record is going to be huge," he said, "but this is the end."

"Of what?"

"This is the end of the line. 50 Cent has crossed a line he doesn't even know he's crossing," he said. "Never in the history of hip-hop has a rapper ever said these three words." I didn't know what three words he meant. I love you? Don't drive drunk? Success breeds success?

"'I'll kill you.'" Rich wasn't saying that he was going to kill me. He was quoting "Heat": "I do what I gotta do, I don't care I if get caught / The DA can play this motherfuckin' tape in court / I'll kill you." And then he was quoting André 3000 from Outkast's "B.O.B.": "'Don't pull that thing out unless you plan to bang.'" Rich's mind always went a million miles a second—not even an hour—so he slowed down to explain. The thing that had always fueled gangsta rap was the idea of the fear. It maintained an air of mystery. "Do you hear them? We're not going to go across the tracks to see if they are dangerous or not." The bluff was always more danger than the threat. Will Eazy-E kill us? We don't know. Will Biggie kill us? We don't know. "The thing is," Rich said, "it's not that you can't say that. But you can't say that if you don't mean it." I was still trying to process this idea that night, when I went back and listened to every threatening rapper: deadpan threatening, comic threatening, East Coast threatening, West Coast threatening, Beasties, Schoolly D, Geto Boys, everyone. And I started to see exactly what Rich meant. That kind of threat was a trump card, and if you played it and it didn't happen, you lost all your capital. That's one of the many times I realized that Rich was a god: of perception, of analysis, of nuance.

The record was huge. It sold nearly a million in its first week and remains one of the ten bestselling hip-hop records of all time. But Rich got so in my head with his understanding of 50 Cent and this lyrical brinksmanship that it affected my perception of everything after that. When the Compton rapper the Game, inserted into the G-Unit by Dr. Dre so that 50 Cent could help out with writing, came out with his own massive debut, *The Documentary*, in 2005, I thought about it. What did it matter to be saying these same things? It was over. They had already been said. When 50 Cent wagered his career on outselling Kanye West's *Graduation* (the two albums were released on the same day in 2006), I thought about it. What did it matter to make a stand? Rich said. It was over. Kanye was going to win by a mile. (I have to admit that I backslid here. No, no, I told Rich. 50 Cent was the biggest rapper of all time. Rich was right.) Even when I found myself enjoying the drama around 50 Cent, especially the angry dissolution of G-Unit and the beef that ensued between 50 and Game—I remember the excitement of "300 Bars and Runnin'" especially—it all felt like smoke and mirrors. I was disillusioned and running myself, for cover.

There were other reasons. I was part of Dave Chappelle's *Chappelle's Show* for its early seasons. My job was music supervision, helping to create music for skits. It was a dry run for some of the parts of the job I would later do at *The Tonight Show*. It was also a hip-hop job, unquestionably. It had that sense of energy in the service of community.

In 2004, Dave had an idea. At first, it floated in the air but then it came into clearer focus, partly because the director Michel Gondry started hanging out with the group. Gondry got famous for very high-concept romantic comedies: *Eternal Sunshine of the Spotless Mind*. When he first became Chappelle-adjacent, it was just out, or maybe even just about to come out. But Gondry was also a music person, or more specifically a music-video person. He had made some of the most visionary, nightmarish, and at the same time childish videos imaginable for Björk, and would go on to work with mostly indie-rock acts like Queens of the Stone Age, the White Stripes, Beck. He hadn't really worked with hip-hop or neo-soul acts. But he and Dave changed that. Dave cooked up a movie idea. In his mind, it would be a modern equivalent of Wattstax, a block party for Brooklyn. He started to book acts. We were one of the acts. Erykah Badu was another. And then there was a young rapper named Kanye West.

Kanye was appearing in the wake of his debut album, *The College Dropout*. It had been, in his mind, at least, a long time coming. For years, he had tried unsuccessfully to convince labels that he could move seamlessly from his production work (most conspicuously for Jay-Z, but also for Beanie Sigel, Cam'ron, Janet Jackson, and others) into performance. He shopped himself around town, took meetings, ran into various roadblocks. At least part of it was the fact that his middle-class background didn't fit the street-cred mold that was popular in hip-hop at the time. Donda, his mother, was a prominent college professor. She had been a Fulbright Scholar, which sent her to China to teach. In the late seventies, she taught at Clark Atlanta University (Kanye was born in Atlanta) and then later, after her divorce from her husband, Ray—a pioneering photographer for *The Atlanta Journal-Constitution*—she moved to Chicago State University, where she helped to establish the Gwendolyn Brooks Center for Black Literature and Creative Writing. Kanye carried himself in a way that was commensurate with his background, which meant that people were taking a look at him with his polo shirts and slip-on shoes and passing hard. Even people close to him felt that way. There's a famous Jay-Z quote where he compared the Marcy Houses of his youth to Kanye's Oak Lawn, Illinois, neighborhood, and all that both places represented: "We all grew up street guys who had to do whatever we had to do to get by. Then there's Kanye, who to my knowledge has never hustled a day in his life. I didn't see how it could work."

But it did work. After failing to connect with other labels, Kanye signed with Jay's Roc-A-Fella and began work on a debut. It took forever, by contemporary music standards. He recorded material starting in 1999 or so, but he didn't really find a focus or a fulcrum until October 2002, when he was coming back from a recording studio in California and got into a car wreck. A bad one: it put him in the hospital with a shattered jaw, a jaw that was still wired shut when he recorded "Through the Wire," his first signature song. The rest, as they say, would be history.

But we had some prehistory with Kanye as well. Rich Nichols, our manager, had met him at a benefit show in New York. Kanye was there, evidently, and approached Tariq and Rich backstage to make a case for himself. I wasn't in on those discussions. To understand why, you'd have to understand the difference in dressing rooms. Tariq has always liked community, noise, fellowship, energy. I get ready for shows in silence and isolation.

Kanye was back for Tariq in LA, with more material to show. He couldn't, in Tariq's dressing room, clear out space to perform. Instead, he had to come in close to Rich and Tariq and start doing his bars quick, at low volume. That's how Rich remembered that night, that Kanye was close-talking Tariq with his lyrics, like some kind of hip-hop *Seinfeld* episode. Riq would listen for a while and then take a few steps, and Kanye would take a few steps, too, a shadow talking, a comer rapping. Rich even said there was one moment when Tariq was in the midst of a clothing change. He was half in and half out of his pants, balanced precariously, and Kanye was still at shadow distance, still calling-carding. Rich could tell a story filled with high volume, high intensity, and high profanity, but he could also lay out at exactly the right moment, because he was a brilliant, funny motherfucker, and that's how he ended that story about Kanye. "He wasn't the Kanye he would become," he would say, "so he didn't yet have that supreme confidence, but he was still"—pause as if searching for a word—"emphatic." (Rich died in 2014. He had no idea who the Kanye Kanye would become would become.)

At that time, Kanye was still very much a practitioner of his first trademark production technique, which involved pitch-shifting old soul samples. Chipmunk soul. Some people called it a "trick," but really, everything's a trick once you see someone do it. Up to that point, it's magic. He did it with Chaka Khan's "Through the Fire" for "Through the Wire," and with Luther Vandross's "A House Is Not a Home" for "Slow Jamz." His third single, "All Falls Down," was a little different. He was using Lauryn Hill's "Mystery of Iniquity," from her Unplugged performance, but it wasn't her singing it anymore. It was Syleena Johnson, the soul singer, the daughter of Syl Johnson, who was a Chicago music legend almost forty years before Kanye. Permissions tangles required Kanye to use her instead of Lauryn Hill. Regardless, I loved the song. It was so simple, so direct. I knew that it would work on the radio, and more than that, I thought that I should have cracked that code. Kanye's lyrics were solid, and sometimes they reached higher heights—I was intrigued with the way that "The New Workout Plan" used sexism to defeat sexism, and the overtly religious "Jesus Walks" was something, even though I hadn't decided yet what it was. But the production was what got me. Kanye wasn't simply sampling. He was fully interpolating. But he was doing it in a completely new way. It was so intuitive but no one had arrived there. It's rare that I think that. It happens once every five years or so. There are parts of Outkast's *Aquemini*, back in 1998, that gave me that same feeling, some kind of tingle on the brain.

I also had been around hip-hop long enough to understand the tingle, which was a Spidey-sense reminder that the genre was largely about life cycles. That's my thesis for history in general, which is why it is also the thesis for this book: ideas are born, run their course, and die, though "die" is a harsh word, maybe too final, for what actually happens, which is that life gives way to afterlife. Leaves fall to the ground and then they sink into the ground, where they are forgotten but also nourish. It happened and happened again and showed every sign of continuing to happen. The way that the Bomb Squad had flat dominated cutting-edge production between 1988 and 1991, say, and then handed the baton to (or had it snatched by) Dr. Dre and *The Chronic* just as 1991 ended—catalyzed, as we've seen, by history, by the beating of Rodney King, by the unrest in LA that followed, which shifted the genre's energy from east to west—was one of those life cycles. The Source Awards back in August 1995, which marked the triumph of acquisition hip-hop, speedboats, and mo' money, was another one. I knew they came around somewhat regularly, as cycles tended to do. There had been a phase after that, in the late nineties, that benefitted the Roots, that swept us higher, that showcased a sharper sense of history, both political and musical, that incorporated the neo-soul movement and produced records like D'Angelo's *Voodoo* and Common's *Electric Circus* and Erykah Badu's *Mama's Gun* and our own *Things Fall Apart*. That was largely a reaction to the there-can-only-be-only-one triumphalism that appeared, partly as a matter of desperation, after the deaths of Biggie and Tupac.

When I heard Kanye's debut, I saw that we were on the cusp of another cycle, and that when it happened, we might cycle out. Partly it was because he was doing something new that was also something old. Partly it was because he had stumbled into or calculated a way into a certain positionality in hip-hop, which combined artistic achievement and materialism. His artistic abilities pulled him to the left of the spectrum, where Outkast had been before. His materialism—his brand-name mentality, his devotion to materialism—balanced that off and complicated it. I had seen it within the Roots a few years before, when Tariq realized that not only were we making money, but that he could spend it on the things that he enjoyed, including clothes. I still had a thrift-store mentality. Tariq suddenly started showing up in outfits that cost as much as a used car. It wasn't superficial. He had come to understand that they expressed an aspect of his personality, genuinely connected with something in him. Rich and I had misgivings about it, if only because we worried that it ran counter to the way the Roots were understood by our audience. We tried to balance it in our image-making. But here came Kanye, with no misgivings at all. He was all-in for a new way of being. When he would talk to the press and try to explain what he was, what Kanye was, he was completely comfortable with every kind of contradiction. He seemed to relish it because he could unfold in the spotlight. So much has happened since then that has amplified certain aspects of that character, but in a way, it was all there from the beginning.

(Part of that character, of course, was a willingness to be hella corny. That same fall that he played for Block Party he appeared on the cover of *Scratch*, an *XXL*-adjacent quarterly devoted to the art of making hip-hop records. During its relatively short life, *Scratch*—subtitle: "The Science of Hip-Hop"—ran features and profiles with producers and DJs. Dr. Dre was on the first issue. Kanye was on the second. He was holding a record, which makes sense for a magazine like that, but the record that he was holding made no sense at all. It was Marvin Gaye's *Let's Get It On*. That's a record you get as a present for your mom's friend. It's not a record to establish your DJ cred. If that was me, I would have been holding Galt McDermot's *The Nucleus* or Eugene McDaniels's *Headless Heroes of the Apocalypse*, and I might have tucked an obscure funk 45 behind it just to let Large Professor know that I had gone to the trouble of ordering it from Japan for $700. Would that have been pretentious, in a sense, a special message for a select few? Sure, but who would be so Captain Obvious to set a tone for his creative life with one of the most famous Marvin Gaye records in history? Maybe the same guy who built songs on Chaka Khan and Luther Vandross.)

The Block Party had lots of live performances. Some of them made the soundtrack album, while some didn't. Record company and rights issues. We had two songs on it, including one called "Boom!" where we brought out hip-hop pioneers Big Daddy Kane and Kool G Rap to perform with us. The live version was a summit, past and present. But the studio version of "Boom!" was an interesting history lesson that enfolded an interesting history lesson on its own. Way back when the Roots were founded, we had several presiding ideas, a kind of mission statement for the band, and some of them revolved around the way that we were living preservers of hip-hop history. This was reflected in the skill sets that fed our reputation. I could play any breakbeat, and Tariq could mimic any MC. In fact, as we got our first major-label record, *Do You Want More?!!!??!*, together, we had a long song that was a favorite of ours that we kept working on, over and over. It was called "In Your Dreams, Kid (I'm Every MC)," and it was a long posse cut that included appearances by Guru, Q-Tip, Ice Cube, Chuck D, Busta Rhymes, and more, except that none of them were on the track. It was all Tariq, impersonating them. It was more than a novelty song, though, or rather it was an extremely high-level novelty song. We matched the production styles and samples for each segment. It was a complete production. When the Kurt Cobain suicide happened and Rich announced to us that we had to pull up stakes and get out of town, that song was hanging in the balance. "But, but, but," we told Rich. "What about 'In Your Dreams, Kid'?" Rich wasn't sentimental that way. He told us we had to go, which meant that the song had to go onto the cutting-room floor. We kept trying to come back to it, year after year, album after album, but the time was never right. Some of the impersonations seemed too passé, or they hadn't cycled around to where they were cool again. And then, for *The Tipping Point*, we wrote "Boom!" Initially, it wasn't just in the style of Kane and Kool G but intended as a collaboration with them. We even had Big Daddy Kane come in to be on the record. He did his verse and left. But Kane 2004 didn't sound like Kane 1988 anymore. Remember: after his first album he changed his vocal style. He went from hard tenor down into a Barry White growl. The sexy tone knocked out the hardcore. I talked about it with Rich, and he agreed. "Not for nothing,' I said, "but I think Tariq as Kane sounds better than Kane as Kane." Rich agreed again. But he had something more: this would be the angle. We would just roll with Tariq playing the role of those other guys. We could represent history the way we wanted and it would make up for lost time and pay off "In Your Dreams, Kid." (We eventually put "In Your Dreams, Kid" out on the twenty-fifth anniversary edition of *Do You Want More?!!!??!*)

We had history on our side. But what did that mean anymore? What was a Kane in the face of a Kanye? I remember the moment that Kanye was set to play "Jesus Walks" there in Brooklyn. That was the fourth single from his juggernaut debut, and it sampled not an old soul song but a performance by the ARC Choir, a Harlem gospel group composed entirely of rehabilitated addicts. Kanye wanted to perform it in a specific way, with a full marching band. I was hanging back a bit, observing, and thinking about the moment. We had a presidential election coming up, one that would bring us a new leader, I was sure—George W. Bush was finishing up his first term, the term he hadn't really even earned (men in suitcoats streaming into Miami-Dade County to make sure that he won the state, and thus the nation), and I was confident that the country would send him back to Texas. That would have meant President Kerry, but out there in Clinton Hill my thought was more about President Kanye. He had a certain bearing, coming in with the band the way he did. Kids in the crowd, especially Black kids, seemed to understand that they were looking at a New World Order.

I went to Rich and expressed my concern. He didn't respond. "Oh, no," I said. "Can you even hear me?" I thought that maybe I had crossed over without knowing it, that I was speaking from a place beyond earthly life. He shook his head. "I hear you," he said. "I just don't know the answer."

Not only was it a time when I was afraid we were disappearing, but everything around us was disappearing also. Take the simplest process: getting new music. It used to be that I would go to a record store. I would go to Sound of Market Street at Eleventh and Chestnut and talk to the youngest person there. He was a kid with my name, more or less, DJ Amir, and he would tell me what records to get. Or I would go to Footwork, Bobbito Garcia's store, or the branch of it that DJ Rich Medina opened in Philly. Or I would go to Fat Beats, a basement spot on the Lower East Side that specialized in underground records. But the internet was growing. I remember getting a demo from Little Brother in 2003 at a North Carolina gig. I loved it and brought it to the attention of the Okayplayer community, only to find that there were people who had already been turned on to it, and records like it, through the internet. They were downloading records. I went to Rich to talk to him about it and he was already on it. He was on Napster and LimeWire and all those places. That shit intimidated me. But I steeled myself. After Little Brother I didn't want to be behind the curve. And this was clearly a way of staying, if not ahead of it, at least on it. I remember making the Roots song "Somebody's Gotta Do It," which was on *The Tipping Point* in 2004. Tariq wanted to have Devin the Dude and Jean Grae on the record. I wasn't really aware of Devin the Dude's history but now I knew about these underground sites, that were posting records. A year after that or so, a site named DatPiff appeared, and that consolidated the underground blogs and became a clearinghouse for mixtapes. That was another evolutionary watershed that may not have changed my tastes, but it definitely changed the way I justified them.

There's a moment on the Roots tour bus that will never leave me. I was listening to a mixtape, which wasn't uncommon, and more specifically to a DJ Drama *Gangsta Grillz* mixtape, which was a little uncommon. I always joke that I am the Gryffindor bus and Tariq is the Slytherin bus, playfully, to draw a distinction between the music-nerd yin of the Roots and the street-cred MC yang of the Roots. But it was my joke, and I didn't always think about how committed he was to his side of the equation. *Didn't always* means *did sometimes*, and this was one of those moments, during a span that stretched from 2002 to 2006 or so when it became clear to me that he was relentless about listening to first-generation trap, all of the Memphis stuff, 8Ball and MJG, Pastor Troy, Project Pat. I got it. I understood that he was on the party side, the crunk side, but I hadn't fully understood the bright line. There were internal identity dynamics at play, of course (we were still only in our early thirties—was he trying to find an identity that I wouldn't taint?). At any rate, he committed to these mixtapes, and they crept into my world, too, competitively, respectfully. I listened. I tried to absorb it all: what DJ Drama was curating, why I had to hear endless Lil Jon tags. As I listened, I thought about why I wasn't quite coming around to the music. Was it not intellectual enough? Was it too repetitive? Was it more about the line that I was drawing, as well, and the fact that in those years I was still knee-deep in Soulquarianism?

Toward the end of that tour I heard Tariq talking about DJ Drama. He was saying something to Kamal about him. "The thing about this tape," he said, "is that Tyree has a theory . . ."

Something caught me up short. "Wait," I said. "Who's Tyree?"

He looked confused now, like I was asking a stupid question. "DJ Drama is Tyree."

"What?"

"Tyree Simmons. You know."

All of a sudden I did know. "Are you trying to tell me that this DJ Drama is Tyree from Philadelphia?" I said.

"Who did you think it was?" Tariq said. I heard only a thick silence in my mind, like my brain had turned to stone. I hadn't thought about who it was, but it definitely had not occurred to me that he was the same Tyree Simmons we had known back in Philly. He was a Germantown kid, half-Black, half-Jewish, had started out as a teenager back in 1995 or 1996 promoting independent rap, brainy rap, underground rap. He wasn't a backpack rapper just yet, because that wasn't a thing just yet, but that was his side of the fence, which was my side of the fence. That's how we knew him at all, because he put us on mixtapes, put out a mixtape in 1996 in fact that was called *Illadelph*, put it out the same year we put out *Illadelph Halflife*, included artists like Tariq, like Dice Raw, like Bahamadia. It was a tour through our world. And that mattered greatly back then, when the ripple effect of the Source Awards a few years earlier meant that there was a difference between underground and mainstream, almost the difference between two countries, and you had to declare yourself when you were traveling between one and the other. Or maybe it was the difference between opposing armies, and the first person that I thought of as a five-star general representative of the underground was Tyree. He would make these underground mixtapes. (It was not new, not exactly. There were records like Slum Village's *Fan-Tas-Tic, Vol. 1* which might as well have been a mixtape, but which I treated more like an independent album that had been bootlegged through the underground.) DJ Drama was a curator and historian of the little circle drawn around us.

Then he went down to Atlanta to attend Clark Atlanta University. While he was there, he met two other Philly products, DJ Sense and Don Cannon. They formed the Aphilliates, a collective that certainly seemed like it was going to use Atlanta as an outpost to keep repping the home city. But a funny thing happened on the way out of Philly. He started to respond to his immediate surroundings, which meant more receptivity to Southern hip-hop acts, and by 1998 he was releasing mixtapes not with Tariq and Dice and Bahamadia but instead with Outkast and Three 6 Mafia and Mystikal, which meant not just Atlanta but also Memphis and New Orleans. That birthed the *Gangsta Grillz* series, which forged associations with some of the biggest artists in the region. Lil Jon began providing tags for the series, and DJ Drama developed a relationship with T.I.

T.I. named this new brand of Southern hip-hop "trap," and the name stuck. Trap was new wine in an old bottle, or new malt liquor in old bottles. It was street-level storytelling, taking stock, slanging rock, power before Power. A music sprang up around it, sped snares, 808s, autotuned vocals. I have read, and believe, that Tyree vibed with it. His parents were Civil Rights vets, and he understood that the advances of the movement didn't necessarily reach deep into the Southern cities where they started.

The DJ Drama mixtapes got bigger and bigger, not just because they were showcasing artists from the ascendant Dirty South, but because he was good at what he did, good at assembling and arranging songs in an almost cinematic way. That's what Tariq was hearing that I was not quite hearing.

Let's go back to the bus for a second. It took Tariq and Kamal seventeen minutes to explain to me what I was hearing. "No, Ahmir," they kept saying, more maddeningly calm each time. "This is the same person." It blew up my mind. It wasn't a sense of betrayal, like he had sold out to the other side. It was more a sense of amazement that he had so flagrantly and so successfully changed horses in midstream. It was like he was in an NBA Finals game and right in the middle of the third quarter, in full view of everyone, with his team ahead by twenty, had taken off his jersey and put on the opposing team's jersey—and then gone on to turn the tide and notch a beyond-improbable-it's-impossible victory. "How do you think I got all these mixtapes?" Tariq said. The thick silence in my mind shifted a bit. I was so closed off to any energy that wasn't pushing the culture forward. But something changed that day in the bus. Part of me asked a desperate question: Do I still have to learn? And another part of me, excited and resigned at the same time, answered in the affirmative.

In the wake of that, I started again to learn. I got familiar with T.I., with Lil Jon, with Yeezy, with Lil Scrappy and David Banner, with Slim Thug and Paul Wall. I made a map in my mind and stuck pins in Memphis and Houston and Jackson and Louisville. One of the biggest pins went into New Orleans, and one of the biggest reasons for that pin was Lil Wayne. He had been releasing records since the midnineties, and mixtapes since just after that (including the Squad Up series), but it wasn't until the midaughts that he really rose into view. The main drivers were his *Carter* albums, on Cash Money, and the *Dedication* mixtapes, which were part of the *Gangsta Grillz* series. Those weren't quite out yet when I was on the bus, but I was set on the path, and by the time those releases started to appear, I was walking down the path with a companion—Solange Knowles, who I befriended and who started trading stuff with me. She was more than happy to show me all the bounce I had missed, all the dope Southern stuff. She was one of the big early backers not just of Southern hip-hop in general, but of Lil Wayne. I remember how she put it: "Wayne is undeniable." She had examples. I considered them.

And yet, even at that relative late date, a few years removed from the bus, a few years with the scales dropped from my eyes courtesy of DJ Drama, I still wondered if she really knew her stuff or if this was a case of a young jawn blinded by the moment. And even as I started to listen to it all, I still felt as though I was supposed to be genetically (and intellectually [and regionally]) predisposed to resist him. What was this Southern sound? Was it neo-minstrelsy? Was it some kind of commentary on stereotypical views toward Black people, or was it somehow trafficking in those stereotypes? I talked about that all the time with Rich Nichols, our manager, not through the prism of Wayne specifically, but through the prism of Project Pat, a Memphis rapper. Rich sent me a song called "Gorilla Pimp." By that time it was a few years old but it had all those hallmarks of Dirty South rap: scenes of criminality, drugs and guns, questionable treatment of women. But buried in it was one moment that Rich wanted me to hear. During a drug scene, there was a threat issued to a woman who was a bystander ("You can be a Jane Doe if you call the po-po"). Rough stuff, right? But right after that, the song let that would-be Jane Doe speak; a female voice said, "I'ma call your momma up," and right after that Pat flinched: "Bitch, that's a no-no." It was rare for street cats to allow any vulnerability, let alone let another voice pop into the song to show up the main narrator. Rich thought it was the funniest shit he had ever heard.

That was when people like Solange started talking up Wayne. I was conflicted. It took a younger brain to move me. Rich's oldest son was traveling with us at the time. He was twelve or so. Everything he loved, I was looking at cross-eyed. He would talk constantly about Lil Wayne but to me he was just another 106th and Park rapper, nothing more. One day he played "Star" on the tour, a Roots song based on a sample from Sly and the Family Stone's "Everybody Is a Star." That shocked me a little. I knew he liked the Roots, but the idea that he would play our music was . . . surprising, at least. You're not supposed to like your dad's band's music. Then all of a sudden I realized that it wasn't really "Star"—it was "Momma Taught Me," from the 2005 mixtape *The Dedication*, and it was Lil Wayne rhyming over our song. ("Our song"—I don't even play my own music.) Self-preservation made me listen to check if he was doing more with it than we had, and I heard lyrics that made me laugh, like "I'm a fly young man / Check my wingspan," or what seemed like a completely random swipe at the NBA player Nick Van Exel for his baldness. (Van Exel had been a star for the Lakers a decade before, and then had bounced around from team to team—best player on a bad Denver squad, diminishing returns in Dallas and Golden State. What was he doing in this song? Though he had also been in Jay-Z's rap verse in Beyoncé's "Crazy in Love" a few years before, rhyming with "next to." Someone should put a pin in *that*—slightly out-of-season sports references in hip-hop lyrics.)

That changed my idea of him, though it didn't change it completely. On the one hand, anyone who rhymed over the Roots had me, especially that year—I was so obsessed with the threat of erasure that it was especially meaningful. On the other hand, that same obsession with erasure meant that I wasn't allowing myself an open heart, especially when it came to artists who were winning. I was constantly seeing a tsunami coming down the path and thinking the only thing I had to do was to save myself. By this point I was getting everyone's record because I needed to keep tabs as a DJ. Even if the Roots didn't make it, I was determined not to fail as a DJ. It was a way of staying progressive in my head with regard to new music.

But the underlying questions weren't being answered: Was I listening to these records in the car? In the gym? In my house in the morning? Wayne wasn't yet there with me, or I with him. The story moves forward. Skip ahead a little to Jay-Z's *American Gangster* album in 2007. He was running Def Jam by then, and we were signed there. We were on good terms, enough so that he let me hear "Hello Brooklyn 2.0" in the office. I was a major Beastie Boys and *Paul's Boutique* fan. "Hello Brooklyn" was the fifth section of the "B-boy Bouillabaisse" suite, that album's version of the end of the Beatles' *Abbey Road*. Jay had reconceived it with Weezy. "Lil Wayne?" I said. "It's hot, ain't it?" he said. That wasn't what I had meant but he couldn't fathom that I had meant anything else. I'm almost certain he would have put every last dime on the fact that I was fully on board. But in my own mind, I was backsliding into us/them-ism. I talked about it with Rich. "You gotta fuck with Lil Wayne," he said. Skip ahead again to the year after that, when Lil Wayne released *Tha Carter III*. People were talking about the record the way I was talking about *It Takes a Nation of Millions to Hold Us Back* twenty years earlier. Did it deserve that kind of praise? My arms were still folded a little bit. I did look into Wayne playing the first Roots Picnic that year, only to be told that he was too expensive. Really? And yet, when I heard "A Milli" in 2009 or so, I knew immediately that the vocal sample was from the Vampire Mix that Fatboy Slim had made for A Tribe Called Quest's "I Left My Wallet in El Segundo." As much as I wanted to resist Wayne, I couldn't resist a deep-cut Tribe sample. The story moves further forward. In 2011, on *Tha Carter IV*, he released what is arguably his most famous song, "6 Foot 7 Foot," not his best or his most important, but arguably his most famous, a status it acquired as a result of one lyric in particular. The song was based around Harry Belafonte's "Day-O (The Banana Boat Song)," which gave it its title (those are sizes of the bunches of bananas that are being lifted from the boat). But toward the end of the second verse, Wayne reiterated a principle of street life: stealthiness. "Paper chasin', tell that paper, 'Look, I'm right behind ya / Bitch, real Gs move in silence like lasagna.'" That line blew up big. It went viral and then some. At the time, I was on a group chat, and it was decided that we would not give him a pass for the lasagna line. It came up in discussion, and someone laid down the law—"he mad corny for that lasagna line"—and one by one everyone started to agree. "It's not what he thinks it is." "Only pretentious idiots would see that as clever." My finger had been hovering over the keyboard ready to give him acclamation. Someone beat me to the assessment and I backed down. By that point I was in another hyperconscious cycle with Wayne. *Pitchfork* was acclaiming him to the heavens, but *Pitchfork* was in a place where they were cosigning extreme Black imagery in a way that seemed like some newly minted kind of hipster racism.

There's a somewhat insane coda to the story—not Wayne's part of it, which drifts into the future, but DJ Drama's. When Drama started his mixtapes, he had an economic model, or at least he had the seeds of one and grew the tree around it. Mixtapes existed in a gray area where Drama didn't have to license samples. He could create physical product for something like fifty cents a copy and could sell a mixtape for ten times that, a bargain compared to commercially produced CDs. If he moved twenty thousand a month without trying, he could double that with effort, word on the street. The money piled up. The money was in piles.

Mixtape culture came right at a time when prestreaming was starting to cut into CD sales. The RIAA shut down Napster. It scared off illegal downloaders—the one case that terrified everyone was a woman named Jammie Thomas-Rasset in Minneapolis who was accused by the record industry not just of downloading music but of sharing it. There was a judgment against her that went from $1.5 million down to $54K back up to more than $200K. The rules were evolving and the punishments with them. The industry had to figure out what to do with mixtapes as well.

Around the same time, Kim's Video in Manhattan, a legendary indie store for CDs, DVDs, and more, was raided. Mixtapes were confiscated, along with a CD burner. Five employees were arrested for piracy. This threw everything into flux. The industry was entirely on the fence with regard to mixtapes. Any executive with eyes open could see how they worked, and how well they worked, when it came to connecting artists to audiences. Drama was effectively a mainstream producer. He was in communication with major labels and, more than that, in cahoots.

As *Gangsta Grillz* grew, so did Drama's operation. He signed with a distributor. Then suddenly they were in the stores. You could buy them as product, which began to unravel the entire philosophy behind them. He continued to move up in the world, working with people like Pharrell and even signing with Atlantic Records for his own solo debut. And then, in January of 2007, he got the raid treatment himself. He was walking toward his car when the forces of the law converged on him. They claimed they were looking for contraband. Had his relationship with artists like Jeezy put him at risk? Was he harboring drugs and guns without knowing it? The contraband they found was CDs, burning equipment, and hard drives. They arrested him and Don Cannon and brought them to the Fulton County Jail, where they were charged with racketeering.

RICO charges—which are accompanied by the seizure of assets—are complex and difficult to explain, but there was a simple truth underneath it, which was that the same record industry that had more or less looked the other way when Drama was making his mixtapes was now dropping the hammer. This exposed a fault line of San Andreas proportions in the hero-villain equation. In the end, the charges were rolled back away from Drama and Cannon, though some of the money seized was not returned.

And there were further fault lines. Some of the artists who had used the *Gangsta Grillz* series to heighten their visibility complained that they had not benefitted financially from the arrangement. But the largest irony comes at the end of the story. Tyree—law-abiding, entrepreneurial Tyree, who had started back in Philly before ever going down to the Dirty South—was now a criminal, an honest-to-badness gangsta. His solo album came out on Atlantic Records, with a lead single that featured Rick Ross. By the time it did, mixtape culture had shifted away from physical product toward downloadable mixtapes as featured on sites like the (Philly-based, but also internet-based, meaning everywhere all at once) DatPiff.com. More on that later.

The two stories that power the opening of this chapter, and this era of hip-hop, seem different. They are different. But they have a common thread, which is that they are both essentially about producers and production sensibility. While the half decade before this had brought stars into the center of the sky, this period (with the exception of Kanye, who literally also proved the rule) was largely about producers. The 1992–1997 period had felt similar—it had stars, but sounds came to the fore, from Dr. Dre's smooth G-funk to Pete Rock's East Coast jazz reinvestment to others—but it was even more true this time around. Think of Swizz Beatz, a New York City native who had first risen to prominence with DMX's "Ruff Ryders' Anthem" and Jay-Z's "Jigga My Nigga" in the late nineties, and had then gone on a hot streak that found him having hits with artists ranging from Styles P to Smitty to Cassidy, the last of whom was the first artist signed to Swizz Beats's Full Surface label. Think of Timbaland, who had come up in Norfolk, Virginia, started out with R&B artists like Ginuwine and Aaliyah, and then sharpened his sound in collaboration with Missy Elliott. (My own private, unpopular theory is that I consider her more of a singer-songwriter than an MC. Just like I consider Arrested Development a pre-neo-soul group more than I consider them a hip-hop group. And the way the members of Stetsasonic consider the Roots a jazz group more than they consider us a real hip-hop group.* Do I harbor a little bit of bitterness over that? Yes, maybe, sorta kinda.) Their records, starting with *Supa Dupa Fly* in 1997, got bigger and better, from *Da Real World* (1999) to *Miss E . . . So Addictive* (2001) to *Under Construction* (2002) to *This Is Not a Test* (2003). Timbaland pulled back a bit for Missy's sixth album, *The Cookbook*, in part because he was busy with every other rapper who wanted a piece of his sound, whether it was Jay-Z or Bubba Sparxxx or Petey Pablo or Lloyd Banks. But his sound was also starting to move through the music world—he had huge pop successes with Justin Timberlake and Nelly Furtado, and then went international by working with acts like the Hives and Björk. He's kind of sui generis, meaning that no matter where he went, he was only ever himself, in sound and sensibility.

From a purely hip-hop perspective, the production stars that meant the most to this era, that changed more things for the better (and a few for the worse), were the Neptunes, composed of Pharrell Williams and Chad Hugo. They were also Virginians, from Virginia Beach instead of Norfolk (Pharrell is a distant cousin of Timbaland's). They had been working since the midnineties, but the first time I heard them knowingly was in 1997, on MC Lyte's "I Can't Make a Mistake." Someone had given me a bunch of singles. I flipped through them, saw a Busta Rhymes title that seemed intriguing, put the rest away. But a few days later they were still there, staring at me. Unheard music will do that. The MC Lyte one elevated a little due to the title, which seemed a little unwieldy to me. The song

* Not Prince Paul . . .

was even more so. It was the oddest sound I ever heard in my life, a really loud clavinet patch. It was weird for MC Lyte and weird for me. When I heard N.O.R.E.'s "Superthug" later that same year, I knew it was by the same guys, because it sounded the same, the clavinet and heavy snare. The same was true of Mase's "Lookin' at Me." I heard, absorbed, and mostly dismissed that first phase. That's not to say that they weren't doing something interesting. It is to say that it arrived in my mind not fully successful, a technique that was both too narrow and too off to the side. It struck me as similar to what Swizz Beats had been doing, these keyboard beats that sounded like they were made by a one-fingered piano player. That's where I classified them for two years, three, four, even as they cut their teeth on hip-hop and bit into pop, producing big songs for Usher and NSYNC and a gigantic crossover hit with Nelly's "Hot in Here."

What finally brought me around to the Neptunes was a remix they did for Jay-Z's "La-La-La (Excuse Me Miss Again)." They had produced the original "Excuse Me Miss" on *The Blueprint 2: The Gift & The Curse*, and I shelved it alongside the other Neptunes productions I had heard. In the remix, though, there was something that caught my ear. It was a drum moment at the thirty-four-second mark, a very understated, blink-and-you-miss-it flam. You turn the snare off and then hit the rim shot and the snare at the same time. Prince had done it on "Under the Cherry Moon" back in 1986. I had done it on D'Angelo's *Voodoo* a few years before. Pharrell did it, just once, and I not only remember hearing it, but remember hearing it with the other Roots and laughing so hard, because it sounded so random and so strange. It was like a noise bursting out of a cartoon. It cracked up the Roots so much that it became an inside joke for us. When someone would fuck up in practice, we would say "bloop," which was our way of referring to that moment in "La-La-La (Excuse Me Miss Again)," and then it migrated into sound check, and even into actual performances.

I am, as I have said a billion times, hyper-analytical when it comes to production choices. When something seems off, I have to create a theory around it. With the RZA's productions for Wu-Tang, I developed an assumption that he hadn't read the owner's manual for whatever equipment he was using, both figuratively and literally, and the amateurishness of the execution was part of the charm. Go back to Raekwon's "Verbal Intercourse," from *Only Built 4 Cuban Linx . . .* , and think yet again why you would sample the part of the Emotions' "If You Think It (You May as Well Do It)" that has talking over it. It's so crazy it just might work! Dilla was the opposite, so blatantly purposeful that every "mistake" seemed like a high-end intellectual riddle that I just hadn't quite figured out yet. For me, Pharrell came to occupy the middle ground. Upon first encounter, his productions felt sloppy, like watching your kid brother make a beat. But then you feel your response evolving from "Ah, whatever, it's just him" to "That part's funny" to "That part's interesting" to "You hear that?" to "Oh my God, what's this??" to absolute 12,000 percent obsession.

After that, I listened harder, which meant that I listened to Kelis's "Milkshake" and Snoop Dogg's "Drop It Like It's Hot" and Gwen Stefani's "Hollaback Girl" and Ludacris's "Money Maker." I also listened to the Clipse. They were a rap duo composed of the Thornton brothers: Terrence (who went by Pusha T) and Gene (who went by Malice). They were a duo rather than two separate artists because of Pharrell, who knew them from Virginia Beach and was involved in their career from the start, not just as a producer but as a consiglieri and label head—after being dropped by Elektra, they signed to Arista, where the Neptunes had their Star Trak imprint. The Clipse's debut, *Lord Willin'*, came out in 2002. This was before I heard the Jay-Z remix that would turn around my sense of the Neptunes. It was also during a time when hip-hop records had stopped mattering to me. As I have said, something broke or fizzled or fell into a well when I heard *Wu-Tang Forever* back in 1997. I had put so much hope in it, and once I saw that the center wasn't going to hold, I sort of gave up on complete albums. I would get them, but I wouldn't experience them the same way I had experienced *It Takes a Nation of Millions to Hold Us Back* or *AmeriKKKa's Most Wanted* or *Midnight Marauders* or *De La Soul Is Dead*. I wasn't sitting down for five hours listening to them over and over and over again, trying to unpack every nuance from every corner. But I was—I am—a DJ, which meant that I had a professional interest in excavating the songs that worked. So I would listen to the record once through but hear only "Grindin'" and "When the Last Time," and then the second time I would listen only to those songs. It made sense to me, in that these producers were thinking like singles artists.

And yet, the arc of the creative universe bends toward irony. In 2006, the Clipse was finishing up their follow-up record, *Hell Hath No Fury*, also produced by the Neptunes. The Roots were down in Virginia, too. It was New Year's Eve, 2005 turning into 2006, and we were trying to get a song from the Neptunes. We had a very specific objective, which was to find a hit song that didn't sound like it was trying to be a hit song. It needed to feel natural, Roots-like. I was, as I have said, judgmental of the early Neptunes sound—though to be fair, also of the early sounds of the other producers at their level. The beats sounded rinky-dink and DIY compared to the complex structures that Dilla was creating for his clients. (As I have also said, I needed time to come around. Now I love both textures. But back then, I was skeptical.) While we were negotiating, fishing for our own hit, they played us "Ride Around Shining." Maybe they picked that one because it featured a Philly rapper named Ab-Liva, who had been in a kind of supergroup called the Re-Up Gang with the Clipse brothers. Or maybe they picked it because it was astonishing. I heard the opening notes, the harp arpeggio that went into sinister mode, and had only one thought, which is that I couldn't remember the last time that hip-hop sounded that dangerous. It was like a window breaking, and not just any window, but a window in my apartment on the seventy-third floor, and after that the shards falling all the way down to the street. I didn't know that it was from a *giallo* soundtrack. I didn't know how they had used it. I didn't know anything except that it was amazing. The rest of *Hell Hath No Fury*, as it turned out, was just as visionary. For the first time since 1997, I listened to a complete album, all the way through, multiple times, without feeling defensive or impatient or like I was being played for a sucker.

The album was also a kind of swan song. It got tons of critical praise. But the praise was frustrating. The *Pitchfork* review, a 9.1, was a perfect example. The Clipse was hip-hop's "meanest" duo (also "smartest," but "meanest" came first), and the record was "unrelenting," with tales of "distribution and desperation," the product of an intelligence that was "malevolent, almost maniacal" in its pursuit of a "simmering executioner's song." I liked the score but I also knew the score, which was that it was a frustrating example of fetishizing Black pain and desperation. It was like Ivan in *The Harder They Come*, an outlaw who became a folk hero, but were they outlaws or artists? I had felt this way before, when N.W.A. had released *Niggaz4Life/Efil4zaggin* back in 1991, but that was a case of the artists self-fetishizing, which didn't make it better necessarily but made it less preventable. If you wanted to make yourself a cartoon, your choice. Here, though, the critics were taking the Clipse and turning them into . . . I wasn't sure what. An object lesson in negative portraiture?

Back when N.W.A.'s record came out, someone had sent me an article from the *New Republic* written by David Samuels. The piece was titled "The Rap on Rap" and subtitled "The 'Black' Music That Isn't Either." It promised to be not promising. But I read on. It opened with the observation that when SoundScan first appeared— when record sales were suddenly tabulated accurately, by machine, rather than through a series of somewhat haphazard phone calls to record stores—the top album was not R.E.M.'s *Out of Time*, as industry-watchers suspected that it might be, but the N.W.A. record. Samuels used that fact to construct a theory of how hip-hop had curdled from being a genuine reflection of Black American experience to a cartoonishly villainous minefield of guns, drugs, and misogyny—and how that curdled world brought in more and more white teenage fans, thrilled by the prospect of connecting to this bleak and lawless world that they believed accurately represented Black reality. At the time, I thought the article was far too reductive. Why would you want to focus so stubbornly on N.W.A. when you also had De La Soul and A Tribe Called Quest and Stetsasonic and P.M. Dawn and Naughty by Nature and Main Source and—even when it came to riskier artists with a more bruising worldview—Cypress Hill and Ice Cube and the Geto Boys and Slick Rick? It seemed to hang a big point on one small nail. Fifteen years later, the insights had gained not cobwebs but resonance.

The producer-centric era had victims as well as victors. A few years back, Tariq and I were having a discussion about hip-hop albums, as we often do, and I came up with a principle that I like to call "When only the best won't do." We were talking about Jay-Z, and the way he left and rejoined his career in the first decade of the twenty-first century. He had left with *The Black Album*, in 2003. It would be his last record, he said, and had promoted the album with that in mind. As release approached, he had given an interview to Touré for a piece in *The New York Times* where he reached back into the midnineties, to the early part of his career, which he remembered as a glory period for hip-hop. That had passed, along with some of the brightest stars from that era. "It's not like it was with Big and Pac," he told *The Times*. "Hip-hop's corny now." Jay-Z insisted to Touré, and by extension to the *Times'* readership, that he was not using a Sugar Ray Leonard–like false retirement to gin up interest in his record. "Give me a little more credit than that," he said. "I could think of other ways to get attention." *The Black Album* seemed to follow thematically from that promise, from the video for "99 Problems" (which ended with Jay being shot down) to the last song, "My 1st Song," which directly addressed the hunger of creation and—it seemed—the way in which it had been lost.

Time passed. Jay-Z reconsidered. It wasn't entirely surprising. In the *Times* article, the last paragraph addresses the possibility that his resolve regarding his retirement might expire. "Well, like Jordan said, 'I've got to leave myself a window,'" he said. "If people take it back to when we were making hot albums and I'm just totally inspired and I'm like, I want in, then that could happen. But I don't foresee it." The stretch after *The Black Album* was largely legitimate retirement, with a cameo here and there, but nothing that suggested that he was ready for a full-scale return. Then word started going out: release on horizon. In November 2006, his ninth album, *Kingdom Come*, appeared. It made a half-hearted attempt to respect the gone-forever narrative. There was a brief moment when he considered releasing it under the name Shawn Carter, to maintain the death/disappearance of Jay-Z. But commercial and maybe other considerations prevailed. Still, the title was not about life, but about the afterlife, the next life. This was another phase.

And it looked from the outside like it might maintain his momentum. On *The Black Album*, he had worked with a slate of producers that included Rick Rubin, Just Blaze, and the Neptunes. Rick Rubin was gone. Just Blaze and the Neptunes were back. There was a song with Kanye. But most interestingly, there were four songs overseen by Dr. Dre: "Lost One," "30 Something," "Trouble," and "Minority Report." The two of them had worked together in the past, of course. Most people don't realize that Jay wrote "Still D.R.E.," from 2001, the first single and the one that got that album up in the air. As recorded, it was a duet between Dre and Snoop Dogg, but Snoop was clear about its origins during an interview on *The Breakfast Club*. "He wrote Dre's shit and my shit and it was flawless. He wrote the whole fucking song." So to bring them back together on *Kingdom Come*, to combine the most magical MC and the most magical producer—you'd think that would be magic.

It was a disappointment. The record songs fell far short of the mark, and they nearly dragged the album down. That was a surprise to me, and a revelation.

I thought about it, not just then, but for years, right up until the moment that it surfaced in one of my discussions with Tariq, along with the when-only-the-best-won't-do formulation. What I meant by it—what I mean by it—is that other kinds of producers were a far better match for Jay-Z than Dr. Dre. Jay's talent, I realized, was that he sucked the air out of a room. He was like Bill Clinton. When he came in, you couldn't see or even sense anyone else. Because of that he needed a musical backdrop that was bland. He needed butter so you could spread on it. I thought back to Jay's early albums. When they came out I thought that the musical backdrops were inferior. And they were, in a sense—I was working with J Dilla, so I was firsthand witnessing sorcery. Compared to that, how could I make sense of other production styles? Take a song like "Jigga My Nigga," which was on the Ruff Ryders compilation and a bonus track on *Vol. 3: The Life and Times of Shawn Carter*. I was left perplexed by the minimalism of the production back then, though I get it now. Or think of "I Just Wanna Love U (Give It 2 Me)," from *The Dynasty: Roc La Familia*. That's a Neptunes production. It shares some DNA with songs like MC Lyte's "I Can't Make a Mistake."

So how does this affect Jay-Z? Well, let's say that an average good song is made up of five entities—lyrics, samples, beats, production, and an MC's performance—each of which represents 20 percent of the overall recipe. A Jay-Z song throws that all off balance. He projects a larger-than-life presence, and so there is no space for him to share that spotlight. Whereas other rappers might fit in nicely around an aggressively brilliant musical backing, Jay-Z needs a backdrop that shrinks back to accommodate his size. That's why certain kinds of productions—Kanye, Neptunes, Swizz Beats— work so well for him. They provide effectiveness and he does the rest. He turns twenty into eighty, but that is also a limiting factor for the twenty that remains.

No account of this era can end without a return to Kanye. And re-turning to Kanye means revisiting some of the history that occurred both to him and around him after *Dave Chappelle's Block Party*.

Since Kanye came to Clinton Hill and ghost-of-Christmas-Future'd me, he had continued his upward trajectory. His second album, *Late Registration*, was largely coproduced by power-pop mastermind Jon Brion and included hits like "Diamonds from Sierra Leone" and "Touch the Sky." It also had "Hey Mama," a tribute to Donda, who had retired from her academic career to help manage Kanye's ca-reer. Oh, and it also had "Gold Digger," a massive hit based on a Ray Charles hook resung by Jamie Foxx, who had just played Ray in *Ray*, and not just played him but won an Oscar for it. (Ray was Kanye's dad's name. Hmm: subject for further research.) The day before the album's release, Hurricane Katrina roared through the Gulf of Mexico and into New Orleans, where it breached levees in more than twenty places, killed a thousand people, and caused well over a hundred billion dollars in damage. Charity began as soon as the storm left, including a nationally televised benefit on September 2 hosted by Matt Lauer and featuring a huge list of celebrities. Kanye, appearing alongside Mike Myers to make an appeal for the hurricane's victims, went off script, and then more off it.

The third album, *Graduation*, took a little longer to put together (it came out in late 2007), but it was another giant, with another number one single in "Stronger" and a broader musical palette, including a collaboration with Chris Martin on "Homecoming." All three of his albums won Grammys for Best Rap Album. It was a streak that at the time seemed historic. And I did my best to avoid it. I listened to the records on the sly. I would get someone to rip them for me. I wasn't buying copies. Or I would get up at one in the morning and sneak to my car. I didn't want anyone in my house to hear me. And there, in the Scion, I would still be critical. I would say to myself, "I don't like these patches" and "this loop seems lazy," but I would also admit that I liked it. It wasn't easy. If I liked it, did that mean that I no longer existed? Around this time, I got myself a new go-to song to replace Jay-Z's "Imaginary Players." It was a Busta Rhymes song, "Legend of the Fall Offs," from his *Big Bang* album, which had come out in 2006. It was produced by Dr. Dre in the spirit of 50 Cent's "Heat," but instead of using gunshots for the beat, Dre used the sound of a shovel, as if the characters in the songs were being buried alive. It terrified me but also clarified what I was feeling. I forced myself to listen to it regularly so I could metabolize the mortal terror I was feeling as the hip-hop world shifted away from my generation toward something new.

Just two months after *Graduation* was released, Kanye's mother went in for cosmetic surgery. I'd say routine cosmetic surgery but they are always warning that no surgery is routine. Still, it was nothing too major, some upkeep for a human in her late fifties (a tuck here, a nip there). The day after, she died. Within a year, Kanye put out another album, *808s & Heartbreak*, which was a far moodier, more electronically processed record that illustrated his melancholy, meditative, and sometimes even tortured state of mind—his mother's death was the major event informing it, but he had also broken up with his long-term girlfriend and was himself cracking a bit under the pressure of celebrity. This engagement with potential unraveling would come to characterize much of the next fifteen years of Kanye's music. In the middle of 2007, though, which is where I mark the end of the Superproducers Resurgent phase of the genre, his unvanquished period had not yet ended. His mother was still with him. He was strong and getting stronger (and getting to "Stronger"). And I was in the car, in the dark, brokering an uneasy peace with what I was hearing.

2007

PULL UP IN THE MONSTER

2012

The old guard takes a break from hip-hop, or is broken by it, takes a breath, and starts to think about how the relationship might be repaired.

I remember going to see *Fela!*, the musical about the Nigerian band-leader and activist of the 1970s and 1980s, in September of 2008. At the time, it was an Off-Broadway sensation. Later on, it would be a Broadway sensation, too. The show had a section in it where the onstage Fela talked about the movie he planned to make in Nigeria, a movie about his ambitions. It was called *Black President*. It was true in his time. Footage exists. But it was also true in the time we were watching. In the theater, a ripple went through the crowd. It wasn't because of Fela himself, but because of what was happening in America: the Democratic nominee, who would face off against Republican nominee John McCain, was a young senator from Illinois, Barack Obama, who happened to be African American. In his case, the word was technically correct: his father was Kenyan and Black; his mother, who was white, had been born in Kansas. Hearing about Fela's *Black President* movie there in the theater, seeing his name on the ballot two months later, seeing him sworn in two months after that—those were moments that rearranged everything I knew about America and the world. Throughout Black America, there was a surge of optimism. Posters of him broadcast a message of hope. In hip-hop, he became an instant icon, mentioned in countless lyrics. (I will count some of them: Common's "The People," Young Jeezy's "My President," Nas's "Black President.") The optimism spilled over to the genre in general, which saw a shift toward optimism and intimacy, toward molly and other party drugs. The stars who appeared were, in general, energetic and up, whether B.o.B or DJ Khaled. Obama's rise led to a rise of visibility for Chicago, his political hometown, and for artists like Chief Keef and G Herbo. The period also shifted the idea of machismo. Obama furnished a new energy, and it was echoed by artists like Kanye and Lil Wayne, who reshaped the idea of machismo in hip-hop. Obama's election opened up everything. For me, personally, this period was a strange one. I was part of the optimism wave, even though the Roots also sensed that any optimism around race could also be seen as the first shoe, with the backlash shoe just waiting to drop. But it was also the first time in my adult life when I didn't track and trace hip-hop with as much care or as much love. I had gotten older, passed through several mini-generations as a fan, a creator, a curator, and so forth. But that was only part of it. In the years just before Obama's election, I experienced some personal and professional downturns. Close friends passed away. The fortunes of the Roots shifted. I felt, at times, profoundly out of step with the new hip-hop that was being made. Where did that leave me? This wasn't a rhetorical question. It was a real one, and one that I didn't always want to answer.

At the beginning of 2006, I went to Los Angeles. Part of the reason was that it was Grammy season. I wasn't nominated that year, but I wanted to be out there for the walkup to the awards. I had friends who were nominated, and some of them were throwing parties or having parties thrown for them. There was a general sense of the industry taking stock of and celebrating itself. Much of my trip was spent with James Poyser. We had some work to do involving Will Smith, so we met and hashed that out. After that, we decided to make another trip to see J Dilla. Since 2004 or so, Dilla and I had been in less regular touch than before, but we had been in touch. He had contributed to Roots work in that period. He had contributed to *Chappelle's Show*. He was working on new music, readying his second solo album. We talked about all those things. But he was on the West Coast and I was on the East Coast. There was also the matter of his health. I had heard through the grapevine that he had been struggling with issues, though no one was very specific about what. I had heard that he had been in the hospital, though no one was very specific about why. When Dilla and I talked, he didn't belabor the matter, and if I asked, he skimmed past it. So I went to his house not just with James but with curiosity.

The curiosity was satisfied, and in the most terrible way. Dilla wasn't alone. His mother was with him. I saw why. The man I had known was gone, and in his place was a shell. He couldn't have weighed more than eighty pounds. He looked ancient even though he was only thirty-two—in fact, his birthday was right around then, the first week in February, a Soulquarian. Later on I knew the reasons—lupus and a rare blood condition called thrombotic thrombocytopenic purpura—but when I walked into the house all I got was the visual, and the visual knocked me down. We talked to Dilla and to his mother, though I don't remember anything I said. I'm sure we talked about *Donuts*, the new album he had coming out. He gave me a rare Stevie Wonder record, a Brazilian gatefold single / EP with four songs from *Where I'm Coming From*, including "Look Around." (To him, it must have been a going-away present. I didn't understand it at the time. I was so honored he was giving me something of value, and of value to him, that it distracted me from what was actually going on.) Mostly what I remember was his diminishment and the diminishment of everything around him. I was accustomed to seeing him at work, surrounded by equipment and dozens of records. This was stark, just a few pieces of electronics and a few records. Whatever was occurring seemed like it had already mostly occurred. James and I stayed for a while and left. When we walked back outside, I felt like there was a thick pane of glass separating me from the rest of the world. The glass slid away. The world resumed, to some degree. But that didn't last long. The next week, I think, Common called to tell me that Dilla had died. He had been thirty-two for three days.

I went to his funeral. It was in Forest Hills, in Glendale, on Valentine's Day. I was with my girlfriend at the time. People filed into the place, and the front row filled up with his nearest and dearest. I saw Common and Tariq down in front. I stayed in the back. My girlfriend didn't understand what I was doing, so I explained: I was protecting myself and protecting my feelings. I have written elsewhere about the complicated history of emotions in Black art, and particularly hip-hop. It surfaced in the Source Awards in 1995, for example, as Nas deflated. I'll return to it as I come closer to the present (the book's present, not this story's present) and address the surprising surge in violence in the community in the late 2010s and early 2020s. But I felt it acutely there in Glendale. I didn't want to be up front because I knew I was going to burst into tears and I didn't want Common and Tariq and everyone else to see me bawling.

We went from there to Hawaii to perform. We checked into the hotel and went to sleep. The next morning, I was up early, and before I knew what was happening, I found myself on the beach running. That wasn't my thing. I was running and crying. I was running and crying and thinking. *Donuts*, the album that came out on his birthday, three days before his death, was in my mind. It had been difficult for me to listen to in the vortex of everything else. I knew that it was a masterpiece, and a different kind of masterpiece than I have ever heard before. It had thirty-one short compositions—one song, "Workinonit," was just under three minutes, but none of the rest even reached two. The dense, layered sampling went all over the map, from Frank Zappa to ESG to Fred Frith to Fred Weinberg to Lou Rawls covering Donovan. The vocal samples were coded messages to his loved ones, like sampling Motherlode's "When I Die" for "Welcome to the Show" or comforting his mother using the Escorts' "I Can't Stand (To See You Cry)" in "Don't Cry." He even cleverly took 10cc's cautionary tale about daredevil motorcycle riding, "Johnny, Don't Do It!" and flipped it to encourage his brother to take over with the lyrics "Johnny, do it" in "Waves." My thinking on the beach was frantic, almost, stabbing deeply and then backing away, but I started to understand that he was doing something revolutionary, creating a new kind of composition. How long did a piece of music have to be before it was a song? Was "Thunder"— a fifty-four-second piece that sampled Martha Reeves, Mantronix, Bobby Taylor, Blinky, Stevie Wonder, and the Originals—a legit new song? Dilla's work asked questions that I couldn't answer. Some of them I still can't answer. I have written about how I inherited the final beat he ever made. It used Funkadelic's "America Eats Its Young" as its spine and stretched out from there. It was dark, bleak, with too much finality. For me, it was almost like he was learning a new language, a purely musical language. Poor health, weakness, terror regarding his mortality—all these things robbed him of the ability to communicate in his native language. He learned. He translated. He transcended.

During this period, there was a distinct shift in tone in hip-hop, as before, though this time it came from within my own world. This idea of unforeseen endings and unforeseeable beginnings, of mourning and relearning, was like a heavy fog that descended after Dilla's death. We had filmed the *Block Party* movie back in 2004, but it was delayed by distribution issues. Movie stuff. When it finally came out in 2006—dedicated to Dilla—it still felt like a changing of the guard. But it felt like more than that. The Roots were in a strange place. *The Tipping Point* had been our least acclaimed album, and it hurt even more because it was supposed to consolidate the gains of *Things Fall Apart* and *Phrenology*. Just to give you one metric—and it was a metric that mattered back then—*Pitchfork* abandoned us. We had been at 9.4 for *Things Fall Apart*. That's nearly ten, which was considered perfect. We could see it. *Phrenology* was an 8.1. *The Tipping Point* was a crater, 5.4, which was mediocre, which was considerably worse than mediocre. And it wasn't the worst review we received. There was tumult in the group, in our sense of ourselves, in our sense of our place in the world. Rich was obsessed with trying to scrub away the skunk of *The Tipping Point*. He envisioned it as a multialbum process. It perhaps could have been faster. By then, Jay-Z was the head of our label, Def Jam, and he didn't want us to make commercial records, not because he wanted to keep us down, but because he didn't want to be seen as the corporate force that turned the Roots into an overly commercial concern. And while it may have slowed us down, we went our own route and got results. *Game Theory* did well as an establishing shot, bringing us back into the sevens. We felt that *Rising Down*, our next album, would be another brick in the wall of rebuilding. It continued our resurgence with critics, coming in a tick above *Game Theory*, even.

Still, it was a low point in the history of the Roots. The records were respected again. They were selling, to some degree—both made it into the top ten. But that wasn't translating. There was a period in which the college gigs stopped coming entirely. That was our bread and butter. Without them, the plate was bare. Rich and Shawn Gee, our business manager, would joke with us. "You guys are too old," they would say. I didn't understand that. We were playing shows with rock groups that were far older but still had an audience. Rich would shake his head. "It's different with hip-hop," he'd say. We had one serious meeting in the summer where we thought about scaling the group back to just a trio. Our price was leveling out, and it was too much to carry the expanded full-scale enterprise. Three albums after *Things Fall Apart*, I started to think that they might.

An answer came in from the sky. It was the most manna from heaven moment imaginable. We ran into Jimmy Fallon on vacation. He had been a friend of the group. That summer, he was planning his next move, which was to take over the *Late Night* franchise from Conan O'Brien. He told us that he had always dreamed of us being his house band. One thing led to another, quickly. We debuted as his on-air band in March 2009.

Late Night was a great job, and a stable one—five years later, we would go with Jimmy when he took over *The Tonight Show* from Jay Leno. One of the best things about it was that it took my head out of hip-hop. The job involved figuring out how to back the musical bookings, which spanned across a wide range of genres. That first few weeks, we had Van Morrison. We had Clap Your Hands Say Yeah. We had Vampire Weekend. And while we also had Ludacris and—an early-in-the-job fantasy fulfilled—Public Enemy, we were suddenly generalists.

That meant that I missed much of what was happening in the rap world. I had always been chronologically unimpeachable, meaning that I tended to get records when they came out if not before. This was different. I sometimes had to cram and listen to bands I didn't know because they were coming on the show, and that meant that I couldn't keep track of new releases (only so many hours in a week), which meant that I might encounter a rap act's second or third album and have no experience with the first. So rather than albums and singles coming to me like clockwork, on Tuesdays (that's when records used to come out), when stores opened, they started to come to me in a multiplicity of ways, jumping off all angles of the clock hands.

That's how I reconnected with Ghostface Killah. In the earliest Wu-Tang years, he wasn't in my top two Wu rappers: I leaned Method Man and then ODB. And I remained intrigued with the RZA for all the obvious production reasons. But as time went on, I kept hearing that Ghostface was the secret weapon, the one whose flow was built to last. I revisited. *Supreme Clientele*, from 2000, was still extremely compelling, and *Bulletproof Wallet* (2001), *The Pretty Toney Album* (2004), *Fishscale* (2006), and *More Fish* (2007) seemed to go deeper into the gonzo lyricism and storytelling without sacrificing Ghostface's unique style. He could work with a variety of producers, too: *Fishscale* had a handful of tracks with MF DOOM, a few with Just Blaze, a few with Pete Rock, and a pair with J Dilla, including "Whip You with a Strap" (a title taken from the same place as the song's sample, Luther Ingram's "To the Other Man"—both the Southern soul original and the hip-hop reimagination talk about self-respect, respect for others, and the importance of discipline). In fact, his output was so consistent that people seemed to be overlooking his records on the grounds that they maintained the same level of quality and, not being notably different, were no longer noteworthy. For me, that was an opportunity. The second a record wasn't grabbing headlines, I went in for truffles, and I dug what I found when I dug. What impressed me most was Ghostface's ability to hold the center no matter who he added in around him, producer or guest, on songs like "Yolanda's House" (featuring Method Man, from *The Big Doe Rehab*) and "Roosevelts" (featuring Raekwon and Trife Diesel and lifted from the B-sides collection *The Wallabee Champ*, named for Ghost's Clarks-brand footwear). No matter where he went, he had a storytelling ability that somehow recalled Slick Rick, Schoolly D, Chester Himes, and Paul Mooney, all at the same time. And no one was better at lobbing in a left-field proper noun—a place name, a brand name, a person's name. Ghostface's actual output, as opposed to the output critics believed they were hearing, remained vibrantly strange. And every few years, he would serve up a record that made this fact impossible to ignore, like *Ghostdini: Wizard of Poetry in Emerald City*, a 2009 album that moved in an overtly romantic direction, with more sex raps and autotuned vocals, but without sacrificing his trademark idiosyncrasy. A song like "Stapleton Sex," pornographically specific, still somehow retained a charm in the telling-of-the-sex-tale that eluded other artists. Why? Maybe because his eye for detail made the whole thing seem intimate, as if it might be happening to real people. Ghost doesn't finish until—and maybe because—the female voice that has been pairing him throughout the song tells him she loves him. And then there's an outro skit where he says he's first going to get himself a cigarette (she reminds him he doesn't smoke, and he laughs) and then reminds her that he's going to put in some studio time, but when he gets back, he's up for another round, nurse-outfit-and-sex-toy assisted. The next song, "Stay," keyed to a sample of Yvonne Fair's "Stay (A Little Bit Longer)," is even more matter-of-factly vulnerable: "I'm not a cold blooded killa, baby, I cry too / The best thing for me is when I'm laying beside you." And that rolls right into "Paragraphs of Love," a sweet and almost innocent flirtation with a pregnant woman (played by the British singer Estelle). It's all a virtuoso performance, unafraid to be silly, filled with confidence but without arrogance.

Sometimes this new practice took me back through time. Sometimes it took me forward. Take Drake. I remember clearly when I first heard him. It was "Best I Ever Had," though I'm not sure whether it was the *So Far Gone* mixtape or the EP of the same name. (I have a feeling it was the EP, because I think it was just after Kanye's onstage rush of Taylor Swift at the MTV Video Music Awards, though that doesn't mean it couldn't have been the mixtape finding its way to me on six-month delay. I also remember the song being pretty high on the track list, and on the mixtape it's down low. Let's say EP.) Rich gave it to me with unspoken instructions: listen to this, tell me what you think, but be sure to think, because I don't want you to come back to me with nothing. That's how Rich gave you a record. The intro to that song was a trigger memory for me. Back when I was a kid, my parents' band was doing a week of performances in Norfolk, Virginia, and we went to the same diner every morning for breakfast. The diner had a jukebox, as diners did back then. I can't say why—maybe someone who worked there needed to start off the day in a certain way, or maybe there was a regular in need of more regularity—but almost every time we were there, the jukebox played Hamilton, Joe Frank & Reynolds's "Fallin' in Love." It's an unwieldy name for such an easy-to-listen-to group: it was a trio, where Hamilton was the guitarist Dan Hamilton, Joe Frank was the bassist Joe Frank Carollo, and Reynolds was the keyboardist Tommy Reynolds. All three sang in soft-rock harmony. "Fallin' in Love" was sampled in "Best I Ever Had," and when I heard it, it returned me instantaneously to Norfolk, to the diner booth, to the excitement and comfort of being on a working vacation with my parents and the recognition, itself a little exciting but also uncomfortable, that Black music ceased to exist the second we left Philly, that with the exception of the occasional Earth, Wind & Fire track this vaguely soulful white soft-rock was the closest we were going to get to it. "Fallin' in Love" struck me as an unusual song for a new hip-hop artist to sample. It wasn't insanely obscure—it was a number one hit—but it seemed to exist in the cracks of cultural memory, and here was this young guy retrieving it. It wasn't unprecedented. Redman had sampled "Fallin' in Love" in "Bobyahed2dis," from *Dare Iz a Darkside*, back in 1994, but he put it into his typically crowded Funkadelic mix. This was a more straightforward use, opening with the piano glissando and then just pushing forward on the melody. It put him in my good graces from the start, or maybe it made me give him a pass on some of the qualities that in another artist I would have hardened against: the lover-boy posing that concealed (but not completely) a misogynistic streak, the not-top-of-the-heap flow, and so on. I knew nothing else about him. Toronto hip-hop wasn't on my radar. I didn't know that he was Larry

Graham's nephew. "Best I Ever Had" (and the "Fallin' in Love" behind it) was all I knew.

After Rich gave me the song, after we talked about it, he put Drake on the short list for the Roots Picnic. That was fine with me. Like I said, I liked the record. But Shawn Gee, our business manager, shook his head. "He's already a star," Shawn said, "and he's going to outprice us." I had been there before—the year before, in fact—with Lil Wayne. I liked the DJ view but not the déjà vu. "I didn't get the memo that this kid was going to be the next star," I said. "You guys don't even want to ask?"

Shawn looked straight at me and even a little through me. "He'll laugh you out the building," he said. That wasn't the first time I felt old, but it was the first time that feeling old started to feel old.

After that I tracked Drake with some interest. I never made fun of what people called Drake's emo-ness, because I didn't think of it that way. Emo was a pose. Drake was, best as I could tell, always sincere. He wore his heart on his sleeve but didn't then keep pointing to his sleeve and saying, "Look, my heart." (See Kanye.) Rich made the observation that Drake was able to pull off what we were not able to pull off with Common, meaning that he was able to foreground his feelings and his honest thoughts without making people feel like he was claiming some special status. Rich was right about that. When *Take Care* came out, I saw Common on Twitter saying that he had been way too early with the emotional stuff. But early Common could be playfully toxic with his stanzas, willing to say the most outlandish shit. Think of "Puppy Chow," when he gets a girl pregnant and then insists the baby's not his, or "Food for Funk," where he "scream[s] fuck the world for having a baby girl sorta cockblock." Even the most earnest, heart-on-sleeve moments, like "Retrospect for Life," are tone-deaf in retrospect—he is taking responsibility for a pregnancy but also taking over his girlfriend's choice. That seemed noble in 1997, playing against missing Black father tropes. Now, not as much. I'm not saying there's anything wrong with it, only that many other rappers would have gotten raked over the coals because they didn't have his ability to balance it off with introspection and intelligence. On *Electric Circus*, he took a big leap forward into a newly realized identity that really showed growth in terms of emotional intelligence. He showed support for the LGBTQIA+ community. He cut the link between emotional honesty and softness. That *Electric Circus* version of Common worked because it was more authentic than the young version. And yet, the album didn't fly with consumers. Here Drake was, flying.

Drake's rise (following Lil Wayne's) had an unexpected beneficiary. I had been interested in Nicki Minaj since her *Sucka Free* mixtape in 2008, which was her second mixtape after *Playtime Is Over*. This was during that DatPiff era of collecting everything and trying to make sense of it. But I didn't take a closer look at her until that period when I started to get priced out of Wayne and then Drake. In a spirit of discovery but also rejection, I took a hard look at the Young Money roster and decided that I was really going to like this Nicki Minaj girl. But I didn't really decide about her until she was on Kanye West's "Monster" in 2010. That was the moment that everyone noticed her, a shot across the bow of hip-hop. But it hadn't happened yet when I made my commitment to her potential.

Rick Ross was achieving altitude at around the same time. I remember looking at the cover of his 2009 album, *Deeper Than Rap*, and thinking to myself "What an imaginative title!" (I did not. It is not.) He was in a blind spot for me, I sort of was in a blind spot. The only thing keeping him in my spotlight was his mysterious beef with 50 Cent. I didn't hear the original insult from Rick Ross: "I love to pay ya bills, can't wait to pay ya rent / Curtis Jackson baby mama, I ain't askin' for a cent." But I did hear 50 Cent's immediate return of fire, "Officer Ricky (Go Head, Try Me)." Officer Ricky, of course, was Ross, who had worked as a correctional officer. The song was mean, but cartoonish, like hothead schoolyard ridicule. (The feud would become consequential a few years later when Lastonia Leviston, Rick Ross's ex-girlfriend and the mother of his child, claimed that 50 Cent had leaked a sex tape of her to humiliate Ross. The consequence? First, that a judge ordered 50 Cent to pay fourteen million 50 cents: or $7 million, if you'd prefer, to Leviston for emotional distress. And second, that 50 Cent then unsuccessfully sued his former law firm for $32 million [why skimp at $7?] for failing to adequately go after Rick Ross in the case.)

The main thing I thought about Rick Ross was about his body. That may sound strange, but think about Black women. That may sound stranger. What I mean is that mainstream America has always had a soft spot—and you could even say a benign obsession—with a certain type of Black woman. Big, soft, a mother figure. For a generation, it reminds them of the nannies or housekeepers who helped to raise them. For another generation, it reminds them of media figures who occupy a version of that same role: Oprah (until recently), for example, or Queen Latifah. But there's also a correlative for Black men. Weight and power, weight and authority, weight and approachability, weight and comedy: all these things are factors. I have always struggled with my own weight. I have gone through phases when I felt I was controlling it, phases when I felt like I couldn't. But I have also watched other overweight Black men who have moved into the public eye. I remember when Biggie Smalls came onto the scene. Rich Nichols called me. "You know what your problem is, Ahmir?" he said. "You're not big enough." I laughed, but I knew what he meant. Weight got lighter when you made it part of your brand. You could go back to the Fat Boys for proof. You could go to Big Pun or Fat Joe. You could go to Heavy D or Bone Crusher or Biz Markie. There was something more approachable about a rapper with the extra pounds. It shifted the dynamics, somehow reducing without eliminating charisma. In 2009, Rick Ross stepped into that spot.

So there I was, enjoying his beef and his beefiness, not thinking in any great detail about his music, and then *Teflon Don* appeared in 2010. I remember the moment specifically. I was at an after-party at a nightclub, which wasn't uncommon, and I was keeping an eye on the younger partygoers, not to ogle, but for research for my life as a DJ. I liked listening to whatever music was coming through the speakers and watching how the younger attendees reacted. If I saw them dancing, I started to think: maybe this was something that I needed to add into my set. That feeling was almost always accompanied by strong FOMO, a sense that what I was listening to (and watching) proved that I was well past my own sell-by date. But that night, I had an entirely different experience, thanks to Maxwell. Maxwell, of course, is roughly my age, a few years younger, and when "B.M.F." came on, he started to *move*. It occurred to me that I needed to revisit Rick Ross, not for DJ purposes but for my own.

I did. I listened to the entire *Teflon Don* record. And the song that jumped out at me was "Maybach Music III." It just did something to my DNA. I was in LA for a few days around that time and I had one day free. I rented a flashy car, rare for me, and drove up the Pacific Coast Highway, playing "Maybach Music III" for an hour straight. It was the perfect accompaniment, the attitude, the verses (not just by Rick, but by T.I. and Jadakiss), the vocals (by Erykah Badu), the sample ("Ancient Source" by Caldera, an afro-jazz-funk band whose debut, which included this song, was produced by Larry Dunn, a keyboard player with golden age Earth, Wind & Fire). The last time I had done that was a decade earlier, with Black Star's "Little Brother." And "Maybach Music III" was a permanent replacement. Even to this day, anytime I am in LA with time off, I do it: car, PCH, MMIII.

In the wake of that drive, I decided to send a DM to Rick and tell him how much I loved the song. I clicked open the window and discovered that he had been DMing me to see if I wanted to work with him on something. Oh, shit. (This was another age-in-life moment. I am sure the kids who were dancing at the club knew not to let their DMs stale. It was only graybeards like me and Maxwell.) I did send Rick a message and he sent one back. He was very gracious and very connected. I went back through his catalog and though I didn't find anything that stuck to me with the grip of "Maybach Music III," I found lots that I did like, including *Rich Forever*, his second mixtape. I didn't consume it all the way through like a proper record, but again, that wasn't Rick's fault. I wasn't doing that with anything in those years.

I have said that the Clipse's *Hell Hath No Fury* was the last album I listened to all the way through, as an album. But the last is never the last. Kanye West resurfaced for me in 2010. After years of sneaking his albums like they were cigarettes, late-night sessions in the car when everyone else was asleep, I came back aboard for *My Beautiful Dark Twisted Fantasy*. It wasn't that I had fewer criticisms. I had the same or maybe more: there were places where I hated the mix, where I hated the patches, where I hated the lyrical excesses (even though they were clearly a feature, not a bug) or the heart-on-sleeve-and-then-some or the fact that, at almost seventy minutes long, this was like a Marvel movie of hip-hop albums, with the same cluttered approach to features and cameos and the same reliance on special effects. I read Pusha T's comments about going to Oahu to record "So Appalled" and how he encountered a creative process that was still very much in process, and I rolled my eyes a little bit. But I also felt the power of the project, and not just on "Power." I heard it on "Devil in a New Dress." I heard it on "Monster," though in that case it flowed as much from Nicki Minaj and Jay-Z as from Kanye himself, and that made sense from a producer's standpoint. Was this a creature of insatiable ego or a generous curator able to deploy other stars in smart and strategic ways? The answer seems like a resounding yes. The deeper I got into the album, the deeper I got into it, and found myself filled with a confusing set of feelings, everything from frustration to enjoyment to intrigue to straightforward enjoyment. It wasn't a five-star experience. It could never be: think of the self-absorption and straight-out woman-blaming of "Blame Game" (people want to call it honesty, but to be respected, honesty includes an element of judgment, or else all you're doing is exposing yourself as a troll). The production is fine, especially the John Legend component, but I can't get behind the appearance of Chris Rock, which is like a disinfectant. Here's something unpleasant. Now it's funny. That makes it pleasant, right? The general lack of self-awareness, made worse by the belief that there is total self-awareness at work, keeps this away from being a five-star album, but the four-and-a-half-star level has always seemed to be more interesting. Messiness is part of the human condition, and sometimes when I call up this record in my mind I change the *F* from "fantasy" to "failure" and think of how that helps the record to succeed.

The world may have been getting healthier in some ways, but it was getting sicker, too. Richard Nichols, the manager of the Roots since the very start, a visionary and a genius who helped steer us through every important evolution, started getting lumps in his arms. At first, he responded with complaints and jokes, most of them originating from him, some from the rest of us. We came up with a scale of citrus fruits to describe their size: not a pomelo, not a grapefruit, not an orange, maybe a lime. Eventually Rich went to the doctor and was diagnosed with chronic myelomonocytic leukemia. The sense of mortality was everywhere, and felt like it would be forever. (Rich would hold on until the summer of 2014.)

One morning in January of 2010, I woke and remembered that it was my birthday. Or rather, I was reminded. People were calling. Some sent gifts. One call spun the opposite direction: Def Jam had dropped us. We were off the label. I had a flashback to high school, when I had been fired twice on my birthday, once from a record store job, once from an insurance job. And here I was at thirty-nine, back in the same spot. "No," I said out loud. I wasn't going to go out like that. I got on the phone and got LA Reid on the line. I told him that he was acting hastily. We had an album ready or nearly ready. He relented. We were un-dropped, though with conditions, which were that we had to turn in a record soon.

We got to work quick and got *How I Got Over* done in time for it to be out in June. It was the first official record of our Fallon career. It incorporated folk and rock artists who had been on the show, like Dirty Projectors, Bright Eyes, and Joanna Newsom. It was innovative but also reflective of the fact that we were still feeling our way through how the Fallon gig would affect our career. Was it a resource? Was it a refuge? Was it a tide that would carry us away from where we needed to be?

I started to look at the long schedule as both an opportunity and a challenge. What did the bookings mean for who we were and, just as importantly, for who we were not anymore? One day I looked and saw an act's name that concerned me: Odd Future. I went to Jonathan Cohen, the booker. "Hey," I said. I kept a careful tone, close to the vest. "This Odd Future I see. Is there a punk band or something named this in Williamsburg? Must be the case, right? They're some rock group."

"No," he said. "This is the LA rap collective."

Even after he said it, I was still praying that there was another group with the same name. They had been active on blogs for a few months. They had a real punky edge, a real sense of danger. It felt like we were heading into Sex-Pistols-on-Tom-Snyder territory, or maybe even Sex-Pistols-on-Bill-Grundy territory.

The day Odd Future came to the show was Odd Present. First, I saw Andy Samberg. Usually he was up on the eighth floor with the rest of *SNL*. What was he doing down on the sixth floor? "We're so excited?" *We?* Suddenly the rest of the Lonely Island guys appeared next to him. "We can't wait for Odd Future." About an hour later, Mos Def appeared on the floor. Had I been living under a rock?

When they went on the show, I was just praying that we would get through it. We did. They were out there, but not so out there that they couldn't get back to here. A little while after that, I went to see them at the Highline Ballroom. It wasn't just them. It was them, Frank Ocean, Hodgy Beats, Domo Genesis. Syd Tha Kyd was the opening DJ. Tyler's *Goblin* album was just coming out, maybe that same day. It was a fully hipsterized crowd. I went looking for other elder statesmen. I found the GZA. He's even older than me. "I'm here with my sixteen-year-old," he said. "You got kids?" I mumbled no. "Then what are you doing here?" I told him the truth, which was that it had been a minute since any music act actually made me fear for my life and that when I encountered entertainment that had a dangerous edge, I moved toward it, moth to flame.

As it turned out, the artist I had the best camaraderie with was Tyler. Right around the first show, he asked me about Justin Bieber's appearance, what it was like. I was sure he was trolling. I mentioned it to a friend and he said, "Ahmir, he's not trolling. He's not even joking. You realize that he's nineteen, right? You're forty. You're looking at this wrong." Maybe the next time Tyler was back he would mention Roy Ayers, and that had me tired in a different direction: Oh, every time you see me you're going to mention someone you think is an appropriate reference for me? But I liked him and I liked following him. He was good on social media, with these random hot takes that didn't add up to anything calculated necessarily but added up. Maybe it's more accurate to say that his entire path was additive. Each record, from *Cherry Bomb* to *Flower Boy*, had something new on it. In some cases he purely reversed what he had done. In other cases, he doubled down on earlier directions.

In 2018, he came onto the show to perform "After the Storm" with Kali Uchis. It was a gentle song, therapeutic, and his verse was quick and inclusive, a Jacksons reference, a little plug for *Flower Boy*. I was shocked because he wasn't being a shock artist. I was expressing my surprise and admiration afterward, and I remember something that Captain Kirk, the Roots guitarist, said. "Maybe he's Bowie," he said. "Maybe every year he's going to reinvent himself." He had some of that, and some of Prince as well, in terms of real evolution, not cynical, not calculated. What else do you want from your artists?

Back in 2008, Tyler was a teenager, sixteen when the year began, seventeen when it ended. At some point during that year, he recorded a song called "Fuck This Election." It was perverse and transgressive, punk in its sensibilities, name-checking and calling out Sarah Palin and John McCain and declaring that "Obama and I is for the ladies." The song didn't come out until 2012, but it was a snapshot both of the excitement that Obama created in hip-hop, the energy that he generated, and a deeper anxiety. I had my own 2008 story, though it ended up in prose rather than on a record. In early 2008, I was out in California for Super Tuesday. For years I hadn't been overtly political. I was an artist. I spoke through my work. My friend, the actress Jurnee Smollett, thought that I was going about things wrong. "You have a platform," she said. "You should use it." At first, I sent sandwiches and water to poll workers or people waiting in line to vote. But she kept the pressure on, and over time I started to participate more directly. In California, we canvassed for Obama, tried to keep his momentum up. We spent a long day trying to get voters on the right track and then went to see a movie in a mall; I snuck away for a minute to get a housewarming present (a Deluxe Scrabble, the edition with the gold letter tiles) and some self-help and psychology books for myself. A few minutes after driving away from the mall, I got a call from Rich, who wanted to discuss our upcoming Grammy jam. I pulled my rental car, a Mini Cooper, into a parking lot. I was a relatively new driver at that point, only three years or so since I had gotten a license, and I didn't want to drive distracted. As I finished up the call, I noticed a police car behind me, and then another. Cops appeared and took me out of the car. The lot where I had stopped was a Mini dealership. There had been thefts from that lot. The cops took me out of my rental and put me in their car. They asked a series of questions, which I answered patiently, though they seemed to interpret my patience as attitude. (I was also a little preoccupied, praying that the cops wouldn't find the Scrabble set and the psychology books—I imagined that they would only encourage their theory that the car wasn't mine.) Jurnee kept trying to slip her phone out of her bag and take video. I kept discouraging her. Eventually, after calling the rental company and verifying that I had in fact rented the vehicle, the cops let me go. I was flustered and furious and, back in the safety of my hotel room in Beverly Hills, also exhausted and sad. I called Rich. "Of course," he said. "And if Obama wins, it's going to get worse. You think it's going to be a kumbaya moment? It's going to license people to admit what they think of us."

I wasn't sure that Rich was right. I may have felt my rose-colored glasses slipping down my nose, but they didn't come all the way off. Partly it was because I couldn't see far enough into the future, couldn't see how odd (and Odd) it would get. That took a first term, and a second one, and then another cycle in which Hillary Clinton got the nomination back but ran into a bizarre, toxic grassroots backlash that changed America in deep, dark ways.

2012

PROMISE THAT YOU WILL SING ABOUT ME

2017

Black America wonders: Was one step forward in fact two steps back?

Obama created hope, but some of that hope was deferred, and that hurt. One result, in the culture at large and in hip-hop specifically, was an era of willful numbing. The drug of choice during this period was pills, and it made its way into the music of the era, not just in the hazy arrangements and mumbled lyrics, but sometimes in the subjects of the songs themselves. Future's 2015 album *DS2* is a kind of manifesto for this period. The title recalls the drugs of an earlier era—DS is "dirty Sprite," meaning sizzurp. The songs on the record are drugged-out and sexed-up, and can come to feel like a joyless exercise in hedonism. For me, the key song is the bonus track "The Percocet and Stripper Joint," which paints the same kind of picture—the pursuit of pleasure without the capacity to truly feel it—and includes one line that's so straightforward that it hurts: "I just need a whole lot of drugs in my system." Or rather, it could hurt, but only if it was allowed to pierce the haze of those drugs, which are worn like armor. The passage of the Obama years isn't the only factor at work in creating this mindset among a younger generation of rappers. Future was born in 1983 in Atlanta, which means that he was raised under the cloud of the crack epidemic that swept through American cities in the 1980s. Danny Brown, another signal talent from this era, was born in Detroit in 1981. You could make the case that these artists were responding, in some kind of epigenetic way, to that legacy. In pain all the time, they sought to be numb all the time. Drugs were portrayed as recreational but only as a feint: within minutes it was clear that they were something more profound, a way of blocking out certain aspects of the society. A promise of a better future led by a Black president that quickly exposed itself as wishful thinking begged to be blocked out.

In addition, the shift in ideas of masculinity that had started a half decade before with artists like Kayne and Lil Wayne went in two directions at once. Drake ascended to the commercial throne—and almost single-handedly established Toronto's contemporary hip-hop bona fides—by projecting a nice-guy persona that concealed some of the same kinds of sexism that had bedeviled hip-hop for years. And Kendrick Lamar rose into view as a kind of anti-Drake: a brainy, introspective lyricist who felt compelled to chronicle the world around him. There was beef between them, though it seemed to be more about showmanship than anything: Kendrick dissed Drake as "the kid with the motor mouth" but later denied that there was any real rift. Still, those two figures marked out the two directions for hip-hop, versions of the have/have not divide that had played out at the Source Awards back in 1995. Was hip-hop a tool for analyzing and ultimately uplifting culture, or was it a way of wallowing in easy pleasures and worrying about what that wallowing would do to your character? In a way, not answering that question definitively was the best answer: it set up current, set up tension, which meant that people had to keep looking. And on top of all that, the record industry was changing in some profound and probably permanent ways. All those factors rolled together and then rolled down the hill of history, flattening what was in their path.

There used to be one way to get a record. You would walk or drive or take a subway train to a record store. You would enter the store. You would go down the aisle to the section that you wanted, thumb through the racks until you found the record you wanted, and then take it to the front counter. Later on, it changed in tiny ways. Cassettes were in racks on the wall. CDs returned them to the bin, first in long boxes, then in plastic lockboxes. But the choreography was still the same: walk or drive or train, enter, aisle, section, counter.

When music first started to appear online, I didn't think much of it. It was snippets of songs, mostly, embedded in reviews at sites like Addicted to Noise. That was in the midnineties, around the time the Roots were first releasing records, and I registered those sites mostly as novelties. Interesting idea, to give readers a chance to listen to a piece of a song, but it didn't change anything about the traditional process (walk, enter, etc.).

Five years later, things started changing. Napster made international headlines in 1999 when it gave consumers the ability to download entire songs that were posted by other consumers. That it couldn't control the songs that were posted and downloaded, and thus couldn't prevent copyright violations, was an issue that resulted in the demise of that original Napster in 2001. But Pandora's box had been opened, and one of the things that escaped was the record industry's sense of how to make money. New models sprang up, at first underground sites and then quasi-official mixtape repositories like DatPiff.

On the heels of that era, there was another massive shift. Rather than downloading, the dominant model became streaming. You wouldn't pull the music down to your hard drive. You would possess nothing. Instead, your computer would just access it, similar to the way a radio pulled waves out of the air. Sites began to appear that would buy up huge libraries of songs and let users search, stream, and listen. Some of them were free with advertisements. Most moved toward some type of subscription model. If you paid eight dollars a month, say, you could have unlimited access to the streaming service's entire library. Spotify was one of the first big services of this type, founded in Sweden in 2006, introduced in the United States in 2011.

As a record-and-radio purist—a former purist—I resisted for a little while. But I watched with interest. I knew the quality was subpar, at least at first, but there were features that appealed to me. It was easier to cross-list artists or albums in different genres, or to sort songs chronologically. You could mark the albums or songs that caught your eye (ear?) and return to them later.

Two things really cinched streaming for me. The first was that I could go back to, and through, the past more easily than ever, for a completely different kind of investment. Let's say that I was reading around the discovered that there was a barrelhouse piano player who had almost the same exact name as J Dilla (James Edwards Yancey versus James Dewitt Yancey). In the past, it would have meant a trip not to the neighborhood place, which wasn't likely to have barrelhouse piano, but to Times Square, to HMV or the Virgin Megastore, down into the basement level where the blues were kept, and then to the end of the section, almost the very end (I don't know of a blues player whose last name starts with *Z*). Maybe I'd find a Yancey record, maybe not. Or I could go down to the Village and start searching, or root around in Colony and pay high prices. The point is that it would be an adventure. Streaming was an entirely different process. Tap in the name, Y-a-n-c-e-y, see if anything comes up . . . Oh, it does? Document Records has three volumes, chronologically organized, that represent most of his recorded output? And I can listen to one after the other at home, for free? I was converted.

The second way that streaming hooked me was that it allowed me to be a full-service curator. Normally when you hear about streaming and curation, it's to criticize video-streaming services for not doing enough of it, for having libraries that are too deep and poorly managed. People want to know which nineties comedies to watch, in order, or how to pick their way through Japanese cinema, the theory goes. But it goes the other way when it comes to music streaming. Curation matters in music, also, in the sense that you might want to get a crash course in Old-School Hip-Hop. But for the most part, music streaming services profit less from top-down curation than from bottom-up curation. It's the reshuffling and surprising connections made by users that create the most exciting environment. In my case, the features of music-streaming services increasingly allowed me to be what I already was, but with a new supersuit.

Take the most basic component, the playlist function. I had always liked pulling together songs from different albums, from different artists, into one place. It was part of early hip-hop, part of being a DJ. Remember "The Adventures of Grandmaster Flash on the Wheels of Steel," which went from a Flash Gordon spoken word record through Chic and Queen into Sugarhill Gang, Spoonie Gee, and more? DJing was like if you took musical intelligence and sculpted it into a person. That was one of my earliest flashes (all puns intended) of inspiration, and the one that stayed with me the longest. Even if I wasn't DJing, I was on the wheels of steel, conceptually speaking. At a party, in a car, hanging with friends at someone's place, other people may have been content just to let a single record play all the way through. I was the hyper one, convinced that juxtaposition made meaning. (I know we're talking about 2012 or so, but skip forward a few years. How could you hear Run the Jewels' "Blockbuster Night, Pt. 1," which begins with "bunches of punches" and "oodles and noodles," and not go back immediately and hear De La Soul's "Oodles of O's," with the echoes in its title and its "lunches of punches"?) Streaming made that simple. You could build playlists across genres, put a Sun Ra song next to an EPMD song next to a Beach Boys song, and do it instantly. Convenience was tipping me away from convention.

These two collided in powerful ways when it came to hip-hop.

I can best explain by talking about Public Enemy. Didn't expect to see them here in 2012–2017, did you? I have written about the group's golden age at length, because I have returned to it repeatedly: in my mind, in my heart, in my bones. "Bring the Noise" and "Don't Believe the Hype" and especially "Fight the Power" will never be far from the top of my mountain. I have also written about October 1, 1991, when I hustled old-style to the record store to buy the new albums from Prince and Public Enemy, which were, respectively, *Diamonds and Pearls* and *Apocalypse 91 . . . The Enemy Strikes Black*. My heart was beating fast as I opened them but it slowed when I played them. To me, the two most important acts of the eighties had suffered missteps. I stayed with them after that, of course. You don't just abandon genius because it forgets where it put its keys. I have written extensively elsewhere about my long journey with Prince. My journey with Public Enemy is trickier. I bought *Muse-Sick-n-Hour Mess Age* in 1994, was displeased by the cover, weathered some confused material, felt some kind of way about what seemed to be a defensiveness on Chuck D's part about the group's place in the current hip-hop scene. Was he feeling pressure from gangsta rap on one side and enlightened pop rap on the other? It was the era of Snoop and Wu-Tang, Arrested Development and Digable Planets. Not to mention that I was trying to find my own way into it. Chuck seemed a little tetchy about the change. Still, I bought the *He Got Game* soundtrack in 1998, a generally stronger and leaner record, though one that had taken four years to put out—I was accustomed to a year between PE records, two at most.

Then I stopped. I knew there were other records coming out—*There's a Poison Goin' On* in 1999, *Revolverlution* in 2002, *New Whirl Odor* in 2005, *How You Sell Soul to a Soulless People Who Sold Their Soul???* in 2007. The titles were always awesome, and sometimes I would hear a single that caught my attention, but I didn't get the records. Around the time that I embraced streaming, Public Enemy had a burst of productivity, putting out two records in 2012 (*Most of My Heroes Still Don't Appear on No Stamp* in the summer and then *The Evil Empire of Everything* on October 1, the thirty-first anniversary of my personal Disappointment Day). Suddenly, I had a new way to listen to them. Instead of putting money on the counter, I could just tap-tap their name into my search bar. I could listen to the new records but also the ones I had missed across the years. And once I searched and listened, I realized that I could make my own albums. I could take the songs that worked and put them in an order that worked and assemble one massive and masterful Public Enemy album from the fifteen years of prolific but scattershot releases. The *Revolverlution* album, for example, was a mixed bag of live tracks, remixes, and new songs. It sounded like a band at loose ends. But the title track, I thought, could go toe-to-toe with their classic period: as they said, "It's a bird, a plane, and the sound remains the same." So that led off the Public Enemy album I was sequencing in my mind.

I soon saw that I wasn't the only one doing this. Streaming unearthed an entire subculture of curators and enthusiastic meddlers, in every corner of the music world. Sites sprang up where people speculated on and reassembled classic albums that never happened. Some of those were classic rock projects, Beatles or the Who projects from the 1960s that were reassembled for release. Some were hip-hop Holy Grails like Dr. Dre's long-rumored *Detox* or the collaboration between Nas and DJ Premier.

Streaming's legacy isn't simple. It had complex and in some ways ruinous effects on the movement of money from listeners to labels, or labels to artists. It also busted apart the idea of the album as a container for songs. There are some people who see it as a scourge.

But there's no question that it energized listeners as well, gave them control (or at least the illusion of it).

If I took to streaming right away, there were other technological developments I resisted. (So much of this book could be subtitled "Old Man Learns Slowly.")

Let's go back to *Dave Chappelle's Block Party*. I snuck down into the audience because I wanted to document the moment that Common and Erykah Badu performed "The Light" together. It would be the first time they had been in close proximity to each other since their breakup. That had been a very important relationship for them both, and I wanted to be in the audience to capture the performance. As it turned out, I was also standing next to J. Cole. He was a teenager at the time, just a kid in attendance. Way later, he got word to me that he had been there next to me, watching me take photos. I went to Shawn Gee and told him. He fixed me with a serious expression. "He's going to be the next Nas." I couldn't understand a statement like that. Why would you burden someone with that expectation? Isn't that doing a disservice to a young artist?

When I started to explore his music, I couldn't get there. It came to me mostly through mixtapes, and even though I was fully engaged with them as a method of distribution, I still harbored suspicion. I wanted artists to have the courage of their convictions. If you are going to make a definitive statement, call it an album, not a project between albums. If you're going to make a half album, I'm going to listen to it with half my attention. (There was also a personal reason. Mixtape DJs, for the most part, were not cosigning us, which meant that they were not acknowledging how dope Tariq was. He wasn't included in that culture enough, even though he was better than 99 percent of the MCs who got put on mixtapes. This was part of a broader anxiety of mine that had me always wondering and often worrying if I was ruining his street credibility. The Roots had been branded as brainy Smurf-rap, or curator-rap, or live-band rap, in a way that means that my nerdiness was 51 percent to the 49 percent afforded his street cred. Occasionally people would recognize, but the rarity of that made me harden my heart toward where hip-hop was going.) I also had, sad to say, regional prejudice. J. Cole was from North Carolina. We didn't think they could live up to our East Coast ethos. That's a sad commentary on how condescending we could be at times. If you lived south of the Mason-Dixon line, we felt that you are from the backwoods. There were many counter-examples, some of which were immensely important to me, like Little Brother, the North Carolina group that had put out a trio of great records. J. Cole was in that tradition, people said. It vetted him some-what. I remember *The Come Up* back in 2010. "Friday Night Lights" was a song that lit people up. Shawn and Rich kept warning me not to miss on him: "J. Cole, Drake," they would say, "Drake, J. Cole."

I was at a strange place, still hurting from the Def Jam situation, so when Shawn stood up for the *Friday Night Lights* mixtape I was not necessarily ready to stand up alongside of him. When "Work Out," the lead single from his first LP, *Cole World*, came out, I was in my dressing room. Someone else who was there, a producer, was angry. "I can't believe that he used that part of the song."

"What do you mean?" I said.

"It's a Kanye sample." When you end a song as a live band, you have a Las Vegas ending, a closing sting. The keyboard player might riff or add a little flourish. This was that, from Kanye's "The New Workout Plan." He took the last seconds and built something new from them. And he wasn't trying to hide it. It's right there in the title. I really respected that as a piece of art. You cleaned your plate. Dilla famously did that for Slum Village's "Hold Tight," which he had to go through twenty minutes of Cannonball Adderley's "Experience in E" just to pick up the last few seconds.

That was one moment. It didn't fully stick. Then we were doing a benefit show for Ron Perlman out in Montauk. We were riding back in the Sprinter, starving. We got to a McDonald's. The line was so long that the driver dropped us to order by foot and went to park across the street at a gas station. We got our food and crossed to the van. Just as I was stepping inside I looked at the blacktop of the gas station and saw something glinting. It was a piece of glass half covered by rocks and papers. But it wasn't a piece of glass. It was an iPhone. This was in 2013, before people learned how to fully lock up their phones, so I was able to click around and find out who it belonged to, and to my surprise it was J. Cole's phone. He had been shooting a video for "Crooked Smile," and he must have stopped for gas and dropped it. I tweeted at him. It was a funny moment on Twitter. But I got cool with him. I found that he was as serious about the production as I had suspected. I resolved to go back and see what I had missed. I realized that he was dope. I really liked "Let Nas Down," which also used a Kanye song ("Big Brother," in this case) and a Fela Kuti sample ("Gentlemen"). It had a backstory, which was that Nas had heard an earlier song and worried that J. Cole was moving away from sharper writing toward a more commercial sound. The earlier song? "Work Out." On "Let Nas Down," J. Cole also sampled a Nas song, "Nas Is Like," which was a 1999 track that found Nas himself moving back from commercialism to creative lyricism. All of this was still aftershock from the earthquake of the 1995 Source Awards. There was a smart version of self-legitimization at work. But it's interesting to me that he made his way into my personal canon not as an MC but as a producer. It confirms my suspicion that I'm the wrong kind of rap fan. I have all kinds of favorite records that I can't vouch for lyrically. I'm not saying they aren't good. I'm just saying that the production is what makes up my mind.

The artists who rose during this period vexed me. Not because they weren't brilliant, but because they were. In fact, the more brilliant they were, the more vexed I felt. Partly it was the wisdom talking. In 2011, a talented newcomer named Nicki Minaj and a talented institution named Lil' Kim started to beef. How had it started? Some said that the trigger was when Nicki first appeared on the scene, wearing colored wigs like Kim had done. Others said that the trigger was Kim's thin skin regarding the mix of homage and competition represented by Nicki; Kim's 2011 *Black Friday* EP was a parody of Nicki's *Pink Friday*. And some (including Kim herself) said that the conflict was more substantive, that Nicki had been assigned to Kim as a mentee early in her career by Cash Money records, and alleged that Kim had shared lyric and rhythmic ideas that Nicki ended up inappropriately appropriating. Whatever the case, it escalated from side-eye to legitimate diss tracks, like Nicki's 2012 single "Stupid Hoe." I didn't like it, not because I think that all women have some chromosomal obligation to be on each other's side—they have the same I'm-angry-at-you privilege as anyone—but because beef involving Kim had ended in tears before (including her own tears). In the late nineties, Kim had fired off (verbal) shots at other female rappers, including Foxy Brown. Foxy fired back (verbally) in her verse on Capone-N-Noreaga's "Bang Bang," where she mocked what she saw as Kim's new "street shit." In February of 2001, Kim and her people ran into Capone outside of Hot 97 on Hudson Street. Shots (nonverbal) were fired, and one of Capone's associates was caught in the back. A few years later, Kim was sentenced to a year in jail for lying about her involvement in the incident.

When it came to the beef between Kim and Nicki, it wasn't just that I was warning against escalation. I also saw it for what it was, which was a distorted form of professional affection. To me, the verbal anger was a way of saying, "I care enough about you to spend my energy on you." If Nicki felt as dismissive toward Kim as she claimed, she could have just ignored her.

It was also sometime during this period that people began to say, decisively, that they had identified the next great talent, the successor to Eminem (in terms of technical ability), or Kanye (in terms of his ability to turn inward in his lyrics), or even Nas (in terms of his talent for portraiture). His name was Kendrick Lamar. Lamar had been spotted early by Anthony Tiffith, the founder of a management company and independent label called Top Dawg. Top Dawg got onto Lamar, then a fifteen-year-old mixtape rapper going by the name K.Dot. Over the next few years, Top Dawg added a number of other rappers: Jay Rock (born Johnny Reed McKinzie Jr.), Ab-Soul (born

Herbert Anthony Stevens), and ScHoolboy Q (born Quincy Hanley). At the suggestion of Hanley, the four briefly tried to organize into a supergroup collective, sort of like the one that Irv Gotti had tried to put together for Jay-Z, DMX, and Ja Rule back in the day. That never panned out, but the Top Dawg artists started to release solo material. Lamar went first, with a record called *Section.80* that generated love among critics, particularly for his intellectual and lyrical agility. (Not for nothing, it's worth mentioning that it included a number of Roots samples: he grabbed from "A Peace of Light" and "Clock with No Hands." The fact that he took from two separate albums gave me hope that younger hip-hop was going to make use of the legacy we were leaving.) His second album, out a year later, was a breakthrough: *Good Kid, M.A.A.D City* was released on a major label (Interscope) and had major guest stars (including Dr. Dre and Drake), but Lamar was the star, unafraid to wade into deep personal waters or unflinching neighborhood portraiture. *Good Kid, M.A.A.D City* outsold *Section.80* in its first week and charted five singles, including "Swimming Pool (Drank)" and "Bitch, Don't Kill My Vibe."

For me, the best track was the most ambitious, the twelve-minute (not a typo) "Sing About Me, I'm Dying of Thirst." In reality, it was two songs stitched together, separated by a skit, though "Sing About Me" still ran out to seven minutes or so. Beginning with a spare beat taken from Bill Withers's "Use Me" and an equally spare sample (tiny pieces, almost like confetti, of the guitarist Grant Green's "Maybe Tomorrow"), as it went, it blossomed, both in its narrative techniques (Lamar inhabited perspectives and voices from elsewhere on the record and even reached back to characters from *Section.80*) and its music (strings entered the picture). He was doing things on the song that were cinematic and surprising, shifting narratives the way that shows like *Atlanta* would do a few years later.

The second part sounded like more traditional hip-hop but also had a jazz backbone, to the point that Robert Glasper—a longtime associate of the Roots—would take a swing at it on his 2015 album *Covered*. At the time, Glasper was also working with Kendrick on the album that followed *Good Kid, M.A.A.D City*. That record, *To Pimp a*

Butterfly, came out in 2015 and took everything up a notch: the ambition, the introspection, the production (Pharrell, Flying Lotus, Boi-1da, and others), the guest stars (here they were George Clinton, Snoop Dogg, Ronald Isley, and others). *To Pimp a Butterfly* was hailed as a Black masterpiece, a mature summation of themes within African American life, African American music, and even African culture (Lamar had visited South Africa and seen Robben Island, where Nelson Mandela was imprisoned from 1964 until 1982). The record was a commercial success, topping the sales of its predecessor, and a critical triumph, earning Lamar his first Grammy for Best Rap Album.

It was also the album where I began to get a feeling about Kendrick. It wasn't a feeling of dislike, or dismissiveness, or any dis- at all. It wasn't even really the fact that it came out the same day as *Black Messiah*, D'Angelo's long-awaited follow-up to *Voodoo*, and siphoned off some of the attention that record deserved. (It's also our fault, to be honest—who takes fourteen years to release a follow-up?) But the records were so demanding and engaging that they drained me. They were great, but it could feel like too much of a good thing, too rich, too deep. Imagine if Cap'n Crunch is your favorite cereal of all time, but then someone tells you that you have to eat seventeen bowls of it. What I learned on *To Pimp a Butterfly*—and confirmed on his next album, *Damn*, which not only won another Best Rap Grammy but brought Lamar a Pulitzer Prize, the first-ever awarded to a musician not in classical or jazz—was that I can only go through a Kendrick album once. I have written about the way that my own listening habits have changed, how I used to put records on heavy rotation multiple times, let them sink in until I heard the nuances of every sample, every breakbeat, every lyrical callback. I can't do that with Kendrick. I treat his records like a heavy movie: while I'm sitting there, I'm totally into it, but going back is overwhelming. I feel like spending multiple hours on multiple days untangling a masterwork is daunting. I find myself talking about Kendrick the way that non–East Coast cats talked about Rakim: too much words, man. I'm not especially proud of it, but it is what it is. Maybe I gave all my brainpower to Eminem. As a DJ, I act differently, of course:

certain songs hit with a crowd independent of their album context, and if they work for a crowd, they work for me.

So, Questlove, curmudgeon. But it's not done yet. Let's tackle Run the Jewels now. A duo formed by the New York–based rapper and producer El-P and the Atlanta-based rapper and political commentator Killer Mike, Run the Jewels (or, if you'd prefer, RTJ) was a sensation with young audiences when they appeared in 2012. They had a sound (bombastic but knowing) and a mission (political statements wrapped in rap attitude) and a look (album covers were variations of the same minimal illustrations: two hands, one in pistol position, the other clutching a chain). Again, I had an issue. Rich once told me something about Outkast that stuck with me. "America will never admit it," he said, "but they only like Outkast because they are from Down South but are not coon." What he meant is that they stood in opposition to what people secretly believed about the South: smart people where you don't quite expect to find them. I felt the same way about Run the Jewels, and especially Killer Mike. I was never entirely in agreement with his politics—to me, his carve-outs for guns, not to mention his take on fairness and equal time, which put him too close to candidates like Herschel Walker, was conservatism in libertarianism's clothing. Still, I saw that because he spoke eloquently, white people were quick to tag him with the "political intellectual" label. I also watched with interest, and some discomfort, as he did the rounds on various political (and political comedy) panel shows. I remembered when Mos Def had been the go-to rap pundit. When he pulled back from it, and networks pulled back from him, I started getting calls. I didn't want to do it because I didn't see the upside. Either I'd say the right thing, which would mark me as the political guy, or I would say the wrong thing, which would make backpedaling a full-time job. Questlove, curmudgeon, or just Questlove, old(er) person who has started to get a clearer sense of his limits and the way that his experience both shifts and reinforces them?

I also don't fully know what my role is anymore. One of my favorite rappers in recent years is Azealia Banks. She has immense talent and such a singular take on things, both musically and lyrically. I spotted her early and never stopped being fascinated by what she would do next, which is the best kind of artist. But I also found myself worrying about the way she was moving through the world—not in terms of her own character or path, but in the way that she was being perceived by others. Every time she was outspoken, which was many times, I would call a kind of war council. It was like one of those scenes in *Star Wars* where people crowd into a conference room overlooking a city of flying cars and decide what to do to bring peace to a certain region of the galaxy. We now recognize Ambassador Questlove. Clears throat: "Which one of us is going to step in as a mentor and be there for her to make sure that she has the best chance of finding her voice and her path as an artist?" I never actually devised a plan or sent out a memo, but I was thinking about it, and I felt like I was trying to help. But as time went on, I realized that it was not that simple, had in fact never been that simple. She had a company where she made soap, Bussy Boy, and at some point I placed a medium-size order just to show support. Who can't use a little extra cash to buy a little extra time to work through the pressure that other people put on you? But someone in her organization—I don't know exactly who, or how—recognized my name on the order and she thanked me. That started to feel too close. Friendships aren't easy to make as you get older, and maybe they're not even an appropriate option: same industry, sure, maybe some long-look wisdom to share, but I didn't really know her, and I certainly didn't know how my help would be perceived. Paternalistic? Tone-deaf? Creepy? A parasocial misstep? The more I thought about it, the more I thought that the best course was to back off, to appreciate and admire her work, but also be an observer as she moved through life rather than any kind of participant. That felt like the best move. Just mind your business. Do an album a year with a legacy artist that you respect. If you have business to mind, mind your business.

———

I have talked about the dissolution of the album form in the streaming era, and how, for me, the last true album artist was Kanye. During this time, Kanye was changing. By now, we know the results of that change, not just in terms of his artwork but in terms of his personality, and his toxic need for attention, and his provocateur moves that seem less and less controlled. Back then, mostly what I noticed was that he was changing as an artist. I liked *Yeezus* (2013) because everyone hated it. Maybe in some sense that's why I liked it, because it showed more of him maybe than even he intended (I tend to like records that do that). I hope it wasn't because I felt it as the first sign of downfall. But it was. The next record, *Life of Pablo*, bummed me out. It was almost like a rap version of *There's a Riot Goin' On*. He seemed tapped out, grasping at straws, but with the intelligence and artistry to turn that tapped-out grasping into a creative artifact.

There was something else happening with that album, which is the way that Kanye unfinished it. Back on his debut, he had been working through the wire. Now he was working right up to the wire—and then across it. Even after *Life of Pablo* was "released," he kept changing arrangements, adding features, altering lyrics. The Def Jam statement seemed visionary. "In the months to come, Kanye will release new updates, new versions, and new iterations of the album. An innovative, continuous process, the album will be a living, evolving art project." At first that struck me as brilliant, a way for the artist to snatch back control from the market. But when I sat with it for a while, it started to feel as depressing as the record's contents. The process of starting to think about something is very different if that thing is a moving target. If I develop an opinion about "The 'Micstro'" or "Grindin'" and then I go back to listen and it's different, what does that mean about my opinion, and the analysis that I built on top of it? It's an anti-critical move but also an anti-historical affront. It's like if Marty McFly, instead of trying to knit things back together at the Under the Sea dance so that he will appear again in the photo, ran from place to place knocking people down, even Marvin Berry.

And history matters. I wouldn't write multiple books about it if it didn't. History is how change gets marked and assessed. It's a communal form of memory and a collective acknowledgment that what we remember matters. A little more than a month after the release of *Life of Pablo* (but was it really released if he kept tinkering? See above), something happened that depressed me far more: Phife Dawg passed away. Or rather, Malik Taylor passed away, and Phife Dawg with him. Phife had been a founding member of A Tribe Called Quest, forever on my short list of best and most important hip-hop groups in history. His death was made more tragic by the fact that the group had started to work on a new record, their first since *The Love Movement*, almost two decades earlier.

Later that year, they released that record, *We Got It From Here . . . Thank You 4 Your Service*. In the Roots, we have always had a three-tier system for titles. When we named a record, we wanted the name to reflect a truth about what was happening within the group, a truth about what was happening in the hip-hop world in general, and a truth about what happening in America in general. The Tribe title, conceived by Phife before his passing, never properly explained to the rest of the group, felt like that. It was an album about going away, about the balance between declaration and dismissiveness, a sad record that kept steel in its spine. But Phife's passing also had a gravitational field that pulled at the meaning of the album: Was it also a memorial for America and maybe even hip-hop? That's out of order, I know, but the whole system is out of order.

Let's go back a year, not from now, but from the album's release: Tribe came on *The Tonight Show* for a reunion performance on the night of November 13, 2015. The occasion was the twenty-fifth anniversary rerelease of the group's debut, *People's Instinctive Travels and the Paths of Rhythm*, which was coming out in a deluxe edition with remixes by Pharrell, J. Cole, Raphael Saadiq, and others. I don't say often that I have waited for something for a lifetime, or even half a lifetime, but this was the exception. To see the whole group onstage together again—Tip, Phife, Ali Shaheed Muhammad, and

Jarobi White—performing "Can I Kick It?" no less, that was trans-formative. (It was also happening against a dire backdrop, though we didn't fully know it at the time. We taped the show in the afternoon, so their performance came at roughly the same time that terrorists stormed into the Bataclan in Paris during an Eagles of Death Metal concert, shooting into the crowd and taking hostages, which was also roughly the same time that suicide bombers detonated their ex-plosives outside the Stade de France in Sant-Denis, which was also roughly the same time that terrorists fired at diners at outdoor cafés in the city. The attacks claimed 130 lives, including ninety at the concert. Word trickled in over the course of the taping, but no one had a complete sense of the chaos unfolding across the Atlantic.)

The joy that I felt was a by-product of the joy that the group felt. It had to be, right? You can't falsify that kind of energy. As happens with real energy, it rolled forward—Tribe started working together again as a full unit, and that resulted in new songs, includ-ing the lead single, "We the People . . ." The song, which included a verse from Phife, took aim at the climate of fear, intolerance, and scapegoating in America and around the world, and specifically the anti-immigrant, racist, and Islamophobic sentiment that was then powering the Trump campaign. And the last song, "The Donald," both paid tribute to Phife—one of his nicknames was "Don Juice"—and tried to reckon further with the rise of Trump and Trumpism. (Back in the nineties, Trump had been a blustery and even comic figure in Black music: think of the Time's "Donald Trump [Black Ver-sion]," where Morris Day's slick loverman drew inspiration from the Donald, or the Coup's "Pimps [FreeStylin' at the Fortune 500 Club]," where Trump was the rude and rough nouveau riche interloper em-barrassing the Rockefellers and Gettys.)

The album proved prophetic, of course: though it was finished long before the election, it was released only three days after it. This chapter has been filled with anxieties about the process of aging, and the way that it separates you from certain kinds of elemental forces, both in the world and within yourself, but it's also true that there is a certain kind of art that can be made only by artists deep in their career, summoning up all that they have learned and wiring a circuit through it that illuminates the world. Tribe's comeback record, their last true record—time has made that a sad certainty—is that kind of art.

2017

THE ROYCE GOT NO ROOF

2022

Everything new is old again, and the nostalgia cycle is peddling a more harmonious relationship between past and present.

Hope deferred is hard. By 2017, the Obama hangover had lifted but the country was in the midst of a Trump bender. The effect on the culture, and hip-hop's corner of it, was complicated. It wasn't that there was less pain in the air, but for the first time in a while, it was being expressed straightforwardly rather than reflected through analysis or repressed with party talk. That had negative effects—more anger in full view, especially on social media—but also some positive ones. There was a renewed interest in protest music, in artists standing up for what they thought was right. The drugs in the culture rolled forward from pills to opioids, but there was a secondary drug as well: nostalgia. For the first time in fifteen years, I found that the younger generation was receptive to absorbing and understanding the music of the past. I can see now how much of that was not only an action but also a reaction, specifically a reaction to Make America Great Again, which was a particularly manipulative way of pulling people from the present to the past. The creative version, Make Art Great Again, suggested that any return to the past wouldn't just bring back problematic policies, but might also connect creative minds to new—well, old, but newly rediscovered—sources of inspiration. If Trump was the first major factor during this period that forced artists to draw a distinction between conservatism and conservation, between reactionary misbehavior and preservationist behavior, the second major factor was even more consequential. That was COVID, and the way that a few cases of a strange new virus that popped up in China and then Italy became, within months, a global pandemic. Those spring months of 2020 changed nearly everything. They shrunk the public sphere and pushed people back inside their homes. The resulting isolation could be a benefit for creative production but a detriment to mental health. People devised new high-tech methods of connection that at first seemed desperate but came to be the new normal. Lockdowns, quarantines, masks, worries about how young children would develop in the years away from classrooms—all of these became frequent topics for hip-hop acts. There was a current-events mentality that complemented the activist strain that sprang up during the Trump years. You could say that the drug during this period was opiates, and in a way that's true, but the drug was also the vaccine. This was accompanied by a sharp change in how business was done. Ten years earlier, the economic structures of the record industry had been battered and bruised by the move to streaming. In 2020 and 2021, they were rocked again by the near-total disappearance of touring. Zoom shows replaced real shows. *Verzuz* battles became appointment viewing. I spent the first months of the pandemic doing live DJ sets on YouTube. Some were tributes to artists who had passed in the few years previous: David Bowie, Prince, and more. But I dedicated at least a few of them to hip-hop deep cuts, songs that I had rediscovered during quarantine. For the first time in a little while, hip-hop seemed sharply focused on both the outside world and the inside one, on both making new things and understanding how to use the things that had been made.

This is the era of Drake, still, unless it's the era of Future. It's the era of Kendrick Lamar, still, unless it's the era of Big Sean. It's the era of when I started listening to new music again, unless it's the era when I realized that I could never listen to new music the same way again, unless it's both.

A decade ago, I wrote a memoir called *Mo' Meta Blues*, though as this book goes on, it's condemned to be more of a metanarrative, too, because nearly every process concerned with art—how I find my way to new music, how I digest it, how I recommend it to others, how I draw lines around it that both protect it and protect me—has become more self-conscious as I have gotten older. As we have established, there will never again be a moment in which I arrive breathlessly at a record store on a Tuesday morning and walk away with a cassette or CD that's about to change my life. Some of that is due to market and technological shifts. Some of it is due to marked psychological shifts. But I remain a person who is obsessed with music and the miracles it can bring about when it works the right way, or the right kind of wrong way.

That brings me to 1982, July, to be specific. In Philadelphia, we were in the middle of a battle over how to desegregate schools. (That I remember.) The University City Science Center office building complex opened, with 100 percent occupancy. (That I had to look up.) Almost four hundred miles northwest of me, a baby had just been born. His name was Alvin Lamar Worthy, and he had a brother, Demond Price, who was actually a half brother, or maybe more like a twin, only a few months younger.

Alvin and Demond got involved in music and street life in equal part. On the music side, they took on new identities. Alvin was Westside Gunn, Demond was Conway the Machine. On the street life side, they took on trouble. A bullet went into Conway's body in 2012, neck and shoulder. He survived it. It gave him partial facial paralysis and a certain vocal sound. Injury has affected voice before. (See the D.O.C., Kanye.) This was the opposite. It became Conway's trademark. That was a wake-up call for Westside, who had been in legal trouble and closer and closer to criminal life for five years or so. They also had a cousin who was killed.

They shaped up. They founded Griselda, a hip-hop collective and independent label. It was named for Griselda Blanco, the Black Widow, a notorious Colombian drug lord who bounced between New York, Medellín, and Miami in the 1970s and '80s, served twenty years in prison in Florida for murder, and was shot, also in 2012 like Conway, but in the head, in Medellín, at a butcher shop by a man on a motorcycle, to death. Before and especially after her death, she became a kind of Scarface figure, an outlaw perfect for hip-hop mythology; you can hear her shouted out in Pusha T's "Pain," the first single from his superstar-studded album *My Name Is My Name*.

Other founding members of the Griselda collective included Mach-Hommy, a mysterious Haitian American rapper from New Jersey, always with a bandana covering his face like a Wild West outlaw, even before COVID. They brought in another cousin, Jeremie Damon Pennick, who went by Benny the Butcher. (His name originally was a sort of acronym for Best Ever 'N New York. I'm not sure it makes sense, but then again, I'm the guy whose name was BROTHER, or B.R.o. The. R, or Beat Recycler of the Rhythm.) Also in the expanding circle were Daringer (Thomas Paladino), who became the house producer; and artists like Boldy James, Armani Caesar, Rome Streetz, and Stove God Cooks. In 2017 they signed with Shady Records for purposes of distribution. I'm not sure when

I first heard the Griselda rappers. But I am sure that when I heard them, I *heard* them.

Technically, the Griselda artists are old millennials, born in the early eighties, but they are right on the edge of that generation. In some ways their throwback move allies them more with Gen X groups like the Lox and Dipset, who were all born around 1975, 1976. In their aesthetic, they are a collective that has a certain looseness and griminess to them, along with a strong sense of place, which means that they can't help but remind me of Wu-Tang. And not in a narrow throwback sense. In the sense that they are advancing the cause, taking the next step.

But the next step from what? Let's go all the way back to the midnineties. The (in)famous Source Awards happened that summer, Nas deflating, Biggie ascending. A week later the Roots left for a two-month tour of Europe. It had us out of the country for June and July, seven weeks total, and seven weeks of hell—there's nothing stranger or more destructive to your sense of self than being broke and touring. We arrived at one of the Swedish venues and learned that Ol' Dirty Bastard had played there the night before. ODB had left a cassette behind. It was Raekwon's . . . *Only Built 4 Cuban Linx*. The album wouldn't officially come out until August 1, which was about a week or two away at that time. This was a rare leak, a golden opportunity. The label was really being secretive and careful with it. I sat on our tour bus with Rich, Riq, and Kelo and we listened to the album, starting with "Striving for Perfection," moving through "Knuckleheadz" and "Criminology" and "Can It Be All So Simple." (Most of the tracks that would end up being the singles were stacked toward the back of the record, "Heaven and Hell" and "Ice Cream.")

Each song was both revolutionary and impossible to absorb. The Wu-Tang had blown apart our sense of things repeatedly, and it was happening again. As before, it wasn't necessarily in a good way. There were so many things about the production that struck me as more than ill-advised, or risky. They struck me as impossible. When we got to "Verbal Intercourse," I think one of us said it, out loud: "Is this allowed to happen?" That song takes a song by the Emotions, the legendary girl group that most people know either from "The Best of My Love" or from their collaboration with Earth, Wind & Fire, "Boogie Wonderland." Before either of these, they recorded a song called "If You Think It (You May as Well Do It)." That was the song that the RZA had used as the bed for "Verbal Intercourse." But the bed wasn't made. There didn't seem to be a real strategy. I had never heard a musical background so carelessly put together. Were you allowed to rap over a loop that already had vocals? Was the RZA a genius or just lazy? On the bus there in Sweden, we had an hour-long debate on that loop. *We* were on a loop.

We solved nothing. What RZA did for Raekwon became an aesthetic that would be taken up over the years by various artists with various levels of talent. Griselda, artists with high levels of talent, brought it back into the light in the 2010s.

But I want to be careful not to skip steps. You know my theory that true pioneers never get noticed? If you are reading this book in order, you do, because I mentioned it when I was speaking about Marley Marl and the Bomb Squad, and again when I talked about *The Chronic* and Wu-Tang. The idea is that true innovators recede as time passes, because people aren't willing or even able to dig through history to find them. The people right behind the pioneer are the ones who perfect, popularize, collect the credit. This is true even when it comes to updating and innovating, picking up a thread from a past moment of genius. Creating a Wu-Tang 2.0 sound a generation later was going to happen. But who was going to do it first, or first best? In my mind that honor goes to Roc Marciano.

Roc Marciano started out his life as Rahkeim Calief Meyer, and started out his rap career as part of Busta Rhymes's Flipmode Squad. On Busta's 2000 album *Anarchy,* Roc featured on a song called "The Heist." I noticed him because he gave me a shout-out: Brother Question on percussion. It was really rare that I got a shout-out like that. Raekwon and Ghostface were on that track, and Roc fit right in with them. He also popped up on the compilation *Wu-Tang Meets the Indie Culture.* But even when there weren't Wu-Tang members around—a feature on a Marco Polo album, an appearance on a Pete Rock record—Roc Marciano carried that same energy with him: grimy without being grim, verbal dexterity without pretention. He also started down the road to drumless production, using loops with minimal or nonexistent percussion.

I heard something there. I heard the future. Back in 2009, when Jay-Z was getting comfortable as president of Def Jam, I tried to convince him that Roc Marciano would be a perfect discovery for him. That became my second misguided Jay-Z recommendation, after the first three tracks of *Kingdom Come*. I wasn't trying to misstep. I always wanted, when I made a recommendation for Jay, to have the aim of a Navy SEAL. I truly believed that Roc was the future. Jay didn't, emphatically. (The year before I had been on him about Odd Future. That, too, was an attempt to find the post–*Cuban Linx* link, though in that case it would have been Earl Sweatshirt. That recommendation wasn't a major misstep. Jay got it. He had dinner with Tyler, the Creator, I think. He just didn't sign them. So no demerit there.)

When Roc Marciano's debut, *Marcberg*, came out in 2010, on Fat Beats records, I was even more convinced that I had been right. *Pitchfork* gave it an 8.1. That was the first time that we had agreed on a rating that I didn't feel had been preordained by the broader culture. They understood the essential grain of the record. The review mentioned Mobb Deep and Raekwon. They said it was "as if Swizz Beats, shiny suits, and rappers in skinny jeans never happened."

Roc Marciano became a footnote in my life—a beloved footnote, but a footnote nonetheless. Some of his songs still flipped my eyes open, like "Congo" in 2018.

But I was waiting, always waiting, for something like that to pop up again. When Griselda finally happened, I loved it.

Westside Gunn was my favorite of the bunch.

From the start, he had a devout commitment to the mixtape format. He released a series under the title *Hitler Wears Hermes* (original, 2, 3, etc.). It was not anything sinister, exactly; it was a play on *The Devil Wears Prada*. The first bunch of *HWH* mixtapes got collected in 2018 on *Hitler's Dead*. I had heard them scattershot but now I could hear them wholesale. I was taken. And it was consistent. I loved songs from the first. I loved songs from the latest. I loved the ones where he was on his own ("Me and My Eagle" and "Eric B.") and the ones where he brought in other Griselda members ("Hall & Nash," which featured Conway, and "Vera Boys," which featured the spoken word artist Keisha Plum).

I wasn't the only one to notice. You can track Griselda's influence in part by how they resurrected the myth of Griselda Blanco. She started to pop up in lyrics by other acts—in NBA YoungBoy's "Slime Belief," in Drake's "Portland"—and a number of film projects entering development, including a Netflix series starring Sofia Vergara. I measured it by how much it kept me connected to artists who sounded as though they had followed a similar path, from "Verbal Intercourse" to Roc Marciano to new inspiration. That included Camouflage Monk, who came from Buffalo but moved to Atlanta; 38 Spesh, from Rochester; and Smoke DZA, from New York. (There were even like-minded collaborations that tied the room together. Roc Marciano worked directly with Griselda artists, producing Stove God Cooks's breakthrough debut, *Reasonable Drought*.)

I liked what Westside Gunn was doing on his own, liked the other artists, and watched with interest as the group released its first official debut as a collective, 2019's *WWCD*. For me, it was a bit of a growing pain. People were still trying to fit in around each other. Still, I got strong Wu-Tang vibes, though a little in reverse: it was like convening a group meeting after everyone had already struck out on their own. Everyone appeared on that, along with guests like Eminem and 50 Cent. The album art was also keyed to a woman who caught the group's eye, though in this case it wasn't Griselda Blanco but rather Clara "Claire" Gomez, a homeless woman from Buffalo. Despite rumors, the title of the record was not an acronym for "What Would Clara Do." It was *What Would Chine Gun Do*, a reference to Machine Gun Black, Benny's brother, who was part of the core crew but died in 2006 in a shooting. (Claire Gomez passed away as I was writing this section, at the age of fifty-eight. Westside paid tribute to her on Twitter.)

Even though *WWCD* wasn't as tight in some ways as the Westside Gunn solo work that had stopped me in his tracks, I still loved the sound, maybe to my own detriment. The best thing about those records are that they feel so Black, so African, and yet, remember drumlessness? All the way back in 1967, in "Cold Sweat," and all the way back at the beginning of this book, James Brown wanted to give the drummer some. Early hip-hop continued on in that tradition. Ultramagnetic MCs even named had a song called that on *Critical Beatdown*. Griselda's style, evolving out of Roc Marciano, gives the drummer none. But this drummer doesn't mind.

When you hear something you like out of a certain spot—a city or scene or collective—it can be tempting to narrow your focus and become an expert, especially when streaming makes everything available to you: I tried to count all the Griselda and Griselda-affiliated projects, and stopped when I was well over a hundred albums.

Still, the pressure remains to be a generalist, and so I try to cast a wider net. I remember exactly where I was when I first heard Danny Brown's "Combat," an amazing burst of lyricism. (Sad reveal: I was in the same chair I'm sitting on now, though working on a different book.) It's also where I was when I first heard Freddie Gibbs's "Babies and Fools." Lots of rappers now set sugar-makes-the-medicine-go-down arrangements and melodies against more difficult lyrics; the work that Gibbs does with the Alchemist is among the best of that type. Take a song like "Babies and Fools," from *Alfredo*, which samples a song from Andrus, Blackwood & Company, a Contemporary Christian group that released its records in the heyday of soft rock. Using music like that as the spine for a song is a different risk than it once was. There was a time that it was corny. In early hip-hop, beats had to be hard, and the samples that went with them had to match. They didn't all have to be straight funk—there was a countermovement that drew on jazz—but they had to be serious. De La Soul ushered in an age of irony, when you could use shit that wasn't taken seriously before, like Steely Dan, like the Turtles. You were covered because here were three dudes that were actually cool building songs around those samples, with an intellectual justification behind it. Now, I feel like this is the standard. If you pull from jazz or James Brown or classic breakbeats, you're just seen as old. "Babies and Fools" is a great example of taking a song that I would never consider and making it work better than I could have ever imagined.

But life is about margins and centers. When I endorse Griselda, I always have a second thought. I see what they are doing. I hear what they are doing. I support it. But I also feel like it has a limit: self-imposed, self-aware, but a limit nonetheless. I am also always looking out for the limitless. I want to put this in film terms. If Griselda is mumblecore, I am also constantly on the lookout for the *Barbie*.

What I have seen in recent years is that the time is right, or at least it's getting righter. For years, the Roots have been on *The Tonight Show*, which means that for years I have watched artists come and go, including hip-hop artists. Because hip-hop changes so regularly—every half decade, I have heard—our status in the minds of those artists also changes. While there are a few rappers who have developed a relationship with us (the Odd Future crew, as I said, Rae Sremmurd, others), there are plenty who don't know who we are. The best example of this is Iggy Azalea. Whenever she's been on *The Tonight Show*, I know that mostly I'm going to see her from the back, because it's rare for her to even turn around and acknowledge the Roots. The first time I felt a certain way about it, edge of offended, but I realized soon enough that it was a condition of her being, creatively. There's so much insecurity in appearing the way she did, being called a flash in the pan, struggling to prove that you have even a few more years in you. All the thoughts are directed inward. Why look outward, let alone toward the past?

But I recently had an experience that worked as a near-total antidote. Doja Cat was on the show. I knew some of her music, liked what I knew, so I thought I would at least go up and say hello. I have a kind of speech prepared for younger artists where I explain the Roots, almost place it in the past, as if I am introducing myself at my own memorial. She started laughing. "I know the Roots," she said. "My mom used to play you guys all the time. I was raised on your records and Slum Village and Little Brother."

She was demonstrating the second half of my drug theory for the period, that it was defined not just by opioids but by nostalgia. Artists like Doja Cat not only know my generation's music but they also know, through transfer, the music that inspired my generation. For years I had a hard time getting younger kids to listen to the kind of music that I felt close to, the music that moved me. It left a number of those microgenerations cold: the ecstasy kids, the molly kids, the sizzurp kids, the pill kids. But the kids coming along in this 2017 to 2022 period seemed to get it. They seemed to want it. (The best example is Doja Cat's newest single "Paint the Town Red," which uses as its main sample Dionne Warwick's "Walk on By," a song that would have been part of my raiding-the-parents'-records process. Nicki Minaj, a decade older, was more likely to go for Sir MixaLot.) It's a cycle of cultural influence, the flowering of seeds that were planted.

Birth and rebirth are part of the cycle, but there's a darker seam to it. There's something more serious moving inside this period. There were deaths in hip-hop, always. Taken as a whole, it was an art form that comprised a large number of people, and of that large number, some did not make it. Eazy-E died of AIDS-related pneumonia in 1994, the same year that Digital Underground's Kenny K died of liver failure. Big Pun died of heart failure in 2000, as did Prince Markie Dee in 2021. Guru died of cancer in 2010, as did Big Bank Hank in 2014 and Bushwick Bill in 2019. Nate Dogg suffered a series of strokes and passed in 2011. Phife from A Tribe Called Quest died of diabetes, tragically. Prodigy died of complications from sickle cell anemia in 2017. MF DOOM died mysteriously in 2020, as you might expect from MF DOOM.

And then, in the summer of 2021, rumors began to circulate about Biz Markie: that he had been hospitalized for complications from diabetes, had fallen into a coma, and suffered a stroke. On July 16, he died. That event hit me harder, for some reason, than the others. Maybe it was the way that Biz carried himself. He was so full of life that he *was* life. How could he be dead? As I mourned him, I thought about the years that Rich Nichols tried to convince me of the wisdom of getting proper health care. I had been reluctant. It's not uncommon among musicians or performers in general. Health insurance is associated with stable jobs, and if you don't have one, it's not an expense that makes sense. I remembered going to the dentist in 2009 and talking to the woman at the desk. "When was your last visit?" she said. I couldn't remember. There were cultural factors beyond the nature of the entertainment industry. Black people have a harder time trusting doctors and science, in part because of the legacy of racist experiments like the Tuskegee Syphilis Study. (It was both racist and misunderstood—there's a persistent belief that the government not only studied the consequences of not treating syphilis but also actually introduced syphilis into men.) We saw during the pandemic how this set of beliefs prevented Black Americans from following the science, which in turn created more of a cultural divide.

Deaths from illness, particularly those that could be mitigated or prevented, are sad. They remind us of the fragility of existence. But they do not remind us of the cruelty of humans toward themselves and others. What does? DJ Screw in 2000, Ol' Dirty Bastard in 2004, Pimp C in 2007. These were drug overdoses, like Mac Daddy of Kris Kross in 2013, Lil Peep in 2017, Mac Miller in 2018, Juice WRLD in 2019, Lexi Alijai in 2020, Shock G and DMX in 2021, and Coolio in 2022. Some of those rappers were old. Some were young. Some were taken by cocaine, some by opioids. Some were taken by violence. We've already talked about Scott La Rock and Paul C and Tupac and Biggie. We haven't talked about Fat Pat, who was shot in Houston the year after Biggie, or Freaky Tah from the Lost Boyz, who was shot in Queens the year after that, or Jam Master Jay, for God's sake. That's about one a year for too many years. Then the pace quickened. XXXTentacion, who had just released his second LP, ?, was murdered in Deerfield Beach in 2018 after years of troubled living. The next year, Nipsey Hussle was gunned down in LA in the parking lot of a clothing store he owned, by someone he knew. Nipsey's killer was convicted of murder in the first degree and sentenced to sixty years in prison. The Brooklyn rapper Pop Smoke was shot and killed in 2020, also in LA, in a home invasion. The Memphis rapper Young Dolph was back home in 2021, visiting his mother and shopping for cookies at his favorite spot, Makeda's Homemade Butter Cookies, when he was assassinated: twenty-two gunshot wounds from two gunmen in a passing Mercedes. And those are just the rappers you may have heard of—there are plenty of others who hadn't made it yet, mostly young.

I heard about each one as it happened. I felt anger, sadness, frustration, and then a numbness that helped me to suppress the rest. And then in November 2022, Takeoff from Migos was shot during an argument about a dice game. Something about the randomness of that act, the trivial cause of a permanent tragedy, broke me. All the feelings that had accumulated over the years poured out of me. I wrote a long Instagram post memorializing Takeoff and asking everyone in the hip-hop community (though mostly the men) to take a long look at the way that Black Americans have mismanaged their emotions. It's been part of our culture for decades, for centuries. When Black Americans lived under the yoke of slavery, they were not allowed to show emotions at all. Crying was decried. Laughing, too. Plantations actually had laughing barrels. This is just as strange and dehumanizing as it sounds. Because enslaved people were not permitted to possess any signs of humanity, they had to stick their heads into the barrels to show their emotions. Some historians have questioned whether this practice was widespread. I hope this practice was more mythical than real. But it is based on something real, and it carried through into the twentieth century in the form of Black cool. It was a way of coping, to bottle up your sadness and rage, and often it took with it displays of joy.

Hip-hop picked up this thread. The genre dissuaded people (especially men) from clearly expressing their emotions, which in turn prevented them from clearly feeling their emotions. Coping mechanisms came on in all forms. Some seemed benign, like workaholism. Some were understood to be harmful but got shoved to the side, like behavior around food. And then there were the numbing agents (drugs) and the desperate attempts to regain control (violence). In my post, I called out all of this behavior. I asked for more accountability, more self-love. Did it make a difference? It did not. BTB Savage, a Houston rapper, was shot and killed, as was Lil Ronald, a fourteen-year-old rapper in Chicago. Gangsta Boo overdosed, as did Boom Pacino. It got to the point where I stopped writing obituaries on social media. I couldn't keep up.

And then it got to the point where I started to feel more philosophical about the entire process, less because of hip-hop proper and more because of the inevitable, unstoppable life cycle. When I directed *Summer of Soul*, one of the beneficiaries of it was the 5th Dimension, the pop-soul music group. For decades I had heard nothing about them. They had faded into the wallpaper. After I directed the movie, people would ask me about them more than I expected. They enjoyed a moment, even with the understanding that their moment was in the past. One day I was looking at music news and saw that Meshell Ndegeocello had a new single out called "The Fifth Dimension." That was interesting, but more interesting were her comments around the song. "Everything moved so quickly when my parents died," she said. "Changed my view of everything and myself in the blink of an eye. As I sifted through the remains of their life together, I found my first Real Book, the one my father gave me. I took their records, the ones I grew up hearing, learning, remembering. My mother gifted me with her ache, I carry the melancholy that defined her experience and, in turn, my experience of this thing called life calls me to disappear into my imagination and to hear the music." The feeling she described was like a supercharged version of what Doja Cat experienced when she remembered the records of her youth, even more powerful because it had the force of finality behind it. I have started to feel those same forces. My father passed in 2016, and my mother is getting older in age. I am not worried about her every day, but it turns out that I am wrong about that. The worry just surfaces in me in strange ways. The other day, I was in some city, getting hungry for lunch, and found myself seeking out a Whole Foods. It makes no sense. I could have gotten a salad and an aloe vera at any healthy grocery. But the way the candle aisle smells there sends me directly back toward the way my mom's apartment smelled in the early aughts. It's not music but it's music of the mind. Meshell chose the record collection as a way of taking her back. I chose Whole Foods. But we both sought out the comfort of knowing that the things that made us, the things that built us and nourished us, are still there for us to find. There's a darker seam to it, but birth and rebirth are part of the cycle.

2023

NO TIME TO
JOKE AROUND

Now it is now.

In the years of the pandemic and the years that followed (in other words, now), I began to think more and more about preservation. Too much culture, especially Black culture, has passed into the past without a second thought. That was a tragedy, an after-the-fact erasure that could almost be a cultural genocide. When I directed *Summer of Soul*, about the Harlem Cultural Festival of 1969, part of the goal was to construct a film essay about what it meant to be a Black artist in 1969—how much white versus Black was a factor, how much the church was a factor, how much youth culture was a factor. Part of the goal was to show an amazing series of performances that answered those questions. But part of the goal was also to fight against time's worst effect, which was to sweep things into the past. That movie won an Oscar, which meant that I started this year, 2023, as an Oscar-winning documentarian of record. That must have meant that at least some people agreed with my idea that the past should be protected. But at least some other people seemed to be moving dangerously in the other direction. In the last few chapters, I have talked about how the main push of the last decade or so was toward numbing, first with pills, then with opioids. I have also discussed how a period of trauma can be followed by a period of hedonism (see the time after 9/11), but also how that hedonism is at least partly the experience of no longer feeling pain. That happened in the wake of the pandemic. But what also happened was a frightening acceleration of the most dangerous drugs, particularly fentanyl. It had been around for a while, but it grew more and more potent, harder and harder to detect. It popped up in other drugs and became a form of pharmaceutical Russian roulette. Fentanyl could end a life in a blink, send a life not just into the past but into oblivion. This happened to famous people like Prince, but it also happened to thousands and thousands of people who never got the chance to be famous. It became a political issue, but to me it was more and more a cultural issue. At a time when I was thinking more and more about the importance of preservation, remembering, and visibility, this kind of erasure was more than a scourge. It was the enemy.

So here we are, at the fiftieth anniversary of this wonderful, bottomlessly creative, meaning-carrying, shape-shifting genre. So what is the state of the art?

At the beginning of 2023, Lil Yachty's *Let's Start Here* came out. It's an ironic title for an album to write about at the end of a book. That was my thought as I went in. I listened to it once and a second time. I needed to process what I was hearing. Then once I had the album in my mind I had to wait again, a full day this time, just so I made certain that I was not putting myself in a position where I would say something that I didn't mean—or, a day later, couldn't mean.

But the record hit me hard. It was a departure record. What does that mean? It's private parlance. Artists establish a certain tone. They have their thing going. Then they take a left turn. It's a sharp left to the point where they are no longer on the same road, but really they are not even on the road at all. They are full-speeding it toward a cliff. A departure record is often a way of dealing with anxiety that you have reached an altitude from which you can only fall.

Sometimes they take an audience and make it smaller by degree rather than kind. They reduce it from the unruly large population to a smaller population that knows what it wants but doesn't just want what it knows. That's what happened with Prince's *Around the World in a Day*. That's what happened with the Beastie Boys' *Paul's*

Boutique. Sometimes they don't work at all. They push everything down the stairs. That's what happened with Miles Davis's *On the Corner* and Marvin Gaye's *Here, My Dear.* (It takes years to get back there but sometimes the tide turns.) Other times the departure doesn't put on any brakes. It blows the band up even bigger. *St. Pepper's?*

But the best effect is when the listener comes in and is blindsided. It's a WTF moment, as the kids say. That happened for me with Radiohead's *Kid A,* with Q-Tip's *Kamaal the Abstract.* Records like that turn your head and then they spin your head. That's what the effect was with Yachty's *Let's Start Here.* But beyond that, it reversed and rethought everything that the artist had done up until that time, and as a result was not only surprising in a pure sense, but a form of productive erasure. I can count on one hand the number of albums that I am still struggling to get into my head because they couldn't fit comfortably alongside what was there before. Divine Styler's second record, *Spiral Walls Containing Autumns of Light,* which came out back in 1992, turned on its head everything that the first album set out on the table, and I am still trying to navigate the hard, aggressive stance of the third Jungle Brothers record, *J Beez wit the Remedy,* thirty years after its release. But this, from a young man, an artist only twenty-five, already making a hairpin turn, turned my hair gray.

But it turns it gray for another reason, too. I saw Yachty during *SNL.* He thanked me for writing the review. That was great, except for how he said it: "That meant so much to me, OG." When he said that, I felt so old, like I was the actor who had played Uncle Remus. I literally went home and ate a can of baked beans. I'm old, might as well have BBQ beans out of a pan. When you hear something like that, you do the things you saw your grandfather do.

Or you pull yourself together and you do things that your grandfather would not do. You go out there and demand evolution of yourself.

Even if finding new music feels as though it is not always top of mind, I have to process records, pass them through my mind, for survival, as a DJ but also for *The Tonight Show*, and for other purposes, too. I used to make playlists for a very select group of people: a curated set of songs, thirty fast ones and twenty slow ones, twice a month. One of those very select people let the cat out of the bag, not maliciously but enthusiastically, kindly, and now I have to send that same list to more than four hundred people. It keeps me on my toes, in the sense that I still have to sift through thousands of songs, new and old, to find the perfect ones. That's a grind, in one sense, but a joy in all the others. What else do I do to stay connected? I try to devote myself to an hour a day of Flex on Hot 97, though I'm fully aware that he has his own thing going. What else do I do to stay exploratory? I look at the list of things I want to listen to—the new Billy Woods, the new Busdriver, the new Conway the Machine, Rio Da Yung OG—and I realize, my heart both leaping up and lying down, that I'll never get to all of it.

I also realize that I'll get to things in my own time, along routes I cannot yet envision. Last night I accidentally stumbled on a new artist, or an artist new to me. I probably follow seventy-five hundred people on Instagram, but I only truly know a thousand or so of them, so I take some time to browse around. There was one account I have followed for a little while, though I wasn't entirely sure if he was a hip-hop artist or a producer or what. He had background music in one of his posts that I liked, and that also seemed to me exactly the kind of trick I would do: bury some music in the background of one of your posts and see if anyone takes the initiative to look (or listen) into it. I went in search of its origins, and that sent me down a rabbit hole. I found some of his songs, and the production lured me in. It had smart samples used in interesting ways, and the deeper I went, the smarter and more interesting they got. The artist's name was Quelle Chris. A light went off in my mind. Wasn't he the guy who did the record with Jean Grae a few years before that had gotten an 8.5 or something from *Pitchfork*? He was, and not only that, but they were married! And that record that I had remembered, *Everything's Fine*—an 8.4 in point of fact—was located on the edge of hip-hop and comedy, with appearances from Hannibal

Buress and Michael Che and others. And it was the follow-up to an album that I then found and loved called *Being You Is Great, I Wish I Could Be You More Often*, which featured Jean Grae, too, but also Roc Marciano and Homeboy Sandman and House Shoes, whom I recognized from his work with Dilla and Slum Village. That alerted me to the fact that Quelle Chris was also a Detroit artist, and that led me to an article in which he recounted that right at the beginning of his career he had played at a record release party for Black Milk, one of Dilla's heirs. And that led me to an interview where Quelle Chris told a website that he had been careful early on not to make anything that sounded too much like Dilla, even though at times he found himself using the same equipment. Staking out his independence led him first into a sound that was "generically boom-bap" but eventually brought him to the music I was hearing on *Being You Is Great, I Wish I Could Be You More Often*.

When my brain settled, I was both gratified and ashamed. Here I was in April 2023 discovering 2018 and 2017. These were records I really loved. I could have used my platform to elevate them, especially during a pandemic, when they could have been a real help to people. But here they were, elevating me, and that was a source of comfort.

Especially during a pandemic . . . I am not alone in believing that the way the world folded up in 2020 and 2021 changed everything. It is one of the ways in which I am least alone. At the beginning of the pandemic, I made overt efforts to connect back to the hip-hop of my youth, the hip-hop that had connected me to others. I DJed YouTube sets on hip-hop deep cuts, talked lengthily between the songs, tried to explain why LL Cool J's "You Can't Dance" or DJ Chuck Chillout & Kool Chip's "I'm Large" meant so much to me. Why? Well, "You Can't Dance" is LL as a master of corn, a song I loved so much that I bought the drum machine that made it from Chung King Studios in New York when it shut down. And "I'm Large" was produced by the very young Salaam Remi, who was still older than he had been when he played keyboards for Kurtis Blow's *Kingdom Come*, and who was part of hip-hop history to the point where I would take any chance to resurface his name.

COVID had me looking back. No one knew what the future would bring. For a while there, no one knew that there would really be a future, especially when it came to live performance. Venues dropped like flies.

In 2023, I read an article in *Rolling Stone*, not about how Run-D.M.C. love their parents, but about Elsewhere, a Bushwick venue that has become one of the focal points for hip-hop performance in postpandemic NYC. Opened by Jake Rosenthal and Rami Haykal, who booked Santos Party House in Tribeca (which means they booked Freddie Gibbs and Big K.R.I.T. and El-P) and then Glasslands in Williamsburg (mostly indie rock). They were pushed out of existing venues and started planning what would become Elsewhere. That's where Roc Marciano was appearing, promoting his new album *The Elephant Man's Bones*. The article made a complex case about why new venues were springing up in the wake of the pandemic, and why they did not appear with as much regularity during the 2000s and 2010s. Nightlife habits changed, first after 9/11, then after the financial crisis. Race and the perception that hip-hop venues would draw a mostly Black crowd was another factor. The third interested me: the kinds of promoters who wanted to start venues in interesting or up-and-coming neighborhoods did not want to be carrying water for the commercial hip-hop that dominated the scene during those decades. COVID reshuffled people's sense of things, as did the ability of social media to identify and inform audiences. Ride-sharing apps were also a factor; they allowed fans to get to and from venues located in neighborhoods farther away from subway lines. All told, the piece painted a rosy picture of the present as it struggled to become the future, and while I felt fairly certain that the road to Utopia was bumpier than most of them understood, I appreciated the idea that there was a virtuous struggle in play.

We are always trading past for future, never quite understanding the terms of the negotiation.

Streaming exposed everyone to everything. Nearly every band

got there. There was one conspicuous holdout, long-suffering. De La Soul, one of the flagships of the Native Tongues movement, weren't able to upload their records to streaming services for years because of the difficulties with clearing samples and the tangle of paperwork and permissions that either had not been done properly or had been done improperly. In the end, after several frustrating delays, De La Soul found their way to streaming. The vast majority of issues with samples were resolved, and those that could not be were resolved through different means. In some cases, producers had to go in with tweezers and lift out little pieces. It was like art restoration, except that it was a bit of destruction, except that it allowed them to join the present.

The De La Soul streaming debut was all set to go. Then in February 2023, Trugoy the Dove (government name Dave Jolicoeur), one of the group's founding members, passed away at the far-too-young age of fifty-four, from congestive heart failure. It was all too similar to what had happened to Phife Dawg in 2016, another Native Tongues pantheon act cruelly reduced by tragedy. As it turned out, Trugoy's death didn't just put a damper on the significance of the group's return to streaming. It also deepened it. A celebration at Webster Hall in early March doubled as a memorial. Pos and Maseo, the other two members of the group, remembered Trugoy in ways that balanced sadness with heard-earned jubilation at the preservation and propagation of De La's music. Everyone showed up, almost as many as the Grammy performance, with plenty of overlap: Busta Rhymes, Queen Latifah, Chuck D, Grandmaster Flash, Monie Love, Large Professor, Prince Paul. Tariq was there. It was a celebration of the way that hip-hop made us, mined us, sustained us, designed us.

The celebration continued. Through the summer of 2023, the Roots went on tour with LL Cool J to celebrate hip-hop's fiftieth anniversary. LL had been wired and inspired by the Grammy show. "Let's tour!" he said. I was beyond exhausted, but LL was a genius at not taking no for an answer. So out on the road we went, to celebrate the genre. We were the core of the show, or the foundation, but everywhere we went we invited other artists onstage with us.

One night it might be Doug E. Fresh and Slick Rick. Another night it might be Jadakiss, or Queen Latifah, or Salt-N-Pepa. Because of the way the tour was structured, each night was a boot camp and more. We would arrive into town in the early morning, set up our dressing room as a rehearsal space, and work for six hours to learn anywhere between sixty and eighty songs that would reflect the city and the special guests. I was no stranger to the three-hour show, but when I played a Roots show, I was playing what I knew, and I didn't get that terror-train, peak-and-valley feeling that brought me within an inch of my life. In those marathon shows we did with LL, I got one three-minute break where I had to run back to the dressing room—we were playing arenas, and we always ended up in the visitors' locker room—and that was it. Every night of that tour felt more physically demanding than anything I had ever done.

They were emotionally demanding as well. I learned so much from those shows. For starters, I learned how wrong I had been about Bone Thugs-N-Harmony. In their day, I had been dismissive of them, even including their work with Biggie. Live, twenty-five years later, I saw the absolute brilliance of their creative project. I am angry at myself and my small-mindedness for not seeing that they were the true inheritors of the legacy of the Cold Crush Brothers. Their performances were among the spiritual and aesthetic highlights of those shows, showing me that I could still sweep away old prejudices and restore artists to their rightful place.

I also learned what it meant for more than a quarter century to pass. We did 2023 shows with Goodie Mob, the Atlanta-based group that came up at the same time that we did—their debut LP, *Soul Food*, was released the same year that we released *Do You Want More?!!!??!* They were not only peers but friends, the first rap group that we connected with socially. When CeeLo left for a solo career in 1999, it felt inevitable. He was the star. It also felt inevitable for the rest of the group to make a record about how they could not only survive without him but thrive (*One Monkey Don't Stop No Show*). But it didn't feel right that CeeLo didn't stay connected to his home base. I am the king of side projects, but they're called side projects for a reason. Why not do "Crazy" with Danger Mouse and do "Fuck You" with Bruno Mars (even performing the cleaned-up version, "Forget You," with the Muppets), while also keeping Goodie Mob a going concern? That didn't happen when CeeLo was flying high, though there was a brief reunion for *Age Against the Machine* in 2013 after he fell back to earth (legal trouble, well-documented) and, long after that, *Survival Kit* in 2020. As I watched them, I saw not only him but his bandmate Khujo, who had a prosthetic leg that was the result of a drunk-driving accident. I saw abundant creative ability and just as much self-sabotage. Did they feel the burden of their talent and try to ruin it? Or was it just what happened as people aged and discovered over and over again that they were fallible and mortal?

The tour also taught me how important it was to get the genre on the proper footing, not just in terms of the music we were making, but in terms of the connections made, broken, and repaired, and also in terms of the messages that were being sent and received. At one point, we got to Madison Square Garden. When we entered the venue, I got word that DaBaby was in the house. DaBaby was a young North Carolina rapper who had been on the scene since 2015 or so but came into my line of vision in 2018 with a mixtape called *Blank Blank* that got him signed to Interscope. He had risen in my estimation in 2020 with a performance at the BET Awards that paid tribute to George Floyd. I had my eye on him as an important new voice. Even my cynical-for-the-future-of-the-culture felt . . . hope? A year after that, he went onstage at the Rolling Loud festival in Miami and made a number of crass and insensitive comments about the LGBTQIA+ community. I didn't feel the need to comment on everything. But I commented on that. I went on Instagram and made it clear that I wasn't trying to create clickbait or artificial controversy. "But right is right & his actions are wrong," I wrote. I wanted to make the point that any hate, whether homophobia or transphobia or xenophobia or misogyny or racism, was wrong. "I had to say something," I wrote, because I had to say something. DaBaby claimed he didn't care about losing me as a fan and didn't even know me, despite the fact that he had performed on *The To-*

night Show with us. People clowned him for this, but to me this was possible, maybe even more than possible—some artists didn't even turn around to look at the rest of the band. His comments hurt him, not because of anything I said (and I wasn't the only one who said it—Madonna spoke out, and Elton John, and others), but because they were indefensible. He was dropped from other festival lineups. He posted an apology on Instagram and then deleted it a few days later. It was a mess.

So DaBaby was in the house. I didn't go over to him right away. But the more I didn't go over, the more the decision not to go over there seemed wrong. This couldn't just be about personal ego and social media, whether one person knew who another person was, could it? This was something bigger. It was about whether there was any such thing as an ambassadorial figure in hip-hop, a person who could reconcile past and present and find a way to send the story of the genre moving forward into the future. And if it was about something bigger, I had to at least try to get up to the high road. DaBaby was in the backstage area, which was packed solid with musicians and comedians. I stood behind the comedian Michelle Wolf, who was with her baby, and then I stepped right toward DaBaby. He extended his hand and then, as he realized who I was, started to draw back a bit. But the shake was still in progress. I leaned in. I explained why I had called him out on social media, told him that he had potential as an artist and that those kinds of comments had no real place in the conversation. I didn't want there to be beef, but I wanted there to be clarity. Behind me, I heard the call to take the stage. I am never late for that moment. When the bell sounds, I'm in the ring. But I stayed a few seconds longer backstage because it was, in its own way, a significant moment.

Way back in the introduction, I told the story of putting together the Hip-Hop 50 tribute for the 2023 Grammy Awards, how exciting it was and also how stressful, to the point where my tooth fell out. As I sat in the dentist's chair, about to go under, I wondered if it had all been worth it. When I woke up, the question had shifted. I wasn't even sure where I was at first. Had I dreamed the whole thing?

I hadn't. Within twenty-four hours of getting back to work and life, Harvey Mason Jr., the CEO of the Recording Academy, reached out. His office wanted to do a postmortem, talk about what had worked and what hadn't. I wasn't ready. I asked for a week to get my thoughts all sorted. They reached back out in a week, and I asked for another week. I kicked the can down the road for five weeks until Shawn Gee told me to stop. "This is a little disrespectful," he said. "It's a congratulations call for you and LL. That's all."

Within a few minutes of the start of the call, it was clear that Shawn was wrong. The praise for 2023 turned quickly to cooking up new plans. One of those new plans was the tour idea. I was already feeling like I couldn't resist that, but I wasn't ready to hear about anything else. And there were lots of anything elses: a proposed prime-time special, maybe a yearly televised showcase. I wasn't on any mind-altering substances, not even dentist's gas, but as soon as the talk turned to new programming, I hung back and zoned out. I may have played Wordle just off-screen. I wanted to flatten out all the conversation to Charlie Brown–teacher sounds, and the desired effect was what I got.

But zoning out is not a permanent solution. At one point, I tuned back in and immediately heard LL's voice. "Right, Ahmir?" he was saying.

Uh-oh. Right, Ahmir, what? Was this the tour he was talking about? I was sure I wouldn't do it, couldn't. I was wrong, of course. Wrong that I wouldn't do it—I did it—and wrong about what he was talking about. As it turned out, in the ninety seconds of the conversation I had missed, LL had taken the idea of a prime-time special and spun it into something much larger: a permanent Hip-Hop Hall of Fame, separate from the Rock & Roll Hall of Fame, managed and promoted by the Recording Academy.

I texted Shawn under the table. "What is this? Did we agree to it?"

The answer came back immediately: "YOU did."

In the days that followed, I told Shawn two things. First, that it was a no-go. I couldn't do something like that again. Second, that if I was to do it, it would only be if we could bring real change to the proceedings. I wanted a hip-hop version of the MacArthur "genius" awards, with real money that would help the prizewinners climb out of the holes where so many rappers found themselves. I wanted an insurance fund. I was trying for something visionary, but more than that I was trying for something impossible. I wanted to set the bar so high that they were certain to call the whole thing off.

That didn't work. The more things I suggested, the more excited they got. We ended the conversation with a blueprint for an institution that would protect and preserve hip-hop, not just keeping the music alive but helping the people who created it. One afternoon, I opened up one of the emails and stared at it. I thought about the trajectory of my career, about the competing pulls I felt from different corners. I knew there was pressure to come back with the Roots and release a triumphant album. I knew there was pressure to inspire new artists. I knew there was pressure to keep writing and making films. But I also knew that a project like this, a way of shepherding hip-hop pioneers through their lives and into the lives of those who follow them, was a more profound and significant legacy. It would ensure the years that have already passed, the fifty and counting, are not erased by ignorance or indifference or inertia. It would ensure that hip-hop is history.

EPILOGUE:
BREAK OF DAWN—
INTRODUCTION TO
HIP-HOP IS STILL HISTORY

2073

just stepped out of my flying car, and I'm walking toward my flying house. How does that work? Flying driveway! I'm about halfway down the flying driveway now. Music is playing up from under my feet. I have the driveway programmed so that it can tell how I feel: it picks up all the health metrics. Depending on what they are, my driveway feeds me music that will either enhance or counter my mood. That's part of a calculation that's too complex to explain concisely, especially while I'm standing here on the flying driveway. Let me get inside the house.

Okay. I'm inside now. When I was contacted earlier today to write the introduction for *Hip-Hop Is Still History*, I had two questions. My first question was "Why didn't you have me write the whole book?" The publisher explained that *Hip-Hop Is Still History*, which celebrates the one hundredth birthday of the genre, isn't a book in the same way as *Hip-Hop Is History*, which celebrated the fiftieth back in 2023. "It's more like a cylindrical tube of cultural analysis with elements of silver-tab annotation," she said.

"Tell me something I don't know," I said.

"What I mean is that we don't really have an author on this one in the same way. We had a source set of contributors curated by a central algorithm."

"But you want me to write the intro?" I said. That was my second question.

"Yes," the publisher said. "We were thinking that maybe you could reflect on some of the ways that the music has changed since you wrote the first edition of *Hip-Hop Is History*."

"I can do that," I said. "How many ways do you want?"

"Five?" I heard a whirring noise behind her. "No. Three!"

"Got it," I said. I knew my first stop: the playlists I have of the best songs from the last few years. I like 2072, though 2071 has a special place in my heart—that's the year I turned one hundred. People who hit that milestone usually talk about the music of their youth (Run-D.M.C., Eric B. and Rakim, De La Soul) or their young adulthood (Jay-Z, Dilla, Clipse). Sometimes, if people are especially interested in a genre, they'll extend their elastic fandom—meaning the part of their enthusiasm that keeps them looking for new acts and new energy—into their fifties (for me, that was Young Thug, A Boogie Wit da Hoodie, Drake) or their sixties (Ten Window, Patroclose, Spilla-X). But it's rare that the ears and the brain behind them keep agile past the century mark. I can't say that I have totally succeeded. There are plenty of hits that whiz right by me these days. "Orange Circle with Two Orange Lines" may have been everyone's jam last summer, but to me it just sounded like warmed-over P.M. Dawn (that's a group from the 1980s and 1990s—sort of ironic, now that climate change has radically destabilized everything, and half the time the sun does rise in the afternoon). But the best songs of 2071, like "Testify to House" and "Foex Need," just plain slap and would have done so in any year.

But I don't want to get down into the weeds. The point of this book—er, cylindrical tube of analysis—is the same as it was back in 2023, which is to celebrate the hip-hop genre in all its diversity and vision, not to mention all its flummery and flaws. When I wrote the first edition of this book a half century ago, I was determined not to be a straightforward cheerleader, partly because I didn't feel like one. I had fallen in love with hip-hop in my twenties and then fallen out of love in my late thirties, only to broker a peace with it as I passed my own half-century mark. I remember sitting in my apartment in New York City (back then, it was one of the largest cities in the world) and "streaming" "songs" on my "laptop," which sounds like nonsense now.

As I am writing this introduction, it's a very different world from that of 2023. Not everything about it is different. I look the same, more or less, except for the giant white hair. I credit the fact that in my fifties, I became very aware of the importance of preserving my health. I fell off a bit when things happened in the 2030s and 2040s, and they happened, you can be sure. (Check out other people's books, like Saana Hutson's *The Great Circus Riots of Space* or Shubhaprada Mehta's *Goodbye, Alphabet* for specifics.) But I got back on track in my seventies and eighties and rolled into my nineties as fit as a fiddle, which leaves me now, at one hundred and three, fully capable of mind-dictating this introduction, in which I address three ways that hip-hop has changed over the past half century.

ENHANCED PROCESSING. EP used to be called AI, which stood for artificial intelligence. Sounds strange to say now, but for decades people resisted this technology. They found it to be inhuman, some kind of violation of an unspoken agreement that artwork would be made only with human hands, human voices, and human minds. But there was a gradual chipping away and then, around 2045, a complete acceptance. The main factor was that EP allowed producers to combine different rappers from different eras. In my youth, people had sports arguments in which they wondered who would win a boxing match, 1966 Cassius Clay (look him up) or 1986 Mike Tyson (yes, the inventor of the T-19 Meditation Chip was once a fighter). EP let you combine 1988 Chuck D and 1994 Biggie, and 1986 Rakim and 2039 Jeffersonian Red Wax. It also let people make new music seamlessly with older artists. Back in the old days, you could find a

Tupac track and update it with new production and features. This was something completely different. I can claim to be a pioneer of this second thing, somewhat. I remember back in the late 2020s, my partner in the Roots, Tariq Trotter, and I tried to patch together a duet with Tariq and the D.O.C.—not the D.O.C. as he was in the late 2020s, but as he had been in the late 1980s, before he was involved in a car accident that changed his voice forever. That was rudimentary, but as the technology improved, the uses of it did, too.

ROOMER HAS IT. You may be surprised that so much of the last fifty years involves going back to the past. You shouldn't be. I have learned in my century-plus that we are a very nostalgic species. During the pandemic—the 2020 one, not the one in 2041 or 2055—I had a key nostalgic phase. I had virtual reality goggles, which is noteworthy, because it was a time when not everyone did. You would laugh at how unwieldy they looked back then. There was a guy who filmed videos on every surface train in Philadelphia. I would recreate my route to school, looking at maps to walk from my house at 52nd and Osage, then following the bus route, then using this guy's videos to get on the Market-Franklin elevated train. That became the second major trend in hip-hop. Not traveling on Philly trains, exactly, but returning to the past, not just by using voices from the past, but by rebuilding past environments entirely. A million years ago, I remember talking to a producer about why it was so hard to capture the sounds of certain decades. The 1960s, I could do. The 1980s, I could do. But there was something about the 1970s that was elusive. He told me his theory, which was that it wasn't just about the microphones being used, or the instruments, but that it was about everything around them: the wood, the rugs, the treated leather of the furniture. Everything in the room contributed to the sound. He had an idea for a company that would build exact rooms and record them for room tone, after which the rooms could be digitally encoded and used as filters. That guy ended up having other good ideas, like making a mint in suspended proteins.

AN-DRÉ DAY. Back when I was writing *Hip-Hop Is History*, I kept extending the deadline, because albums kept coming out, and I wanted to comment on them. Then one day I got *New Blue Sun*. We all know this record now, of course, but back then it was a bit of an oddity—the comeback record after nearly two decades by André Benjamin, then mostly known as André 3000 and one half of the classic Atlanta hip-hop duo Outkast. (The other half, of course, was Big Boi, former governor of Georgia.) André had stopped rapping, more or less, and learned woodwind instruments, and in 2023 he surprise-released an album of longish instrumentals. The second I heard the record, I knew that I had to add in an essay about it to *Hip-Hop Is History*. "No," my coauthor said. "Just because a rapper made an album doesn't mean it's hip-hop. Also, we're way past our deadline. They're going to press." Deadline! Press! And yeah, this was well before mind-dictating became a thing. That guy's long gone now, obviously. Good riddance, really. But the publisher also said no. Anyway, I wanted to say that the record, though sure, was not hip-hop at all, it was fundamentally hip-hop in that it took a stand against everything that was dominant. Sounds funny to say this now, of course, but it was rebel music, a middle finger, and because André did it with such focus and purpose, he put it across. It even sold pretty well, even at the beginning, better than albums by people like Nas that came out around the same time. But I think we can all agree that the album was most noteworthy for the kinds of sounds it introduced. When I was forty years old, or fifty, I would get ready for making music of my own by listening to J Dilla for three hours. I wanted to fill my system up. André's album replaced that, not because it filled me up in the same way, but because it emptied me out and made me fill myself back up. That album opened the door to people listening to tones, white noise, binaural beats. But I don't have to tell any of you that. When "Dreams Once Buried Beneath the Dungeon Floor Slowly Sprout into Undying Gardens" became the new national anthem in 2048, it was a bigger moment even than that of Kendrick Lamar winning the Pulitzer Prize twenty years before. DAMN. Between this sentence and the last, I stood with my hand on my heart for seventeen minutes and eleven seconds. Meditative and good exercise both. (But still, pour a little out for Francis Scott

Key. That song was definitely not hip-hop, but it didn't deserve its ignominious fate.)

There we are. Three ways hip-hop has changed. Except that I have one more. Here I am, breaking the rules, rebelling. Hip-hop, you know? This last one is a little bit sad and a little bit hopeful.

About twenty years ago, I had a big Thanksgiving dinner at my house. It wasn't the floating one yet. This one was on the ground like houses used to be. Still had that souped-up DeLorean in the garage. Lots of people came over. I used a caterer and had them re-create the Thanksgiving meals of my youth, the ones that my grandma and aunt and mom made. We were talking about the meal, and how the expensive catered version was re-creating a meal that was made for nearly nothing by women who were stretching their means over an entire family in the name of love. This led somehow to a discussion of soul food, and I said something about how it had a fundamental connection to Black pain. That stopped some of the younger people in the room. They didn't know what I meant. I explained that soul food grew out of the cooking done by enslaved people, both in terms of the ingredients (which had been discarded by the people in the plantation house) and the preparation (which had to be done without fancy equipment). They were surprised, and I was surprised that they were surprised.

Then about ten years ago I was DJing a party, something I still did regularly until I got second-generation robotic fingers about five years ago. They work fine. They just somehow don't have the right feel. Anyway, I was DJing and I played James Brown's "It's a New Day." Toward the end, he really screams. A kid came up after that—by kid, I mean maybe a guy in his forties—and said, "What's with all the screaming?"

I flashed back to the Thanksgiving conversation. "That scream is pain turned into art," I said. "If he didn't scream there . . ." I trailed off. "If he didn't scream there after all he went through, maybe he's a mass shooter. Alternatively, every mass shooter might be a screamer who didn't get to make art."

He looked confused. I explained further. "Even though it's entertainment, the release in the song is preventing James Brown from doing something more violent." He looked at me kind of funny and walked away, but I had meant what I said, so I hit the memory disc behind my ear to make sure I recorded that conversation, and I've been thinking about it regularly for the last few years. I was thinking about it today when I started writing this introduction.

So much of hip-hop is a reflection of pain, even the joyful parts. It only existed in the first place because public school music education was so woefully underfunded. Black kids wanted to play the trombone or the violin, but they weren't getting instruments. That forced them to use the equivalent of food scraps, and ingenuity and genius turned those sonic scraps into a new genre. Hip-hop got diluted over the years, but the pain was still there in its DNA. It was trauma music. Even early on, people said that because Blondie rapped, and the Beasties, and Eminem, how could hip-hop be about Black pain? But that was obviously just wrong, and it's just as wrong to write it off now. Just the other day, listening to "Foex Need," I was thinking that maybe we have to give up everything we have known in Black culture to be free of the pain that sits at its source.

And so I want to end on that note, sad and a little hopeful, by saying that even though I've been an old man for a long time now, I plan to live for a while longer. I have all my nutraceuticals and nootropics lined up on the windowsill. I have the best organs that money can buy, from heart to lung to kidneys, right on to the organs of perception. My eyes are only eight years old. My ears are maybe twelve. There's no real reason to go gentle into that good night. But even given that, I don't want to write the introduction for *Hip-Hop Is Still, Still History* in 2123. I'm not sure that I want there to be any more hip-hop in 2123. I want it to truly be history. Breakbeats are evidence of how we were once broken, and I want nothing more than to bring about a healing.

—QUESTLOVE
Floating Palisades CrossPlane 11, 21:08 p.m.

HIP-HOP SONGS I ACTUALLY LISTEN TO

How do you make a list of hip-hop songs that avoids the Captain Obvious selections, but that preserves all the joy and energy and hope and humor and intelligence and attitude and flash that the music has generated over its first half century? You make this list. What appears below is a snapshot that represents my current thinking. "Current" meaning now, and not necessarily . . . now. In my mind, this playlist is continually evolving, and I try to update the online version of it accordingly. If you check that list tomorrow, or next week, or next year, there may well be shifting and settling: I might take a step back from certain aspects of 1985 or make a turn toward Rap-A-Lot and the Houston scene. And beyond this list, of course, there are thousands and thousands of songs that move the needle. Listen to mine. Find your own.

1979–1982

"Busy Bee & Jazzy Five 1980"	Chief Rocker Busy Bee	1980
"The 'Micstro'"	Radiänce	1980
"The New Rap Language"	Spoonie Gee and the Treacherous Three	1980
"Sugar Hill Groove"	The Sugarhill Gang	1980
"The Adventures of Grandmaster Flash on the Wheels of Steel"	Grandmaster Flash	1981
"Okay Okay"	Pino D'Angiò	1981

1982–1987

"Chi-C-A-G-O (Is My Chicago)"	Light Touch Band	1982
"Funky Soul Makossa"	Nairobi	1982
"The Escapades of Futura 2000"	Futura 2000	1983
"Break Dance—Electric Boogie"	West Street Mob	1983
"The Original Human Beat Box"	Doug E. Fresh	1984
"Here We Go (Live at the Funhouse)"	Run-D.M.C.	1984
"It's Yours"	T La Rock and Jazzy Jay	1984
"La-Di-Da-Di"	Doug E. Fresh and Slick Rick	1985
"Larry's Dance Theme"	Grandmaster Flash	1985
"You Can't Dance"	LL Cool J	1985
"Hardcore Hip-Hop"	Mantronix	1985
"Gucci Time"	Schoolly D	1985
"P.S.K. What Does It Mean?"	Schoolly D	1985
"Paul Revere"	Beastie Boys	1986
"Roaches"	Bobby Jimmy and the Critters	1986
"Freelance"	Grandmaster Flash	1986
"Go See the Doctor"	Kool Moe Dee	1986
"I'm Chillin'"	Kurtis Blow	1986
"Music Madness"	Mantronix	1986
"Beat Biter"	MC Shan	1986
"Son of Byford"	Run-D.M.C.	1986

1987–1992

"Small Time Hustler"	The Dismasters	1987
"Ahh, Let's Get Ill"	LL Cool J	1987
"Bring the Noise"	Public Enemy	1987
"This Beat Kicks"	T La Rock	1987
"Funky (Original 12 Version)"	Ultramagnetic MCs	1987
"Put It 2 Music"	Audio Two	1988
"Set It Off"	Big Daddy Kane	1988
"D-Nice Rocks the House"	Boogie Down Productions	1988

"I'm Still #1"	Boogie Down Productions	1988
"Nervous"	Boogie Down Productions	1988
"Live at Union Square, November 1986"	DJ Jazzy Jeff and the Fresh Prince	1988
"Still Talkin'"	Eazy-E	1988
"Because I Got It Like That"	Jungle Brothers	1988
"B-Side Wins Again"	Public Enemy	1988
"Show 'Em Whatcha Got"	Public Enemy	1988
"Straight Up"	Three Times Dope	1988
"Rhymes"	Too $hort	1988
"Detonator"	Tuff Crew	1988
"Mentally Mad (Original 12)"	Ultramagnetic MCs	1988
"Caught in the Middle of a 3 Way Mix"	Beastie Boys	1989
"Egg Man"	Beastie Boys	1989
"Your Sister's Def"	Beastie Boys	1989
"Can U Keep a Secret"	De La Soul	1989
"I Can Do Anything (Delacratic)"	De La Soul	1989
"Then She Bit Me"	DJ Jazzy Jeff and the Fresh Prince	1989
"Portrait of a Masterpiece"	The D.O.C.	1989
"Knick Knack Patty Wack"	EPMD	1989
"Size Ain't Shit"	Geto Boys	1989
"Done by the Forces of Nature"	Jungle Brothers	1989
"Kool Accordin' 2 a Jungle Brother"	Jungle Brothers	1989
"Nitro"	LL Cool J	1989
"Jingling Baby"	LL Cool J	1989
"Fast Peg"	LL Cool J	1989
"No Kid"	Urban Dance Squad	1989
"Rhythm (Devoted to the Art of Moving Butts)"	A Tribe Called Quest	1990
"Edutainment"	Boogie Down Productions	1990
"All for One"	Brand Nubian	1990
"Step to the Rear"	Brand Nubian	1990
"Doowutchyalike"	Digital Underground	1990

"Hit Squad Heist"	EPMD	1990
"No Omega"	Eric B. and Rakim	1990
"AmeriKKKa's Most Wanted"	Ice Cube	1990
"Trivial Pursuit"	JVC Force	1990
"Hey Lover (Street Mix)"	LL Cool J	1990
"Murdergram"	LL Cool J	1990
"I Got Ta"	Masta Ace	1990
"Livin' Like a Star"	Special Ed	1990
"Ya Wish Ya Could"	Special Ed	1990
"Al'z A-B-Cee'z"	3rd Bass	1991
"Come on Down"	Big Daddy Kane	1991
"Have U.N.E. Pull"	Black Sheep	1991
"How I Could Just Kill a Man"	Cypress Hill	1991
"Shoot 'Em Up"	Cypress Hill	1991
"Tres Equis"	Cypress Hill	1991
"Who Stole The DJ"	DJ Jazzy Jeff and the Fresh Prince	1991
"Tear It Off"	DJ Quik	1991
"Homicide"	Godfather Don	1991
"Bitches 2"	Ice-T	1991
"Fried Chicken"	Ice-T	1991
"M.V.P.s"	Ice-T	1991
"Mr. Hood Gets a Haircut"	KMD	1991
"Mr. Hood Meets Onyx"	KMD	1991
"Feminine Fatt"	Leaders of the New School	1991
"Sound of the Zeekers"	Leaders of the New School	1991
"Large Professor"	Main Source	1991
"Peace Is Not the Word to Play"	Main Source	1991
"The Dayz of Wayback"	N.W.A.	1991
"Each One Teach One"	Poor Righteous Teachers	1991
"Are You Wit Me"	Son of Bazerk	1991
"N-41"	Son of Bazerk	1991
"What Could Be Better Bitch"	Son of Bazerk	1991
"Your Mother Has Green Teeth"	Stetsasonic	1991
"Ain't Got Nuttin'"	Terminator X	1991

"Juvenile Delinquintz"	Terminator X	1991
"Game"	Tim Dog	1991
"Traci"	Young Black Teenagers	1991
"Loud and Hard to Hit"	Young Black Teenagers	1991

1992–1997

"A to the K"	Cypress Hill	1992
"True Fuschnick"	FU-Schnickens	1992
"Daily Operation"	Gang Starr	1992
"The Place We Dwell"	Gang Starr	1992
"Soliloquy of Chaos"	Gang Starr	1992
"Come and Get Some of This"	House of Pain	1992
"Put on Your Shit Kickers"	House of Pain	1992
"On the Run (Untouchable)"	Kool G Rap and DJ Polo	1992
"Soul Brother #1"	Pete Rock and CL Smooth	1992
"Young Girl Bluez"	Biz Markie	1993
"Hand on the Glock"	Cypress Hill	1993
"The Return of the Crazy One"	Digital Underground	1993
"Streets of the Ghetto"	Ed O.G. and Da Bulldogs	1993
"Erick Sermon"	Erick Sermon	1993
"Female Species"	Erick Sermon	1993
"Hostile"	Erick Sermon	1993
"Addicted to Danger"	Ice-T	1993
"That's How I'm Livin'"	Ice-T	1993
"Cash in My Hands"	Nice and Smooth	1993
"Can I Get It, Yo"	Run-D.M.C.	1993
"What's My Name?"	Snoop Dogg	1993
"Let 'Em Know"	Souls of Mischief	1993
"Only When I'm Drunk"	Tha Alkaholics	1993
"If Papes Come Home"	A Tribe Called Quest	1994
"Fried Chicken"	The Beatnuts	1994
"Get Funky"	The Beatnuts	1994
"Show & Prove"	Big Daddy Kane	1994

"Jettin'"	Digable Planets	1994
"6 Feet Deep"	Gravediggaz	1994
"Brooklyn Took It"	Jeru the Damaja	1994
"The World Is Yours (Tip Mix)"	Nas	1994
"Jam on Revenge (The Wikki-Wikki Song)"	Newcleus	1994
"Let's All Get Down"	Nice and Smooth	1994
"O-Zone"	O.C.	1994
"Let's Organize"	Organized Konfusion	1994
"Da Journee"	Redman	1994
"Rockafella (R.I.P.)"	Redman	1994
"Rockafella Remix"	Redman (with Erick Sermon)	1994
"Behind Bars (Dum Ditty Dum Mix)"	Slick Rick	1994
"Get the Girl, Grab the Money and Run"	Souls of Mischief	1994
"Mo Money, Mo Murder (Homicide)"	AZ	1995
"Vital Nerve"	Company Flow	1995
"Killafornia"	Cypress Hill	1995
"Spark Another Owl"	Cypress Hill	1995
"Buck-Buck"	Das EFX	1995
"Man Above"	Erick Sermon	1995
"Rock On"	Funkdoobiest	1995
"Intro"	Group Home	1995
"Investigative Reports"	GZA	1995
"Hold"	KRS-One	1995
"Masta I.C."	Mic Geronimo	1995
"On the Air"	The Nonce	1995
"My Man"	The Pharcyde	1995
"Brooklyn Zoo"	Ol' Dirty Bastard	1995
"The Stomp"	Ol' Dirty Bastard	1995
"Verbal Intercourse"	Raekwon	1995
"Bucktown"	Smif-N-Wessun	1995
"Broken Language"	Smoothe da Hustler	1995
"Heartz of Men"	2Pac	1996

"Word Play"	A Tribe Called Quest	1996
"Keep It Movin'"	Busta Rhymes	1996
"Tried By 12"	The East Flatbush Project	1996
"Undastand"	Heltah Skeltah	1996
"Heart Full of Sorrow"	House of Pain	1996
"Physical Stamina"	Jeru the Damaja	1996
"The Rhyme"	Keith Murray	1996
"101 Things to Do While I'm with Your Girl"	Kwest tha Madd Ladd	1996
"The Rap World"	Large Professor	1996
"Get Dealt With"	Mobb Deep	1996
"Mainstream"	Outkast	1996
"She Said (Jay Dee Remix)"	The Pharcyde	1996
"Pick It Up"	Redman	1996
"Escape From New York"	Sadat X	1996

1997–2002

"1'2 Many . . ."	Common	1997
"Imaginary Players"	Jay-Z	1997
"Ten Crack Commandments"	The Notorious B.I.G.	1997
"Beej N Dem"	Slum Village	1997
"Fantastic 2 (Interlude)"	Slum Village	1997
"Fantastic 3 (Alternative Mix)"	Slum Village	1997
"Hoc N Pucky"	Slum Village	1997
"Keep It On (Remix)"	Slum Village	1997
"Pregnant"	Slum Village	1997
"Deadly Melody"	Wu-Tang Clan	1997
"Three MC's and One DJ"	Beastie Boys	1998
"Body Movin' (Remix)"	Beastie Boys (with Erick Sermon)	1998
"Back Up off the Wall"	Brand Nubian	1998
"Gimme Some More"	Busta Rhymes	1998
"Horse & Carriage"	Cam'ron	1998
"A Day Like No Other"	Company Flow	1998

"Damien"	DMX	1998
"Gutta Butta"	Goodie Mob	1998
"You Never Knew"	Hieroglyphics	1998
"If You Think I'm Jiggy"	The Lox	1998
"SpottieOttieDopaliscious"	Outkast	1998
"Pre-Game"	Sauce Money	1998
"Slam Pit"	The Beatnuts	1999
"A to G"	Blackalicious	1999
"The Onslaught"	Black Moon	1999
"Two Turntables and a Mic"	Black Moon	1999
"Tramp"	Foxy Brown	1999
"The Legacy"	Group Home	1999
"Word on the Street"	Inspectah Deck	1999
"Great Solar Stance"	Jeru the Damaja	1999
"Speaker Smashin'"	Lootpack	1999
"Ghetto"	The Madd Rapper	1999
"Rhymes Like Dimes"	MF DOOM	1999
"Tick, Tick . . ."	MF DOOM	1999
"The Realest"	Mobb Deep	1999
"Out There"	Project Pat	1999
"Let's Ride"	Q-Tip	1999
"Table of Contents (Parts 1 & 2)"	The Roots	1999
"S.O.U.L."	Slum Village	1999
"Bizarre"	U-God	1999
"Die"	Beanie Sigel	2000
"Stop, Chill"	Beanie Sigel	2000
"Laughing at You"	Big Pun	2000
"Nigga Shit"	Big Pun	2000
"Little Brother"	Black Star	2000
"Check It Out Y'all"	Bumpy Knuckles	2000
"Bang, Bang"	Capone-N-Noreaga	2000
"Heat"	Common	2000
"The Light (Remix)"	Common	2000
"Retreat to This"	Dice Raw	2000
"Thin Line (Between Raw & Jiggy)"	Dice Raw, Black Thought	2000

"We Came 2 Play"	DJ Quik	2000
"Stroke of Death"	Ghostface Killah	2000
"1-900-Hustler"	Jay-Z	2000
"Where Have You Been"	Jay-Z	2000
"Toilet Tisha"	Outkast	2000
"Tight"	Rah Digga	2000
"Fall in Love"	Slum Village	2000
"What's That All About"	Slum Village	2000
"Return of the Diaz Bros."	Tony Touch	2000
"It's Da Nuts"	The Beatnuts	2001
"Genesis"	Busta Rhymes	2001
"The People"	De La Soul	2001
"Jealousy"	Ghostface Killah	2001
"Don't Play"	J-Live	2001
"Interlude 1 (I'm a Rapper)"	J-Live	2001
"Them That's Not"	J-Live	2001
"2nd Childhood"	Nas	2001
"Doo Rags"	Nas	2001
"Gorilla Pimp"	Project Pat	2001
"Uzi (Pinky Ring)"	Wu-Tang Clan	2001

2002–2007

"Originate"	The Beatnuts	2002
"Routine"	The Beatnuts	2002
"Make You Feel That Way"	Blackalicious	2002
"Imaginary Places"	Busdriver	2002
"Soul Power"	Common	2002
"Love Me"	Eminem, Obie Trice, 50 Cent	2002
"A Charmed Life"	J-Live	2002
"Like This Anna"	J-Live	2002
"If You Only Knew"	Jurassic 5	2002
"A Day at the Races"	Jurassic 5	2002
"Luv U Better"	LL Cool J	2002
"The Come Up"	Ms. Jade	2002

"Purple"	Nas	2002
"Zone Out"	Nas	2002
"VIP In"	Slum Village	2002
"Heat"	50 Cent	2003
"Giantz Ta This"	DJ Premier	2003
"As Serious as Your Life"	Four Tet	2003
"The Exclusive"	Jaylib	2003
"Anti-Matter"	King Geedorah	2003
"Next Levels"	King Geedorah	2003
"The Yo-Yo"	Little Brother	2003
"A Day in the Life of Benjamin André (Incomplete)"	Outkast	2003
"Reset"	Outkast	2003
"Gotta Have It"	Beanie Sigel	2004
"Brrr Stick 'Em"	Beastie Boys	2004
"We Don't Give a Funk"	The Beatnuts	2004
"Verbal Clap"	De La Soul	2004
"I Do What I Like"	Dice Raw	2004
"Young & Sexy"	Fabolous	2004
"Freak Like Me"	Heather Hunter	2004
"Spaceship"	Kanye West	2004
"Every Sip"	LL Cool J	2004
"Accordion"	Madvillain	2004
"America's Most Blunted"	Madvillain	2004
"Hoe Cakes"	MF DOOM	2004
"One Beer"	MF DOOM	2004
"Fallback"	Peedi Crakk	2004
"Leisure Rules"	Prozack Turner	2004
"Star"	The Roots	2004
"Web"	The Roots	2004
"Pastor Skillz"	Skillz	2004
"We Both Think Alike"	50 Cent	2005
"Window Shopper"	50 Cent	2005
"Duck"	Black Milk	2005
"The Movement"	Common	2005

"Caught Up in the Hype"	Consequence	2005
"The Main Event"	Freddy B and the Mighty Mic Masters	2005
"Late"	Kanye West	2005
"Cheatin'"	Little Brother	2005
"Shotgun Intro"	Platinum Pied Pipers	2005
"Trill"	Clipse	2006
"Clipse of Doom"	Ghostface Killah	2006
"Underwater"	Ghostface Killah	2006
"Whip You with a Strap"	Ghostface Killah	2006
"The Prelude"	Jay-Z	2006
"Workinonit"	J Dilla	2006
"Universal Magnetic (Live)"	Mos Def	2006
"Still Dreaming"	Nas	2006
"Where Y'all At"	Nas	2006
"The Jump Off"	Plastic Little	2006
"Margarita"	Sleepy Brown	2006

2007–2012

"Callin' Me"	Consequence	2007
"Belt Holders"	Ghostface Killah	2007
"Milk Crates"	Ghostface Killah	2007
"The Champ"	Ghostface Killah	2007
"The Sun"	Ghostface Killah	2007
"The Watch"	Ghostface Killah	2007
"Wise"	Ghostface Killah	2007
"Aunt Jackie"	Jason Fox	2007
"American Gangster"	Jay-Z	2007
"Fuck Them Muthafuckas"	Peedi Crakk	2007
"My Gun"	Peedi Crakk	2007
"Torture"	Peedi Crakk	2007
"Welcome to the Terrordome"	Pharoahe Monch	2007
"Don't Nobody Care About Us"	Phat Kat	2007
"ABC"	Raekwon	2007
"Tr(n)igger"	Saul Williams	2007

"Hot Thing"	Talib Kweli	2007
"In the Mood"	Talib Kweli	2007
"Punch Drunk Love"	Common	2008
"Don't Beg"	Diamond D	2008
"Be Out RMX"	Ghostface Killah	2008
"Charlie Brown"	Ghostface Killa	2008
"Roosevelts"	Ghostface Killah	2008
"Yolanda's House"	Ghostface Killah	2008
"Dr. Carter"	Lil Wayne	2008
"Feel My Heart Beat"	LL Cool J	2008
"You Better Watch Me"	LL Cool J	2008
"Beat Provider (Through the Years)"	Madlib	2008
"Do You Know? (Transition)"	Madlib	2008
"Floating Soul (Peace)"	Madlib	2008
"J.B. and J.D. (Interlude)"	Madlib	2008
"The Main Inspiration (Coltrane of Beats)"	Madlib	2008
"Rzaview (Live on WFMU)"	MC Paul Barman	2008
"We Roll"	Pete Rock	2008
"Click"	Torae	2008
"The Feature Heavy Song"	Wale	2008
"Exhibit C"	Jay Electronica	2009
"The LP"	Large Professor	2009
"Surf Swag"	Lil Wayne	2009
"Hot Guacamole"	MC Paul Barman	2009
"Power"	MC Paul Barman	2009
"Casa Bey"	Mos Def	2009
"History"	Mos Def	2009
"Child Seek 'Em"	Ol' Dirty Bastard	2009
"Cloud 9"	Slum Village	2009
"Next Time (Just Right Version)"	Common	2010
"In tha Park"	Ghostface Killah	2010
"Superstar"	Ghostface Killah	2010
"Tigallo for Dolo"	Little Brother	2010

"Maybach Music III"	Rick Ross	2010
"Fake I.D."	Consequence	2011
"Sorry 4 the Wait"	Lil Wayne	2011

2012–2017

"The Reunion"	Beanie Sigel	2012
"His Pain"	BJ the Chicago Kid	2012
"BFK"	Freddie Gibbs	2012
"Dilla's Mix"	J Dilla	2012
"Let's Take It Back"	J Dilla	2012
"Make 'Em NV"	J Dilla	2012
"Shouts (Alt)"	J Dilla	2012
"Wild"	J Dilla	2012
"Dreams and Nightmares"	Meek Mill	2012
"Trillmatic"	A$AP Mob	2013
"Burgundy"	Earl Sweatshirt	2013
"Let Nas Down"	J. Cole	2013
"Bound 2"	Kanye West	2013
"Seasons Change"	Quasimoto	2013
"456"	Roc Marciano	2013
"The Sacrifice"	Roc Marciano	2013
"Art Imitates Life"	Talib Kewli	2013
"Point Blank"	Jeru the Damaja	2014
"The Waters"	Mick Jenkins	2014
"Lunch Money"	Pusha T	2014
"Break the Bank"	ScHoolboy Q	2014
"Paperwork"	T.I. (feat. Pharrell)	2014
"Know Yourself"	Drake	2015
"Extradite"	Freddie Gibbs	2015
"Hood Politics"	Kendrick Lamar	2015
"Classic"	Meek Mill	2015
"Got 'Em Covered"	Pusha T	2015
"All Day, Always"	Skyzoo	2015
"2000 Seasons"	Talib Kweli	2015

"Nasty's World"	A$AP Mob	2016
"The Gospel"	Alicia Keys	2016
"AAAHHHH!!!"	Busta Rhymes	2016
"Jay Dee 45"	J Dilla	2016
"Jay Dee 51"	J Dilla	2016
"That's O.K."	Jonwayne	2016
"Young Black Intelligent"	Masta Ace	2016
"And I Go"	Slum Village	2016
"Fly Girl 1"	Slum Village	2016

2017–2022

"Things Ain't the Same"	Frank 'n' Dank	2017
"LAUDER"	JID	2017
"Shea Stadium"	Meyhem Lauren	2017
"Rollinem 7's"	N.E.R.D.	2017
"One Life to Live"	Pete Rock	2017
"Buddies"	Quelle Chris	2017
"Popeye"	Quelle Chris	2017
"Jocelyn Flores"	XXXTENTACION	2017
"The E Train"	DJ Muggs	2018
"Secrets of the Sandz"	Donte the Gr8	2018
"Red Water"	Earl Sweatshirt	2018
"Shattered Dreams"	Earl Sweatshirt	2018
"1985 (Intro to *The Fall Off*)"	J. Cole	2018
"Gold Purple Orange"	Jean Grae	2018
"Ohsh"	Jean Grae	2018
"Ye vs. the People"	Kanye West	2018
"2009"	Mac Miller	2018
"Breukelen 'Brooklyn'"	Masta Ace	2018
"Gold Man"	Maxo	2018
"Going Bad"	Meek Mill	2018
"Gotta Love It"	PRhyme	2018
"Congo"	Roc Marciano	2018
"Burn"	Slum Village	2018

"Living It Up"	Slum Village	2018
"Eric B"	Westside Gunn	2018
"Hall & Nash"	Westside Gunn	2018
"Me & My Eagle"	Westside Gunn	2018
"Never Coming Homme"	Westside Gunn	2018
"Vera Boys"	Westside Gunn	2018
"Background"	B. Cool-Aid	2019
"Combat"	Danny Brown	2019
"4N"	Earl Sweatshirt	2019
"Freestyle Shit"	Freddie Gibbs	2019
"So Many Rappers"	Gang Starr	2019
"Mittrom"	Mach-Hommy	2019
"QueensBridge Politics"	Nas	2019
"You Mean the World to Me"	Nas	2019
"Nasa"	Nowaah the Flood	2019
"Nah!"	Slum Village	2019
"Capoeira"	Action Bronson	2020
"Golden Eye"	Action Bronson	2020
"MANNA"	Babyfather	2020
"It's Over"	Black Soprano Family	2020
"When the Gods Meet"	Blu and Exile	2020
"Yah Yah"	Eminem	2020
"Babies & Fools"	Freddie Gibbs	2020
"itkanbe[sonice]"	Knxwledge	2020
"Story"	The Lox	2020
"DOLOMEALS"	Medhane	2020
"Covid Cough"	Roc Marciano	2020
"Pimps Don't Wear Rabbits"	Roc Marciano	2020
"The Best Natural Face"	Vic Spencer	2020
"Loose Change"	The Alchemist	2021
"Two Kevlaar"	Bronze Nazareth	2021
"Glowing Mics (Founders Remix)"	Gang Starr	2021
"Woman"	Little Simz	2021
"Two Worlds Apart"	Little Simz	2021
"Nobody"	Nas (feat. Ms. Lauryn Hill)	2021

"Bing Bong"	Nems	2021
"RIGHT NOW"	Westside Gunn	2021
"Jaguar"	Action Bronson	2022
"Subzero"	Action Bronson	2022
"Tongpo"	Action Bronson	2022
"Turkish"	Action Bronson	2022
"Zambezi"	Action Bronson	2022
"usedtoo"	B. Cool-Aid	2022
"So Cool"	Big K.R.I.T.	2022
"Walkin"	Denzel Curry	2022
"BLACK THOUGHT FREESTYLES"	DJ BomaNdoki	2022
"Power Power"	Duckwrth	2022
"Knee Brace"	Eshu Tune	2022
"Gorilla"	Little Simz	2022
"Block List"	RXK NEPHEW	2022
"Peace Flygod"	Westside Gunn	2022

2023–2024

"MAILBOX FREESTYLE"	Baro Sura	2023
"Brandy, Aaliyah"	B. Cool-Aid	2023
"ChalkRoundIt"	B. Cool-Aid	2023
"Lovely How I Let My Mind Float"	De La Soul	2023
"Hustle, Repeat"	Godfather of Harlem	2023
"Risking It All at Wegmans"	J Scienide	2023
"From Vailsburg To Vaudeville"	Mach-Hommy	2023
"Szechuan Capital"	Meyhem Lauren	2023
"Chapter 6: Hard 2 Kill"	Sideshow	2023
"Traffic"	Solo Jones	2023
"Introduction"	Westside Gunn	2023
"Fork in the Pot"	Westside Gunn	2023
"Mamas PrimeTime"	Westside Gunn	2023
"née-nah"	21 Savage	2024

GENERAL INDEX

DeMann, Freddy, 62
departure records, 279–80
Devin the Dude, 194
Diamond, Michael, 60–61
Diamonds and Pearls (Prince), 115
Diary (Scarface): *Source* five-mic rating, 177
Dice Raw, 195
Digital Underground, 88, 112
Dinkins, David, 159
Dirty Projectors, 230
Divine Styler, 280
disco, watering down of, 27
Disco Dave and the Force of the Five MCs, 34
Disco Fever, 40
disposable culture, 8
Dixon, Troy, 121
DJ Drama, 14, 194; Black Thought on, 195; mixtapes by, 195–201; raid on, 201–202
DJ E-Z Rock, 77
DJ Jazzy Jeff, 79–82, 114–15
DJ Junebug, 40
DJ Polo, 100
DJ Premier, 122–23
DJ Screw: death of, 270
DJ Sense, 196
D.M.C.: on daily rituals, 43–44
DMX, 165; death of, 270
DMX, Davy, 52
D-Nice, 64
D.O.C., 124, 176
Doctor Dré, 84
Documentary (The Game), 186
Doggystyle (Snoop Dogg): *Source* five-mic rating, 177
Doja Cat, 269, 273
Dolby, Thomas, 78
Domo Genesis, 231
Donuts (J Dilla), 218–19
Do the Right Thing (film), 87
Do You Want More?!!!??! (Roots), 132, 138–39; twenty-fifth anniversary of, 192
Drake, 4, 223–24, 266; emo-ness of, 225; Lamar dissing, 238

Dr. Dre, 6, 123, 125–27, 145, 177, 209; productions by, 124
Dread, Mikey, 88
DS2 (Future), 237
Duke Bootee, 38
Duke Williams and the Extremes, 90–91
Dunn, Larry, 228
Dust Brothers, 91
Duvall, Robert, 100

E-40, 169
Eagles of Death Metal, 254
Earth, Wind & Fire, 228
East Coast jazz, 76
Easy Mo Bee, 128–29, 144
Eazy-E: death of, 269
ecstasy era, 21
Edutainment (Boogie Down Productions): *Source* five-mic rating, 175
ego: Hip-Hop 50 and, 7–9
8Ball, 194
8-Mile (film), 172
808s & Heartbreak (Kanye West), 212
E.L.E. (Busta Rhymes), 170
Electric Circus (Common), 190, 226
Elephant Man's Bones (Roc Marciano), 283
Elliot, Stro, 11
El-P, 250
Elsewhere, 283
E Mike C, 34
Eminem, 170–71, 185; influence of, 172–73
Eminem Show (Eminem), 172
emotions, 271–72
Emotions, 264
Encore (Eminem), 172
Enjoy Records, 34
Enter the Wu-Tang (Wu-Tang Clan), 129, 132–33, 136; sampling in, 130; *Source* five-mic rating, 177
EPMD, 79, 104, 169, 175–76; formation of, 101–102; sampling and, 103; vocal delivery of, 103
Eric B., 68, 70–71, 175–76
Escape (Whodini), 78

INDEX OF SONGS

AFTER THE CREDITS . . .

Back in the epilogue, I imagined a world where hip-hop was one hundred years old, playing out the tail of its life cycle. But the reality is that I'm in the present, in 2024, and in the present we are still celebrating the fiftieth anniversary of hip-hop.

"Still celebrating the fiftieth anniversary of hip-hop" is a polite way of saying that we're still in a period that's like the running of the bulls. Over the last year, everyone has been gunning to be seen as the definitive punctuation mark on this sentence. Nas created the Paid in Full foundation, which set up a fund to support hip-hop pioneers, including Rakim and Scarface. Run-D.M.C., Snoop, and others performed at Yankee Stadium. There were museum shows and benefits and everything. And there I was, with the group of coworkers and collaborators (Shawn Gee, LL Cool J, and the rest) that had created the Grammys tribute back in February 2023, re-upping for a prime-time special to be aired in December. Which meant that I had to take stock of my schedule and all the work in it, which had suddenly become distractions, to do a ten-week sprint to coordinate a two-hour version of that original fifteen-minute segment, which stressed me out so much that one of my teeth fell out. Fifteen minutes to two hours—what is that, eight teeth?

The first thing I did was get someone to handle the music: a fall guy, you could say. I enlisted the services of DJ J.Period and gave him a disclaimer: "I'm not responsible for the stress. And there will be stress." But I still had to fill out the lineup, which meant that I was making the same phone calls I had made earlier in the year, and then some.

The first order of business, of course, was to try for the impossible, and that was to convince Dr. Dre to put together an N.W.A. reunion. You know when the Three Stooges are in the army? When the drill sergeant says, "Whoever wants to be on the front lines, step forward," and they all step back except one guy? I was that guy, which meant I was tasked with setting up a Zoom call to ask Dre. The one thing everyone told me was that Dre doesn't play with punctuality, that he always shows up fifteen minutes early to every meeting. Hearing that not just once, not just twice, but maybe ten times got me a little angry. I wasn't angry that they were insinuating that I might be late to a meeting. I was angry that they knew me well enough to be right about it. Who wants people around who know you that well? So the night before, I decided to shock the world. If Dre was going to show up fifteen minutes early, I'd be an hour early. I did my meditations, showered, put on clothes, and set my alarm for early in the morning. It was the same thing I did the morning of the nomination readings for the Oscars. You don't have to be in-person ready. You only have to be Zoom ready.

I woke up, got my head together, had some breakfast, and checked the clock. It was 7:55. I set my computer up. At exactly 8:00 a.m., I clicked on the meeting link and . . . Cotdamnit!! Dre was already there. "What the hell you doing here? Aren't we talking at nine?"

"I learned this a long time ago," he said. "Get there way before everyone else to get the lay of the land." It had a *Miami Vice* feel, like he was sweeping for weapons.

When I looked at his background, it was sort of like a studio, but sort of not. "Where are you right now?" I asked.

He repeated my question to someone off-screen, and I realized he was on his yacht. Timbuktu? Morocco? South of France? They were scrambling to determine. "Just taking it easy," he said. Behind him now I saw people I recognized, and also what looked like an orchestra. One of the people was . . . well, let's say an A-list artist whose name would surprise you. We did a little small talk, but I instantly knew I couldn't get through the hour like that. Seeing him on that yacht was like opening the door to a chamber of imagination. I needed to get off the call so I could keep working until I got my orchestra-and-A-list-artist-whose-name-would-surprise-you yacht.

"Uh," I said. "I have to go pick up a package, but I'll hop back on right at 8:59 for the meeting with the rest of them." There was no package, but you channel your inner Larry David when necessary.

"Cool," he said, drinking the most expensive wine in the world from the most expensive glass in the world. "Yeah, okay then."

I sat in the room silently. I was in my luxury apartment feeling like I was in my old bedroom in West Philly. Was I doing enough with my life or not doing shit? I popped back into the meeting and Dre immediately spoke. "Who all gonna be there?" he said. Flashbacks to February. I explained the event and its historical importance. "Nope," he said. "I'm passing." I thought I had given an irresistible pitch, but he had made his decision and I had to respect it. The call ended. (A little later, I was asked to go back one more time and ask him to reconsider, and he said the greatest, scariest thing ever. "You know, Quest," he said, "the one thing in the world that I hate most is having to say 'no' twice." In the silence that followed, I thought about my dad seeing three Fs on my report card when I was a kid and understanding in my bones what was coming next. I have taken to using Dre's line, and it works.)

So, no N.W.A. But the show must go on, which means that the planning for the show must go on. I was hearing that we didn't yet have the quote-unquote Big Celeb to satisfy CBS and the producers of the Grammys. They all said the same thing: "You know who you're going to have to call."

I knew. (Gulp.)

Will Smith.

It would have been a tough call to make anyway, and then there was THE THING that had HAPPENED (see Oscars 2022), which made it even tougher. My heart started trembling. It felt like the pressure of a prom ask, but a million times more intense.

At the time Will was in a kind of soft relaunch. He had engineered a few calculated appearances across the globe to test the waters, but he hadn't done much in the US. The first person I called was Jazzy Jeff to gauge where Will's mind was. Jeff was excited. "Yes," he said. "Please ask him to do this. It's the perfect thing to get him out of this spiral."

I wrote a text, simple but complex. It was one word and a few dots: *Look . . .*

That ellipsis represented it all: hey, I remember what happened, and hey, remember when you said you'd owe me one in the future, and hey, let's not talk about THE THING that had HAPPENED but let's talk about this.

I stared at it for a good thirty-five minutes and then pressed send, then stared at that for an equally good forty-five seconds before I sent a follow-up explaining my pitch. *Remember the Grammys with Jeff? Well, now we're doing a full-blown prime-time special, and I was wondering . . .* I thought it was only a sentence or two but nerves pushed it out to a paragraph. It sat there for an hour without a reply. Ah, man, I thought. Rejection. I knew it. Oh, well.

An hour later my phone buzzed. It was Will. "I'd love to," he said. I could have cried on the spot.

At the taping for the special, I was asked to introduce Will and Jeff before they came out. I weighed it. Did that make sense? Could I do it without feeling too much at once? I decided to go for it.

The rest of the taping was a blur. Did we have a show that was doing justice to hip-hop? Were all the parts of it working the way they were supposed to? When I looked around at the faces of the crew, I could tell they were thinking the same thoughts.

That night when I got home. I must have been wearing the stress on my face, because my girlfriend didn't say much for a while, and when we were finally in bed, she asked me a question. "Was it worth it?"

I thought back to the moment when I had introduced Will, and to all the moments before that. So much had come full circle: hip-hop, Philly, THE THING, everything.

Exhausted beyond belief, finally sliding into relief, I managed a one-word answer:

"Absolutely."

A NOTE ABOUT THE AUTHORS

Questlove is a six-time Grammy Award–winning musician, Academy Award–winning filmmaker, drummer, DJ, producer, director, culinary entrepreneur, *New York Times* bestselling author, cofounder of the Roots, and the musical director for *The Tonight Show Starring Jimmy Fallon*, where the Roots serves as the house band. He is the author of the *New York Times* bestsellers *Mo' Meta Blues*, *Creative Quest*, *Music Is History*, and his first children's book series, *The Rhythm of Time*, as well as the James Beard Award–nominated *somethingtofoodabout*, *Mixtape Potluck*, and the Grammy-nominated audiobooks *Creative Quest* and *Music Is History*. Questlove made his directorial debut with the Academy Award–, Grammy Award–, and BAFTA Award–winning documentary film *Summer of Soul*, which broke the record for the highest-selling documentary to come out of the Sundance Film Festival. Questlove is a cofounder of Two One Five Entertainment. He is the publisher of AUWA Books, an imprint of MCD / Farrar, Straus and Giroux.

Ben Greenman is a *New York Times* bestselling author and *New Yorker* contributor who has written both fiction and nonfiction. His novels and short-story collections include *The Slippage* and *Superbad*. He has been Questlove's collaborator on a series of books, including *Mo' Meta Blues*, *Creative Quest*, and *Music Is History*, and he has written memoirs with Sly Stone, George Clinton, and Brian Wilson. His writing has appeared in numerous publications.